Art and Archaeology of Orissa

Recent Perspectives

ART AND ARCHAEOLOGY OF ORISSA

Recent Perspectives

Edited by
Sadasiba Pradhan

POST GRADUATE DEPARTMENT OF HISTORY
SAMBALPUR UNIVERSITY
Sambalpur

ARYAN BOOKS INTERNATIONAL
New Delhi

ART AND ARCHAEOLOGY OF ORISSA

ISBN-81-7305-316-2

This monograph has been published with the financial assistance of UGC under Departmental Research Support made available to the PG Department of History, Sambalpur University.

First Published in **2006** by:
ARYAN BOOKS INTERNATIONAL
Pooja Apartments, 4B, Ansari Road, Darya Ganj, New Delhi-110 002 (India)
Tel.: 23287589, 23255799; Fax: 91-11-23270385; E-mail: aryanbooks@vsnl.com

Computer Typeset and Printed in India at
ABI Prints & Publishing Co., New Delhi.

PREFACE

Archaeology is a neglected discipline in Orissa despite its vast treasure of archaeological wealth that can be compared with any other state in India. In the recent years the Post Graduate Department of History, Sambalpur University through its UGC-DRS financial assistance have made some pioneering efforts to unravel the rich archaeological potential of the middle Mahanadi Valley that was traditionally considered *terra incognita* or an area of isolation. The area roughly extends from the Hirakud dam in Sambalpur district up to the Satkosia in Angul district. But the present volume entitled "Art and Archaeology of Orissa – Recent Perspectives" with a collection of three important research papers contributed by three senior teachers of the Department based on their field works negate this long-standing hypothesis that culturally this was an area of isolation or of recent human penetration. Rather, it was an important geo-cultural region right from the pre-historic times.

P.K. Behera's extensive and intensive explorations along with a series of trial excavations conducted in the middle Mahanadi Valley have brought to limelight a large number of ancient settlements, ranging in date from the Mesolithic to the Early Historical Periods. The paper through material evidences tries to highlight how the egalitarian hunter-gatherer adaptations of the Mesolithic Period gradually shifted towards permanent settlement and food production and finally to complex urbanization of the Early Historic Period. It has also been observed that human occupation of the valley and its contiguous areas saw no major periods of abandonment right from the Mesolithic to the Early Historical Period.

Sadasiba Pradhan, editor of the present volume, presents the results of trial excavation conducted at Nuagarh, a proto-historic site in the Middle Mahanadi Valley. Locally known as Asurgarh, the site yielded material evidence from the Chalcolithic to the Early Historic Periods. The author discusses about the archaeological significance of Asurgarh sites as a host of ancient sites in Western Orissa are locally known as Asurgarh. Except Nuagarh all other Asurgarh sites were fortified settlements of the Early Historic Period with a material culture characterized by the use of large-sized bricks, iron, punch-marked coins, and potteries of Black Slipped Ware and Black-and-Red Ware. At Nuagarh, a pre-iron Chalcolithic Phase atop the natural soil is quite discernible.

P.K. Nayak in his extensive study of the temples of Western Orissa tries to focus the regional variations and peculiarities in the domain of temple building, an important cultural trait of the Medieval Period. Starting with the twin temples of Gandharadi, Nayak tried to document all types of temples such as the stellate temples of Baudh, hypethral temple of Chausathi Yogini at Ranipur-Jharial, temples with pillared *mandapa* and lateral transepts as noticed at Baidyanath, Charada, Ranipur-Jharial, Patnagarh, Sauntpur and Narasinghnath; temples without *Jagamohana* at Baud, Narla and Surda; brick temples at Ranipur-Jharial and Budhikomna; and finally, a hybrid construction as noticed at Samaleswari, Patanesvari and Anantesayya temples in Sambalpur.

This volume would not have been possible without the financial support received from the UGC through Departmental Research Support grants for undertaking the field works as well as for its publication.

I am thankful to both the contributors P.K. Nayak and P.K. Behera for their scholarly work and providing necessary help and co-operation in publication of this volume.

I put on record the generous help and co-operation extended by Prof. S.C. Panda, Coordinator, UGC-DRS, Post Graduate Department of History. He has been a source of inspiration and the man behind the successful completion of the DRS project.

I must record my appreciation to my friend Dilip Kumar Padhi, for his help in designing of cover page and other details.

Sri Vikas Arya of Aryan Books International deserves our sincere thanks for publishing the volume with great care and in a record time.

Sadasiba Pradhan

CONTENTS

Preface *v*
List of Illustrations *ix*

1. **Investigations into the Mesolithic and Post-Mesolithic Settlements in the Middle Mahanadi Valley, Orissa** **1**
   — *Pradeep K. Behera*
   Introduction 1
   The Mesolithic Sites 3
   Beginning of Sedentism: The Neolithic Evidence 22
   The Chalcolithic Settlements 33
   Iron Age and Early Historic Settlements 41
   Concluding Remarks 57

2. **Excavations at Nuagarh-Asurgarh : A Preliminary Report** **63**
   — *Sadasiba Pradhan*
   Excavation 63
   Stratigraphy 65
   Pottery Assemblage 67
   Graffiti Mark Pottery 73
   Culture Sequence and Chronology 73
   Discussion 75

3. **Temples of Western Orissa** **79**
   — *Prafulla Kumar Nayak*
   Introduction 79
   Phase – I: Early Temples 80
   Sankushgarh Site 98
   Somesvara Temple of Ranipur-Jharial 98
   Somesvara / Kosalesvara Temple of Patnagarh 100

Kosaleshwar Temple of Baidyanath 103
Kapileswara Temple of *Charada* 111
Kosalesvara of Sauntpur 117
Narla Siva Temple 119
Narasinghnath Temple 119

Phase – II: Medieval Temples: Temples of Sambalpur 123
Temples of Suvarnapura 137
Saiva Temples 142
Vaishnava Temples 144
Shakta Temples 146
Temples of Sundargarh 147
Temples of Patnagarh 150
Temples of Khariar 151
Temples of Kalahandi (Junagarh) 152
Temples of Bhawanipatna 153
Conclusion 155

LIST OF ILLUSTRATIONS

INVESTIGATIONS INTO THE MESOLITHIC AND POST-MESOLITHIC SETTLEMENTS IN THE MIDDLE MAHANADI VALLEY, ORISSA

Figures

1. Map showing the position of the Middle Mahanadi Valley in Orissa highlands.
2. Showing distribution of Mesolithic sites in the upper part of the Middle Mahanadi Valley.
3. Excavated section (facing north) in Trench-I at Burla. *Layer-1*: Reddish-brown, loose, silty-sandy; *Layer-2*: Very loose, whitish fine-sand; *Layer-3*: reddish-brown, compact, sandy-silty-clayey soil mixed with ferricrete pellets; *Layer-4*: yellowish-brown, comparatively hard, sandy-silty-clayey soil mixed with calcrete nodules and sparse ferricrete pellets.
4. Re-touched tools from the Mesolithic industries of the Middle Mahanadi Valley. Backed points (1-8), typical microlithic forms (9-23), burins (24-29), end scrapers (30-34) and awl (35).
5. Showing various scrapers (1-5), denticulates (6 & 7), notches (8-11) and blade/bladelet cores (12-17).
6. Re-touched thin pebbles from the Mesolithic sites of the Middle Mahanadi Valley.
7. Anvils (?) with flat ground face/faces with or without a dimple at the middle (1-3), bored stones (4 and 5).
8. Narrow, elongated choppers of "Group-A".
9. Choppers of "Group-B".
10. Choppers of "Group-C".
11. Distribution of Black-and-red ware settlements and excavated sites in the central part of the Middle Mahanadi Valley. The excavated sites are 1-Khajeriapali, 2-Hikudi, 3-Manamunda, 4-Khameswaripali, 5-Kumersingha, 8-Nuagarh, and 7-Kurumpadar.

12. Excavated section (facing south) in Trench-I at Hikudi, *Layer-1*: light-brown, loose sandy-silty; *Layer-2*: compact, greyish-black, silty-clayey soil; *Layer-3*: same as above; *Layer-4*: compact, yellowish-grey, silty-clayey soil with sparse distribution of ferricrete pellets.
13. Excavated section (facing east) in Trench-II at Hikudi. *Layer-1*: compact, yellowish– grey, silty-clayey soil with loose ferricretes; *Layer-2*: same as above but more dark in colour.
14. Representative shapes in the cord-impressed potteries from Trench-II at Hikudi.
15. Cord-impressed potteries from Trench-II at Hikudi.
16. Representative shapes in the white-painted (1-19) and plain (20-24) Black-and-red ware potteries of *Period-IA* (Chalcolithic) from Khameswaripali.
17. Ceramic types of *Period-IB* (Chalcolithic) from Khameswaripali. Black-and-red ware (1-14), black slipped ware (15), burnished Black ware (16 and 17), Red slipped ware (18-27) and plain Red ware (28-31).
18. Shapes from *Period-II* (Late Chalcolithic) at Khameswaripali. Black-and-red ware (1-6), burnished Black ware (7), Red slipped ware (8-11), and plain Red ware (12-13).
19. Various small finds from the Chalcolithic levels at Khameswaripali. *Period-IA*: bone points (1-4), stone disc (5), ground axe (6), terracotta spindle whorl (7), stone bead (8), shell pendant (9), shell blade (10); *Period-IB*: tanged bone points (11-13), ivory bangle (14), pottery disc (15); *Period-II*: bone spear-head (16) and pottery discs (17 and 18).
20. Excavated section (facing west) in Trench-II at Khajeriapali. *Layer-1*: dark-grey, compact, sandy-silty-clayey soil; *Layer-2*: greyish-yellow, sandy-silty-clayey soil.
21. Excavated section (facing north) in Trench-II at Kumersingha. *Layer-1*: greyish-brown, loose, sandy-silty soil; *Layer-2*: compact, dark grey, sandy-silty-clayey; *Layer-3*: same as above; *Layer-4*: slightly compact, greyish-yellow, sandy-silty-clayey soil with patches of ash and charcoal; *Layer-5*: same as above; *Layer-6*: loose, yellowish-brown, sandy silty soil with patches of ash and charcoal; *Layer-7*: same as above but very loose in texture.
22. Important pottery shapes of *Period-IA* from Kumersingha. Black-and-red ware (1-9), black slipped ware (10-22), Red slipped ware (23-32), and plain Red ware (33 and 34).
23. Graffiti marks on potteries from Kumersingha. *Period-IA*: 1-3 on black slipped ware; *Period-IB*: 4 and 5 on black slipped ware, 6 on Red slipped ware and 7-15 on Black-and-red ware; *Period-II*: 16-21 on Black-and-red ware.
24. Representative potteries of *Period-IB* from Kumersingha. Black-and-red ware (1-5), black slipped ware (6-16), Red slipped ware (17 and 18), and plain Red ware (19-23).
25. Select shapes of *Period-II* from Kumersingha. Black-and-red ware (1-4), black slipped ware (5-8), Red slipped ware (9-11) and plain Red ware (12-15).

26. Excavated section (facing south) in Trench-I at Kurumpadar. *Layer-1*: brownish, loose, sandy-silty soil; *Layer-2*: brownish-grey, slightly compact, sandy-silty; *Layer-3*: same as above; *Layer-4*: dark-grey, compact, silty-clayey soil; *Layer-5*: same as above; *Layer-7*: yellowish-grey, slightly compact, sandy-silty; *Layer-8*: ashy-grey, loose, sandy-silty soil.
27. Representative shapes of *Period-I* from Kurumpadar. Black-and-red ware (1-7), Red slipped ware (8-10) and plain Red ware (11 and 12).
28. Graffiti marks on potteries from Kurumpadar. *Period-I*: 1 on burnished Black ware, 2 on Black-and-red ware; *Period-II*: 3-12 on Black-and-red ware, 13-16 on black slipped ware; *Period-III*: 17 on plain Red ware.
29. Representative potteries of *Period-II* from Kurumpadar. Black-and-red ware (1-3), black slipped ware (4-6), Red slipped ware (7-10) and plain Red ware (11-13).
30. Select shapes of *Period-III* from Kurumpadar. Black-and-red ware (1-3), black slipped ware (4 and 5), Red slipped ware (6-9) and plain Red ware (10 and 11).

Plates

I. A cluster of Mesolithic artefacts lying exposed on the erosional surface at Burla.
II. A cluster of Mesolithic artefacts lying exposed on the erosional surface at Burla.
III. A chopper knapping spot, lying exposed on the erosional surface at Burla.
IV. A chopper knapping spot, lying exposed on the erosional surface at Burla.
V. Showing a dense cluster of celt-dressing waste and semi-finished celts near a dolerite dyke at Lahanda site.
VI. A general view of the exposed granodiorite rock at the Neolithic quarry-based celt production site of Hirakud.
VII. A closer view of the quarry area of milonitic rocks for celt production at Hirakud.
VIII. A Neolithic pottery from Hikudi, showing vertical cording pattern on its outer surface.
IX. A Neolithic pottery from Hikudi, showing slanting cord marks on its outer surface.
X. Neolithic sherds from Hikudi, showing cord impressions on the inner surface.
XI to XVI. Neolithic cord-impressed potteries from Hikudi, showing various types of decorative patterns on their shoulder part.

EXCAVATIONS AT NUAGARH-ASURGARH : A PRELIMINARY REPORT

Figures

1. Map of Orissa showing excavated Asurgarh sites.
2. Excavated section facing west to trench NGH-I.
3. Red slipped ware: 1- Layer (1), 2-9 Layer (2), 10-12 Layers (3), 13-14 Layer (4), 15-16 Layer (5).

4. Red ware: 1-7 Layer (2), 8-11 Layer (3) & 12-15 Layers (4).
5. Black slipped ware: 1-8 Layer (2), 9-13 Layer (3) & 14-15 Layer (4).
6. Black-and-red ware: 1-6 Layer (2), 7-11 Layer (3), 12-14 Layer (4) & 15-16 Layer (5).
7. Painted pottery: 1 & 2 white painting on Red ware, 3, 4, 5, 9 white painting on Red slipped ware, 6 white painting on black slipped ware, 7 black painting on Black-and-red ware & 8 ochre painting on Red ware.
8. Graffiti marks in potteries: A - Red slipped ware, B - black slipped ware, C - Black-and-red ware.
9. Knobbed lids.

TEMPLES OF WESTERN ORISSA

Figures

1. Kartikeya, Charada Temple.
2. Ground plan of Kosalesvara Temple, Baidyanath; Courtesy-Prof. D.R. Das, Calcutta.
3. Ground plan of Kosalesvara Temple, Charada; Courtesy-Prof. D.R. Das, Calcutta.
4. Profile of Kosalesvara Temple, Charada; Courtesy-Prof. D.R. Das, Calcutta.
5. Ganesa, Charada Temple.
6. Sectional Elevation of Somesvara Temple, Ranipur-Jarial; Courtesy-Prof. D.R. Das, Calcutta.
7. Ground plan, Somesvara Temple, Ranipur-Jarial; Courtesy-Prof. D.R. Das, Calcutta.
8. Nataraja, Charada Temple.
9. Harihara, Charada Temple.
10. Alasakanya, Charada Temple.
11. Ground plan of Narasimhanath Temple, Narasimhanath; Courtesy-Prof. D.R. Das, Calcutta.

Plates

1. Leaning Temple of Huma.
2. Ganesa, Gopalji Temple.
3. Gopalji Temple, Sambalpur.
4. Nrisimha, Gopalji Temple.
5. Ten armed Nataraja, Gopalji Temple.
6. Kapilesvara Temple, Charada.
7. Twenty armed Durga, N.K. Sahu, Museum.
8. Goddess Samalai, Sambalpur.
9. Samalai Temple, Sambalpur.
10. Narsinghnath Temple, Narsinghnath.
11. Indralath Temple, Ranipur-Jharial.
12. Baudh Temple, Baudh.

13. Ananta Sayana, Gopalji Temple, Sambalpur.
14. Statue of Bansigopal, Gopalji Temple, Sambalpur.
15. Khakhara Temple, Ranipur-Jharial.
16. Liyahari Temple, Ranipur-Jharial.
17. Lingam, Baudh Temple, Baudh.
18. Tapasvini Parvati, Patnagarh.
19. Somesvara Temple, Ranipur-Jharial.

INVESTIGATIONS INTO THE MESOLITHIC AND POST-MESOLITHIC SETTLEMENTS IN THE MIDDLE MAHANADI VALLEY, ORISSA

Pradeep K. Behera

INTRODUCTION

Physiographically, the Middle Mahanadi Valley lies between the northern uplands and the south-western hilly regions of Orissa highlands[1] and stretches from the Hirakud dam reservoir to about the Tikarparha gorge (Fig. 1). Geographically, it is a transitional zone between the Chhattisgarh plains and the coastal plains of Orissa. The area, characterized by sub-tropical climate with medium to high annual rainfall (average, 1500 mm), is a self contained geographical entity which probably had sufficient range of ecological variability providing the year-round requirements of the nomadic hunter-gatherers and sedentary communities of the Late Quaternary Era. Even today the area provides an extensive and varied resource base to the present populations for its diet and other consumption requirements. A review of archaeological literatures, however, revealed the region to be largely *terra incognita*. Although a few Pre-historic and Early Historical sites had been reported earlier,[2] no systematic investigation in the Middle Mahanadi Valley had ever been attempted from a regional perspective. In view of this, the recent archaeological investigation conducted by the author during 1995-2000 in the Middle Mahanadi Valley of Orissa with evidence for cultural succession right from the Mesolithic to the Early Historical Period becomes significant. The study, backed by systematic exploration and a series of test excavations, resulted in the discovery of a large number of Mesolithic open air sites, Neolithic celt production and habitation sites, and settlement sites of Proto-historic, Iron Age and Early Historical Periods. Since detailed studies from multi-disciplinary perspectives are underway, only a preliminary account of the results obtained so far, is being presented in the following pages.

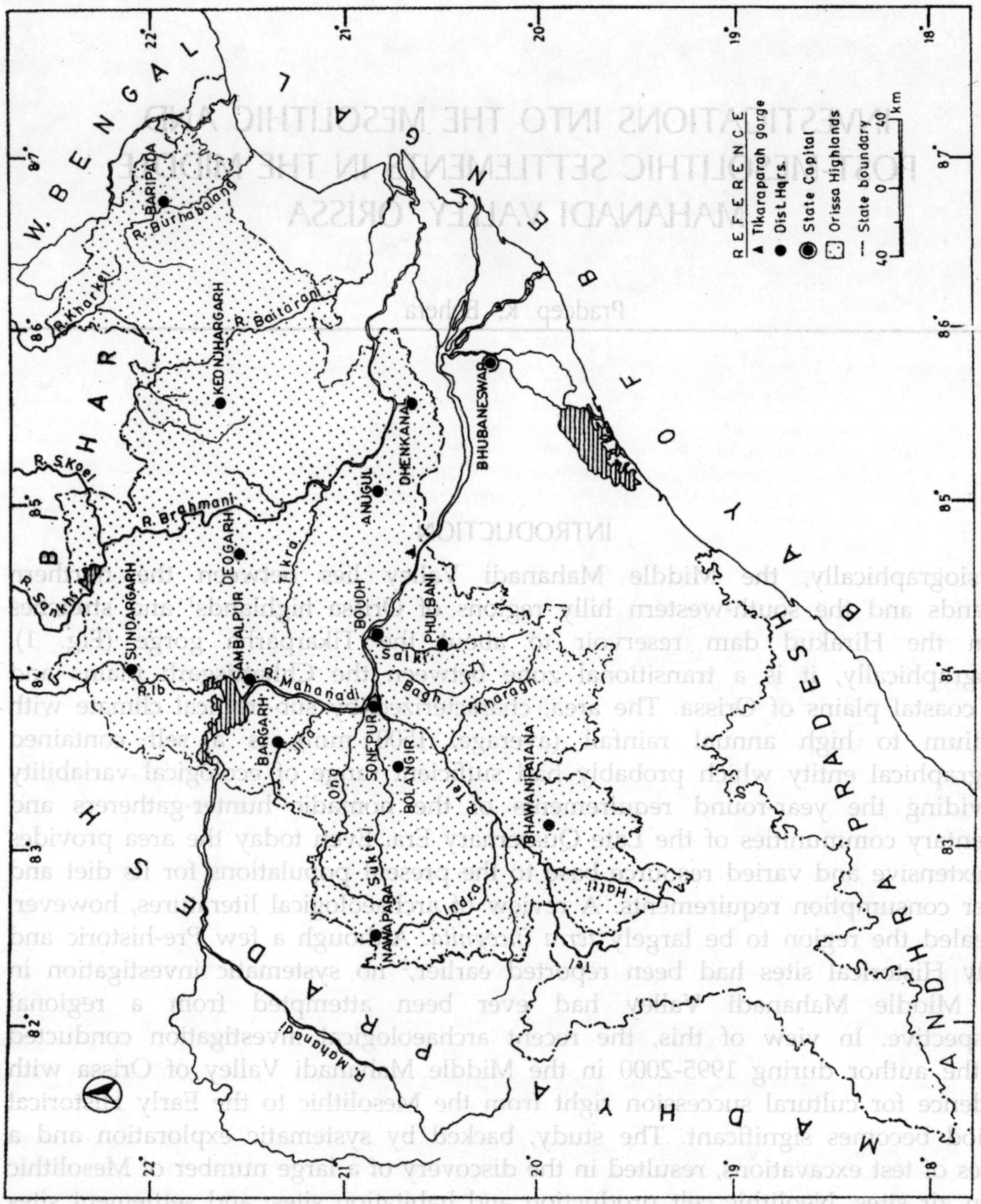

Fig. 1 Map showing the position of the Middle Mahanadi Valley in Orissa highlands.

THE MESOLITHIC SITES

Systematic exploration in the upper part of the Middle Mahanadi Valley (between Hirakud and Binka towns) for over four seasons have led to the discovery of a large number of open air sites with evidence for varying concentration and dimension of lithic artefact scatters, representing temporary as well as base camps of the Mesolithic people. Located mostly on the cliff surface of the Mahanadi and its major ancillary tracks, the majority of the sites discovered is primary in nature and still preserve habitation deposit. There are also a few open air sites located at the foot of the hills lying close to the Mahanadi. Our investigation reveals the existence of two different lithic components within the Mesolithic assemblages of the area. They are represented by microliths (both geometric and non-geometric) and heavy-duty artefacts like various types of pebble-cobble choppers, retouched thin pebbles, querns, hand-stones, ring-stones, anvils and hammers.

In order to determine the nature of the Post-Pleistocene lithic industries of the area and their geo-stratigraphic context, assemblages form seven major localities, viz, Burla, Hirakud, Kirba, Durgapali, Jharapali, Kardola and Bajpur (Fig. 2) were subjected to detailed study. Of the seven localities, trial digging was carried out at Burla to determine the stratigraphic context of the Mesolithic assemblages. The site-wise description of lithic assemblages is briefly outlined below.

I. Burla

Located on the cliff surface of the right bank of the Mahanadi, Burla is an extensive Mesolithic site. The site is situated little less than half a kilometer south-east of the Hirakud dam and about two kilometers north-west of the nearest Burla town. It is indeed a factory-cum-base camp site, littered with thousands of artefacts lying on the undulating erosional surface of a compact reddish-brown, sandy-silty-clayey soil (Pl. I & II). The artefactual scatters spread over an area of about one square kilometer and occur in the form of small to large clusters, each of which contains varying number of cores, core-dressing flakes, blades, bladelets, finished and semi-finished tools, hammers, anvils, heavy-duty tools, a good number of unmodified raw materials and large debris. Almost all the exposed artefacts are in mint fresh condition and it appears from the presence of several conjoinable specimens that the site has not undergone any major post-depositional disturbances.

With a view to ascertain the stratigraphic context of the surface scatter, a small trench, measuring 2 m x 2 m, was excavated on the undisturbed surface of the site. The objective was fairly achieved and a total of 23 artefacts was recovered at a depth of 58 cm from the upper part of a thick deposit of reddish-brown coloured, compact, sandy-silty-clayey soil mixed with loose ferricretes (Fig. 3). The thickness of this deposit measures between 15 cm to 20 cm. This layer is overlained by a 3 cm to 5 cm thin cover of whitish fine sand, over which lies 44-54 cm thick layer of reddish-brown coloured, loose silty-sandy soil. The dense concentration of ferricretes in the implementiferous stratum gradually

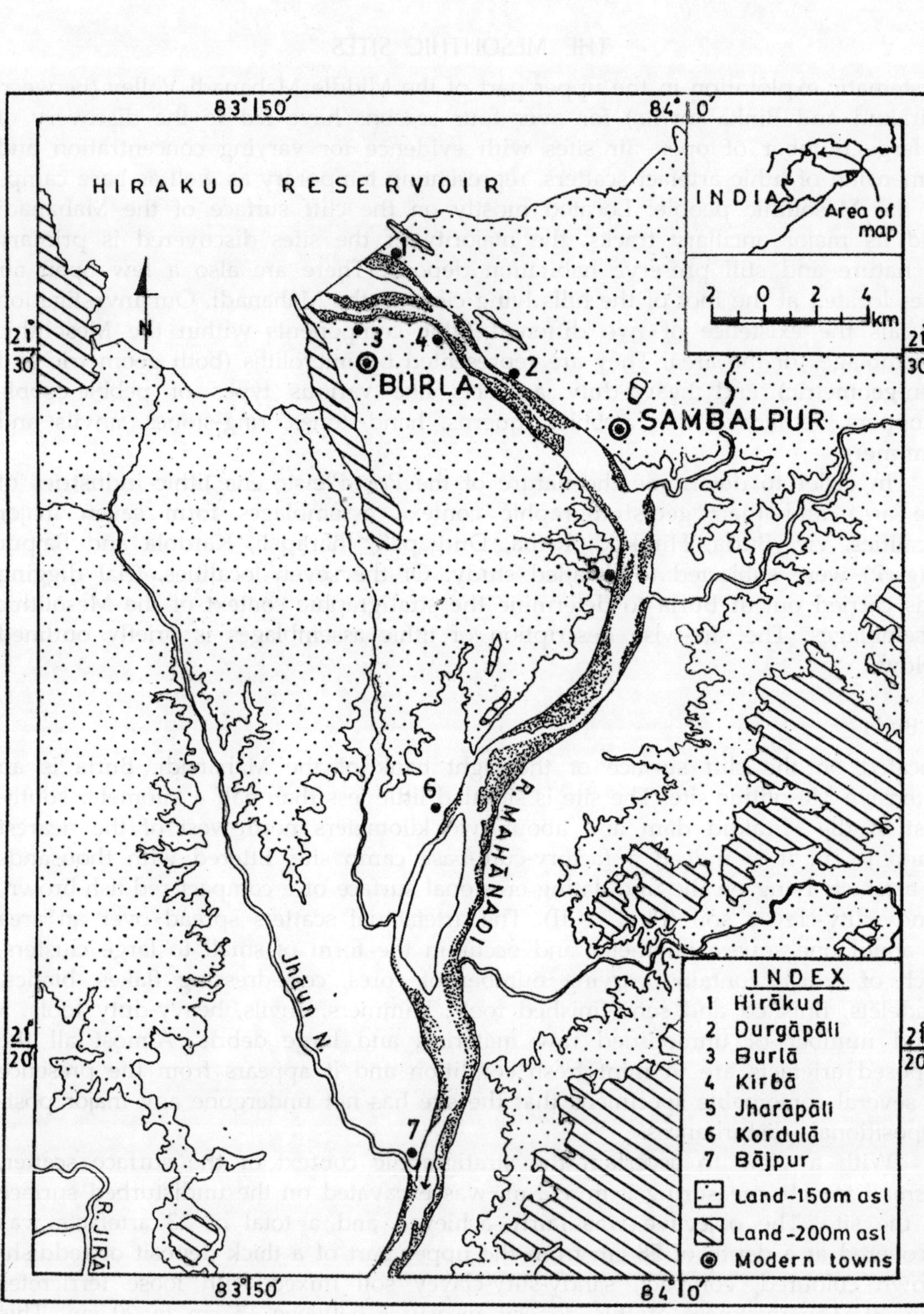

Fig. 2. Showing distribution of Mesolithic sites in the upper part of the Middle Mahanadi Valley.

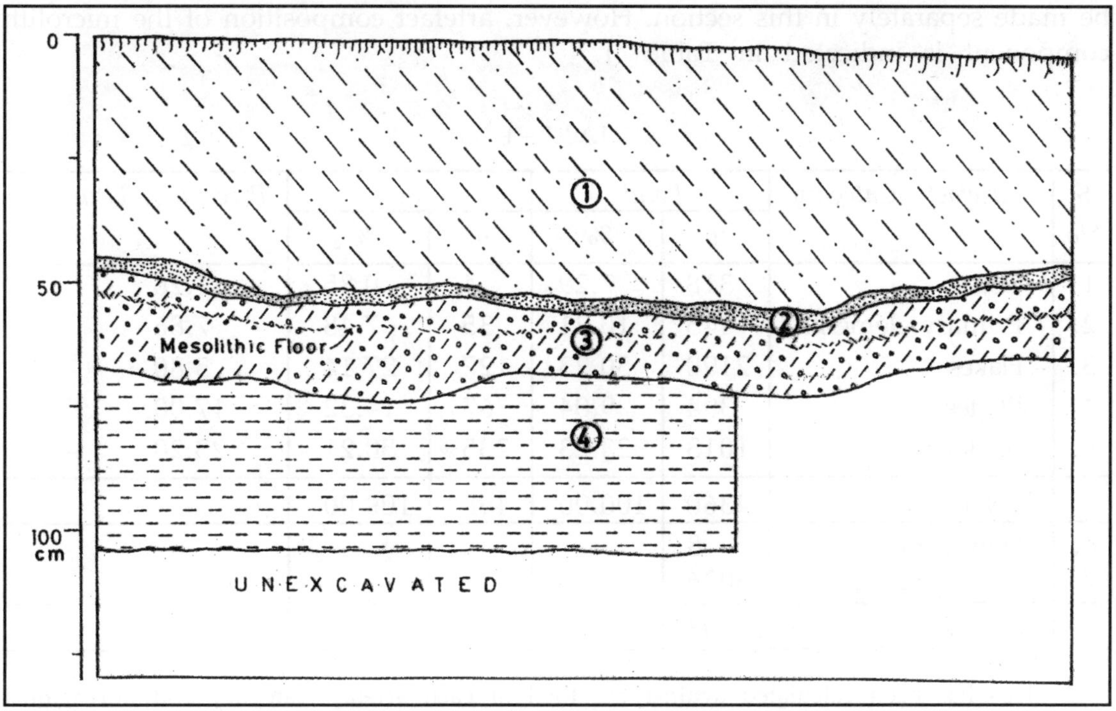

Fig. 3. Excavated section (facing north) in Trench-I at Burla. *Layer-1*: Reddish-brown, loose, silty-sandy; *Layer-2*: Very loose, whitish fine-sand; *Layer-3*: reddish-brown, compact, sandy-silty-clayey soil mixed with ferricrete pellets; *Layer-4*: yellowish-brown, comparatively hard, sandy-silty-clayey soil mixed with calcrete nodules and sparse ferricrete pellets.

decreases when one goes deeper into the underlying thick deposit of yellowish-brown, sandy-silty-clayey soil mixed with calcium carbonate nodules. It is worthwhile to note here that the nature of the implementiferous stratum found at this site, is to a large extent similar to that found at the Mesolithic site of Khomananta in the Boudh district of Orissa.[3]

The assemblage recovered from the trench comprised two bladelet cores, six flakes, eight bladelets, one cobble chopper, one hammer and five chips. Besides the above, the floor also contained two post-holes. The trial digging at Burla not only provided the stratigraphic context of the surface scatters, it also firmly confirmed the co-occurrence of microliths and pebble-cobble chopper in the Mesolithic industries of the Middle Mahanadi Valley. Sites with similar composition have also been reported from other localities of Orissa highlands.[4]

Since the number of artefacts acquired from the limited probing was too small for any meaningful analysis, artefacts were randomly sampled from a small part (measuring 150 m x 150 m area) of the exposed surface of the site for a detailed techno-typological study.

A study of 7653 specimens were collected from the surface of the sampled area. Two hundred fifty nine specimens of these belong to the heavy-duty tool category and the rest 7394 fall in the group of microlith component. General discussion on the techno-typological features of both the above components will be made separately in this section. However, artefact composition of the microlith component is indicated in Table – 1.

TABLE – I

S. No.	Artefact Category	Total		Tool		Percentage Utilized*
		n	%	*n*	%	
1.	Cores	318	7.29	4	0.85	1.26
2.	Primary elements	445	10.21	35	7.48	7.86
3.	Flakes	2190	50.23	127	27.14	5.80
4.	Blades	394	9.04	67	14.32	17.00
5.	Bladelets	1013	23.23	235	50.21	23.20
	Total	4360	100.00	468	100.00	
6.	Hammers	8				
7.	Chips/wastes	3026				
	Grand total	7394				

* This has been calculated against the total of each artefact category and not against the total number of artefacts of the assemblage.

The vast majority of the chipped stone artefacts of this site was produced on various types of rock, belonging to the group of crypto-crystalline silica, viz, chert, chalcedony, agate, milky-quartz and rock crystal, which are readily available in the gravel spread of the river Mahanadi. However, coarse-grained rocks like quartzite, argillite and dolerite were exclusively employed for manufacturing heavy-duty tools and hammers. Our study also reveals that almost all the stages of lithic reduction sequence, starting from raw materials selection to the tools production, were carried out at the site itself.

2. Hirakud

The Mesolithic site of Hirakud is located on the left bank of the Mahanadi and it is about half a kilometer east of the Hirakud Dam and about the same distance north-east of the Hirakud town. The site spreads over an area of about half a square kilometer. A total number of 2413 artefacts were randomly collected from the exposed surface of the sampled area, measuring 100 m x 100 m. Though the number of artefacts from this site is much less than those found at Burla, yet as far as techno-typology and stratigraphic context are concerned both the industries show striking similarities. Of the total number of specimens collected from Hirakud, 46 belong to pebble-cobble chopper category, while the rest fall in the microlith component. The macro-assemblage composition of the later component is indicated in Table – 2.

TABLE – 2

S. No.	Artefact Category	Total		Tool		Percentage Utilized*
		n	%	*n*	%	
1.	Cores	132	15.44	—	—	—
2.	Primary elements	131	15.32	—	—	—
3.	Flakes	349	40.82	29	43.94	8.31
4.	Blades	39	4.56	4	6.06	10.26
5.	Bladelets	204	23.86	33	50.00	16.18
	Totals	855	100.00	66	100.00	
6.	Hammers	3				
7.	Chips/wastes	1509				
	Total	2367				

Almost all the artefacts collected are in mint condition. The pattern of raw material exploitation and their use in the blank production are same as at Burla. While the heavy-duty tools are made of coarse-grained rocks like quartzite, argillite and dolerite, crypto-crystalline silica group of rocks are extensively used in the production of microlith component.

3. Kirba

The site is situated about four kilometers west of Burla on the right bank of the Mahanadi. Here, clusters of artefacts were found on the undulating, eroded surface of the cliff, which rises to a height of about seven meters from the surrounding plains. The lithic scatters spread over an area of about 300 square meters, of which only 50 m x 50 m surface area, selected for random sampling. A total of 2415 specimens were collected, of which 63 are pebble-cobble choppers and the rest fall in the category of microlith component. The macro-assemblage composition of the latter component is shown in Table – 3.

TABLE – 3

S. No.	Artefact Category	Total		Tool		Percentage Utilized*
		n	%	*n*	%	
1.	Cores	155	11.68	—	—	—
2.	Primary elements	173	13.04	17	11.33	9.83
3.	Flakes	534	40.24	47	31.33	8.80
4.	Blades	134	10.10	14	9.33	10.45
5.	Bladelets	331	24.94	72	48.00	21.75
	Total	1327	100.00	150	99.99	
6.	Hammers	5				
7.	Chips/wastes	1020				
	Grand total	2352				

The above table clearly reveals the factory site character of the assemblage. The artefacts have been fashioned out of locally available nodules and pebbles of crypto-crystalline silica group of rocks. But, in the manufacture of heavy-duty tools, including hammers, argillite and quartzite rocks were preferred.

4. Durgapali

The site of Durgapali is located about three kilometers south-east of Kirba, on the left bank of the Mahanadi. Here, artefacts were found on the eroded surface of a compact, sandy-clayey deposit mixed with loose pisolites. The lithic scatters, which occur in the form of several clusters, are spread over half a square kilometer area. Random sampling of artefacts was done from a small area, measuring 70 m x 70 m, which yielded a total of 2180 specimens. Except 21 cobble-choppers, the remaining lithic artefacts belong to the group of microlith component, the assemblage composition of which is shown in Table – 4.

TABLE – 4

S. No.	*Artefact Category*	*Total* n	*Total* %	*Tool* n	*Tool* %	*Percentage Utilized**
1.	Cores	202	15.07	—	—	—
2.	Primary elements	147	10.97	12	12.50	8.16
3.	Flakes	432	32.24	26	27.08	6.02
4.	Blades	76	5.67	4	4.17	5.26
5.	Bladelets	403	36.04	54	56.25	11.10
	Total	1340	99.99	96	100.00	
6.	Hammers	1				
7.	Chips/wastes	818				
	Grand total	2159				

All the specimens, barring cobble-choppers, which are of argillite and quartzite, are made of fine grained materials of the quartz group, like chert, chalcedony, agate, rock crystal, quartz and opal.

5. Jharapali

Situated at a distance of about eleven kilometers south-east of Durgapali, it is an extensive Mesolithic site spread over an area of little less than one square kilometer. The site is located by the side of the confluence of a streamlet and the right bank of the Mahanadi. Thick brownish coloured sandy-silt top-soil of the site has been completely eroded, leaving extensive patches of artefact-bearing stratum associated with loose pisolites. Artefacts were randomly collected from the surface of a small portion of the site, measuring 100 m x 100 m. The collection included 31 cobble-choppers, 3 ring stones and 4656 artefacts belonging to the microlith component. The assemblage composition of the latter component is indicated in Table – 5.

TABLE – 5

S. No.	Artefact Category	Total		Tool		Percentage Utilized*
		n	%	n	%	
1.	Cores	184	8.29	—	—	—
2.	Primary elements	252	11.35	23	9.20	9.13
3.	Flakes	1013	45.63	74	29.60	7.31
4.	Blades	228	10.27	31	12.40	13.60
5.	Bladelets	543	24.46	122	48.80	22.47
	Total	2220	100.00	250	100.00	
6.	Hammers	4				
7.	Chips/wastes	2432				
	Grand total	4656				

Once again it is a very rich factory-cum-base camp site with substantial evidence for the on-site production of tools. While there is hardly any difference between Jharapali and the preceding assemblages in the use of raw materials, particularly interesting is the occurrence of a ring stone made of Khondalite rock, the nearest source of which is located about 130-140 km south-west of the site in the upper Ong River Valley, a tributary of the Mahanadi. In all probability the ring stone appears to have been imported from the Ong Valley, which has also produced evidence for wide occurrence of Mesolithic sites.[5]

6. Kardola

The village Kardola is located about 12 km south-west of Jharapali on the right bank of the Mahanadi. The exact site is situated about half a kilometer north-east of the village. The exposed sections of the river at this place contains a gravel deposit of 50-80 cm thickness, lying directly on the weathered and undulating surface of the granite bed-rock. It is overlain by a thick and compact deposit of brownish coloured sandy-silty-clayey layer of 170-175 cm thickness with calcium carbonate nodules. The eroded surface of this deposit has exposed a large chunk of area with artefactual scatters spreading over an area of about 70 m x 70 m. The artefacts were found associated with loose ferricretes as at other sites. A total of 891 specimens were randomly collected from a small area, measuring 30 m x 30 m. These include five cobble-choppers made of quartzite and argillite. The macro assemblage composition of the microlith component is shown in Table – 6.

On-site production of microliths is sufficiently evident from the occurrence of a sizeable number of primary elements and waste products besides other artefact classes. At this site also the artefacts of the microlith component are made variously on chert, chalcedony, agate, red jasper and quartz.

TABLE – 6

S. No.	*Artefact Category*	*Total* n	*Total* %	*Tool* n	*Tool* %	*Percentage Utilized**
1.	Cores	76	16.31	—	—	—
2.	Primary elements	21	4.51	5	8.93	23.81
3.	Flakes	234	50.21	24	42.86	10.26
4.	Blades	56	12.02	8	14.29	11.29
5.	Bladelets	79	16.95	19	33.93	24.05
	Total	466	100.00	56	100.01	
6.	Chips/wastes	420				
	Grand total	886				

7. Bajpur

The Mesolithic site of Bajpur is located near the right bank of the Mahanadi and the left bank of a perennial stream called Jhaun. It is situated nearly 14 kilometers south of the site of Kardola and about two kilometers north-east of the village Bajpur. It is an extensive site spread over an area of little less than a kilometer. The artefactual scatters in the form of small to large clusters were found exposed on the eroded surface of the compact, brownish coloured sandy-silty-clayey deposit mixed with loose ferricretes. In respect of general topography, raw materials, and techno-typology, this industry closely resembles the preceding industries. A total of 2172 specimens, including 17 cobble-choppers, were randomly collected from the undulating surface (measuring 50 m x 50 m area) of the site. The assemblage composition of the microlith component in indicated in Table – 7.

TABLE – 7

S. No.	*Artefact Category*	*Total* n	*Total* %	*Tool* n	*Tool* %	*Percentage Utilized**
1.	Cores	87	8.81	—	—	—
2.	Primary elements	109	11.04	9	10.98	8.26
3.	Flakes	478	48.43	29	35.37	6.07
4.	Blades	76	7.70	17	20.73	22.37
5.	Bladelets	237	24.01	27	32.93	11.39
	Total	987	99.99	82	100.01	
6.	Hammers	5				
7.	Chips/wastes	1163				
	Grand total	2155				

Barring 17 cobble-choppers, which are made of argillite and quartzite, the specimens of the microlith component are manufactured out of crypto-crystalline silica group of raw materials.

The foregoing accounts bring out the general characteristic features of the Post-Pleistocene lithic industries of the Middle Mahanadi Valley of Orissa. The discussed assemblages represent factory-cum-base camp sites of the Mesolithic communities. The occurrence of heavy-duty pebble-cobble tools, mainly choppers, appears to be a typical feature of these assemblages. Industries with comparable features have a wider geographical distribution in the Orissa highlands.[6] Accessibility to the abundance of raw material for lithic tool production, suitable ecological niche, and environmental condition were some of the determinant factors which attracted the attention of the Mesolithic folks to inhabit the riverine tracts of the Mahanadi. Unfortunately, near absence of scientific data on the Post-Pleistocene environment and ecology of this region seriously impair reconstruction of Mesolithic adaptation in the Middle Mahanadi Valley. In view of this, our observations on the Mesolithic adaptation in the area of present study is largely based upon inter- as well as intra-site variability in lithic assemblage composition and data on present-day environments. We believe that variability in assemblage composition reflects different requirements felt by members of a single technological tradition as they carried out their varied task.

Our study of the assemblage composition from the seven select sites reveals the existence of two distinct typological components, viz, microliths and heavy-duty tools. We propose to describe both the components briefly in the following pages with a view to emphasize their techno-typological features.

The microlith component

The artefacts of this component are well represented in all the seven Mesolithic localities of the area under discussion. Despite some amount of intra-site displacement through natural erosion processes, most of the investigated sites are still in their original sedimentary context where the artefacts were fashioned and/or used and discarded. This is evident from the occurrence of several re-fitted specimens and concentrations of micro-flakelets (less than 5 mm in size), and also from the general mint fresh condition of the artefacts. In this respect, localities like Burla, Jharapali and Bajpur are the most well preserved ones.

The tables indicating macro assemblage composition (Table 1 to 7) clearly reveal that almost all the stages of lithic reduction sequence, starting from the selection of suitable raw materials to the tool production, were carried out at all the seven localities. This is evident from the occurrence of cores, core-dressing flakes, primary elements (flakes with 100% cortical portion), various types of blanks, raw materials and large amount of debris. The vast majority of the specimens were produced on the locally available nodules, pebbles, and cobbles of chert, chalcedony, agate, jasper, milky quartz and quartz crystals. These are generally seen on the gravel spread of the river Mahanadi. Probably, there were no constraints on the Mesolithic knappers for procuring raw materials. However, cores are seldom found fully exploited and very often they were discarded with slight or without any visible defects on their blank removal surface.

The blank detaching techniques adopted in the discussed assemblages are reflected by the presence of numerous blanks and cores. The lithic production is focused on bladelets, although flakes predominate the blank group. The large majority of the flakes seem to have been produced during the process of core reduction. This is particularly evident from the study of core types, among which bladelet cores form an overwhelming majority. There are only a few cores meant for true flake and blade production. Cores are typically single platform blade/ bladelet types, but those of opposed platform types are also fairly represented. In majority of the cases, nodules of varying sizes have been used as blanks for both bladelet and blade/bladelet cores. However, in certain other cases thick flakes or chunks have also been used for the above purpose.

Prepared unfaceted platforms are most common among the available core samples. The low incidence of core tablets is important in this context, since most of these unfaceted platforms were prepared by the removal of a simple flake, with the result that these platforms formed an acute angle with the blank removal surfaces and did not need any rejuvenation. The angle ranges mostly between 50° and 80°, suggesting thereby that the indirect percussion method was adopted for blank removal.[7] It should also be noted here that a sizeable number of cores in most of the localities were abandoned before the total periphery of the platform had been utilized. This appears to have occurred because of imperfections in either the core itself or in the flaking techniques, which mostly resulted in step or hinge fractures just below the platform on the blank removal surface.

Metric observation of length and width were taken on unbroken blanks of the discussed assemblages. While general length of blanks varies from 15 mm to as high as 85 mm, the mean length is microlithic (35.50 mm) and 92.7% measure less than 50 mm in length.

The vast majority of the retouched tools (Figs. 4 & 5) were produced on bladelets followed by flakes, blades and primary elements. Most retouched tools, although complete, do not accurately reflect original blank form because of intensive modifications made to length or width through retouch. The most striking typological feature is the predominance of larger tools, such as burins, notches, scrapers and denticulates, though the assemblages are Mesolithic (Table – 8). Among the backed tool variants arch-backed points are fairly well represented. The typical microlithic forms comprise lunates, triangles, trapezes and a solitary tranchet. Besides, there are a good number of elongated flakes, blades and bladelets containing marks of sickle gloss (?) along their lateral margins.

Heavy-duty tool component

This component comprises pebble-cobble choppers, retouched thin pebbles (Fig. 6), anvils with flat ground faces/face with a bored dimple at the middle (Fig. 7: 1-3), ring stones (Fig. 7: 4-5), hammers with battered ends, saddle querns and pestles/hand-stones. There is, however, considerable variability between sites. Among the heavy-duty tools unifacially-flaked choppers made on water worn

TABLE – 8

Sl. No.	Tool Types	Hirakud		Durgapali		Burla		Kirba		Jharapali		Kardola		Bajpur		Total	
		n	%	*n*	%	*n*	%	*n*	%	*n*	%	*n*	%	*n*	%	*n*	%
1.	Denticulate	2	3.03	4	4.17	49	10.47	13	8.67	22	8.80	9	16.07	6	7.32	105	8.99
2.	Retouched Notch	—	—	12	12.50	44	9.40	20	13.33	42	16.80	6	10.71	14	17.07	138	11.81
3.	Burin	14	21.21	21	21.87	59	12.61	17	11.33	34	13.60	8	14.29	23	28.05	176	15.07
	Totals	**16**	**24.24**	**37**	**38.54**	**152**	**32.48**	**50**	**33.33**	**98**	**39.20**	**23**	**41.07**	**43**	**52.44**	**419**	**35.87**
4.	End Scraper	7	10.61	9	9.37	24	5.13	9	6.00	20	8.00	4	7.14	3	3.66	76	6.51
5.	Side Scraper	2	3.03	6	6.25	13	2.78	7	4.67	3	1.20	1	1.79	3	3.66	35	2.99
6.	Transverse Scraper	—	—	—	—	11	2.35	—	—	1	0.40	1	1.79	—	—	13	1.11
7.	Unilaterally retouched margin	2	3.03	3	3.12	28	5.98	11	7.33	21	8.40	2	3.57	2	2.44	69	5.91
8.	Bilaterally retouched margins	1	1.51	1	1.04	30	6.41	—	—	2	0.80	—	—	—	—	34	2.91
9.	Bilaterally retouched point	1	1.51	—	—	3	0.64	2	1.33	—	—	—	—	—	—	6	0.51
	Totals	**13**	**19.70**	**19**	**19.79**	**109**	**23.29**	**29**	**19.33**	**47**	**18.80**	**8**	**14.29**	**8**	**9.76**	**233**	**19.95**
10.	Truncated Element	1	1.51	5	5.21	25	5.34	1	0.67	2	0.80	—	—	2	2.44	36	3.08
11.	Backed Point	12	18.18	11	11.46	41	8.76	23	15.33	36	14.40	8	14.29	7	8.54	138	11.81
12.	Other Backed Tool	3	4.55	2	2.08	18	3.85	3	2.00	7	2.80	2	3.57	2	2.44	37	3.17
	Totals	**16**	**24.24**	**18**	**18.75**	**84**	**17.95**	**27**	**18.00**	**45**	**18.00**	**10**	**17.86**	**11**	**13.41**	**211**	**18.06**
13.	Lunate	5	7.58	5	5.21	17	3.63	16	10.67	19	7.60	5	8.93	3	3.66	70	5.99
14.	Triangle	—	—	1	1.04	11	2.35	2	1.33	13	5.20	1	1.79	4	4.88	32	2.74
15.	Trapeze	1	1.51	—	—	6	1.28	1	0.67	4	1.60	1	1.79	1	1.22	14	1.20
16.	Tranchet	—	—	1	1.04	—	—	—	—	—	—	—	—	—	—	1	0.09
	Totals	**6**	**7.58**	**7**	**7.29**	**34**	**7.26**	**19**	**12.67**	**36**	**14.40**	**7**	**12.50**	**8**	**9.76**	**117**	**10.02**
17.	Borer/Awl	3	4.55	3	3.12	11	2.35	3	2.00	2	0.80	1	1.79	1	1.22	24	2.05
18.	Partially Retouched	8	12.12	10	10.42	50	10.68	19	12.67	13	5.20	4	7.14	10	12.19	114	9.76
19.	Partially Backed	4	6.06	2	2.08	28	5.98	3	2.00	9	3.60	3	5.36	1	1.22	50	4.28
	Grand Totals	**66**	**99.99**	**96**	**99.99**	**468**	**99.99**	**150**	**100.00**	**250**	**100.00**	**56**	**100.01**	**82**	**100.00**	**1168**	**99.99**

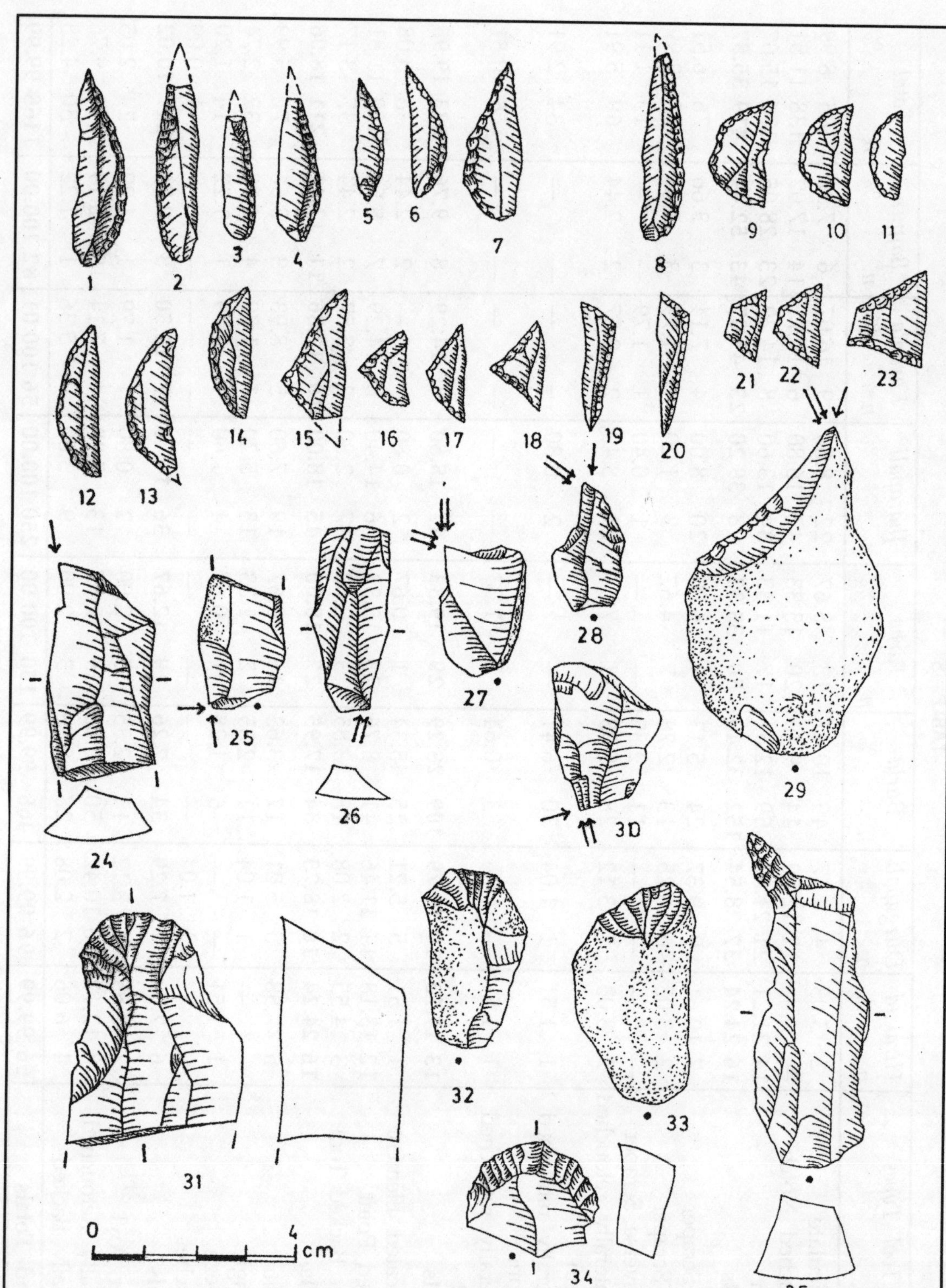

Fig. 4. Re-touched tools from the Mesolithic industries of the Middle Mahanadi Valley. Backed points (1-8), typical microlithic forms (9-23), burins (24-29), end scrapers (30-34) and awl (35).

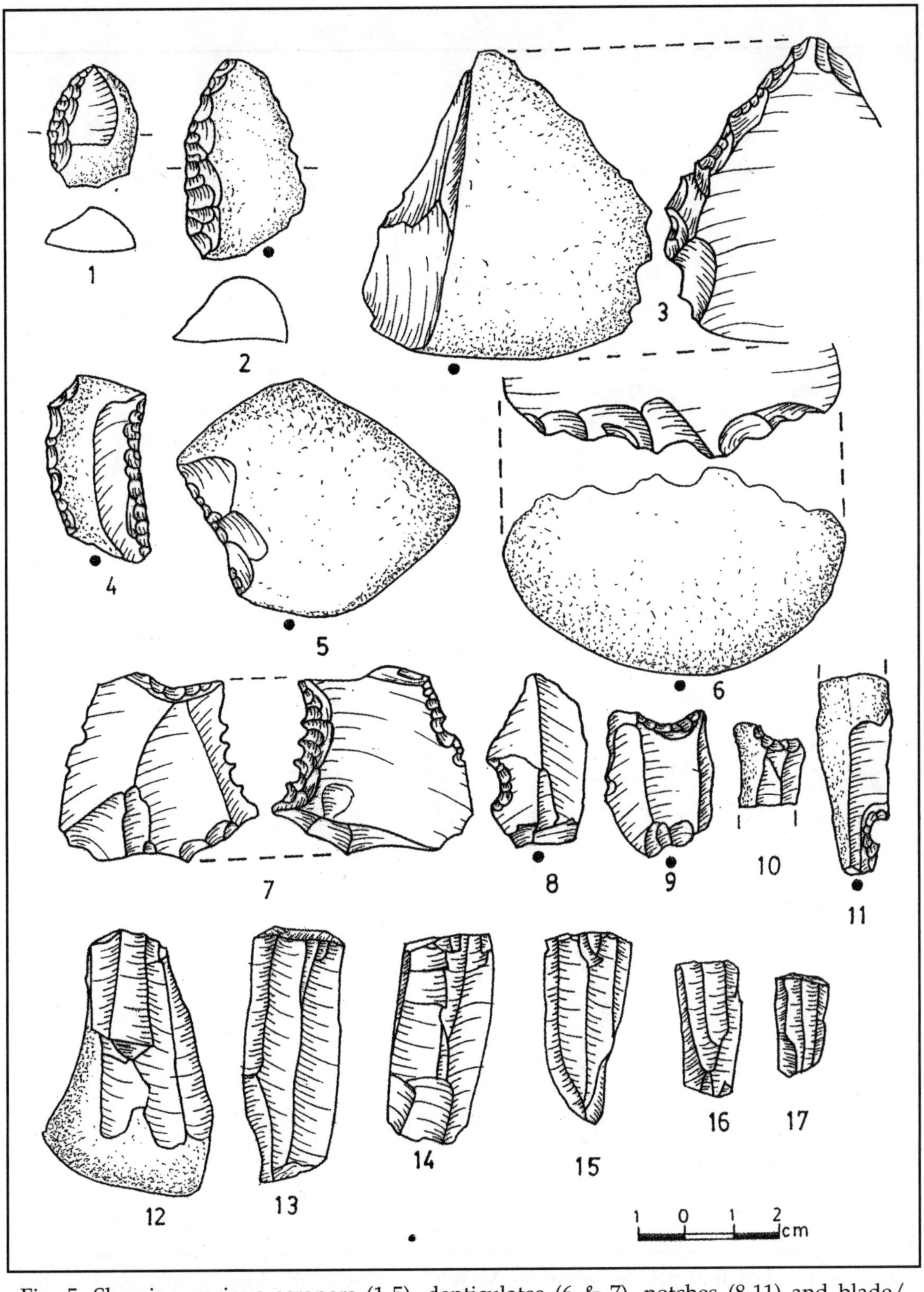

Fig. 5. Showing various scrapers (1-5), denticulates (6 & 7), notches (8-11) and blade/bladelet cores (12-17).

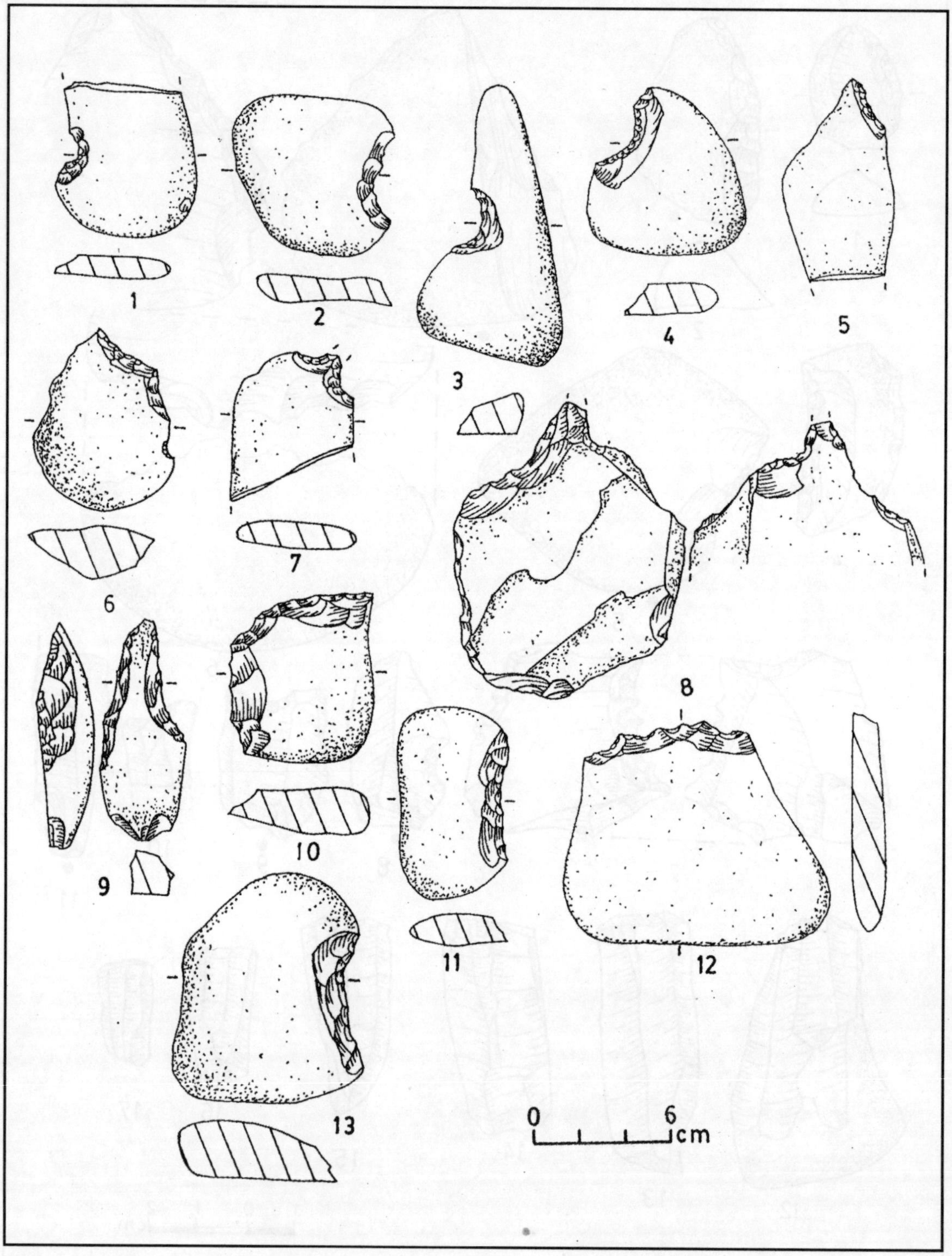

Fig. 6. Re-touched thin pebbles from the Mesolithic sites of the Middle Mahanadi Valley.

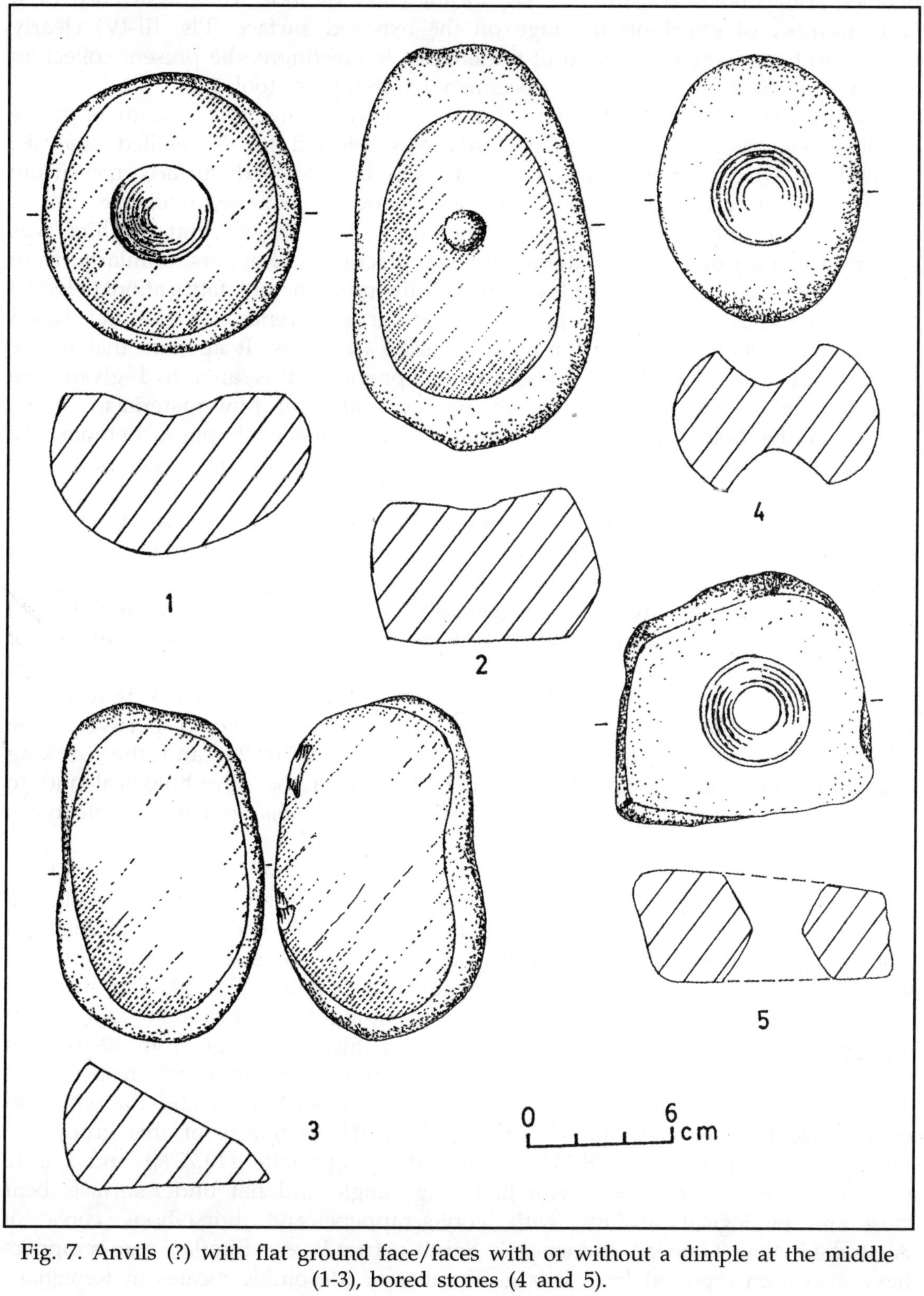

Fig. 7. Anvils (?) with flat ground face/faces with or without a dimple at the middle (1-3), bored stones (4 and 5).

pebbles and cobbles constitute a significant class of tool. The occurrence of a large number of struck-off debitage on the exposed surface (Pls. III-IV) clearly testifies to the on-site production of these tools. Interestingly, the present collection does not include even a single specimen of chopping tool.

With a view to elucidate the techno-typological characteristic features of the pebble-cobble choppers, the site of Burla was selected for a detailed analysis. A total of 231 specimens were sampled from the exposed surface, measuring 150 m x 150 m area. Of these 78.65% are made of argillite, while 18.18% of quartzite and only 2.16% of quartz materials. This shows that argillite was preferred against other raw materials for manufacturing choppers. Similarly, from the point of view of size, cobbles were mostly used in tool fabrication (89.61%) than pebbles (10.39%). There is also particular preference for the flat based cobbles and pebbles (70.13%) for manufacturing choppers. It appears that in the selection of blank forms, the Mesolithic knappers of this area had given due consideration to the type, form, size and suitability of raw materials.

From the point of view of technique, the available choppers demonstrate sophisticated workmanship and clever manipulation of the raw materials. Our study reveals variation in the size, shape, weight, cutting-edge angle and shape, and butt-end shape among the choppers. However, on the basis of breadth/ length ratio, the available choppers may be categorized into four broad groups as follows.

The choppers of Group-A are generally narrow-elongated in shape (Fig. 8) and their B/L ratio varies between 0.29 and 0.70. Out of a total number of 56 samples, as many as 53 are made of argillite, 2 of quartz and only 1 of quartzite. Their length, breadth and thickness vary from 86-173 mm (mean 121.91), 43-109 mm (mean 70.02) and 18.76 mm (mean 39.93), respectively. The weight ranges between 80 gm and 1930 gm (mean 509.23) and the working edge angle between 30° and 85° (mean 60.14). From the morphological and to some extent, functional points of view, most of these tools appear as proto types of Neolithic adzes and chisels.

In comparison to other chopper types, the percentage occurrence of tools belonging to Group-B is far more in almost all the Mesolithic sites investigated in the region. A total number of 147 specimens of this category were sampled from Burla. Their B/L ratio varies from 0.71 to 1.30. These are generally ovaloid to sub-rounded, rectangular and sub-triangular in outline (Fig. 9). The shape of the working edge varies from convex to straight, denticulated and rarely convergent or pointed. The length, breadth and thickness range from 40-160 mm (mean 90.23), 42-163 mm (mean 86.31) and 17-91 mm (mean 41.50), respectively. The weight varies between 72 gm and 2005 gm (mean 471.33) and the working-edge angle between 34° and 90° (mean 65.95). The artefacts of this group are mostly made of argillite (78.23%), followed by quartzite (19.73%) and quartz (2.04%). Many of these tools with high edge angle and flat under-surface, bear close morphological affinity with core-scrappers and horse-hoof cores of Australia,[8] New Guinea,[9] Indonesia,[10] South Africa,[11] etc. Similar core-scrappers have also been reported from a large number of Mesolithic locales in Keonjhar[12] and Phulbani[13] districts of highland Orissa.

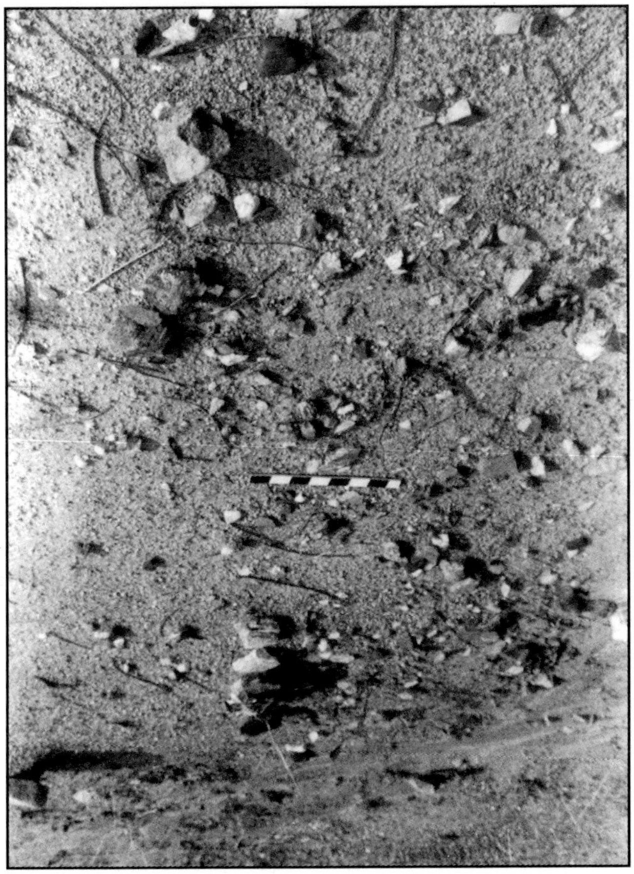

Pl. I. A cluster of Mesolithic artefacts lying exposed on the erosional surface at Burla.

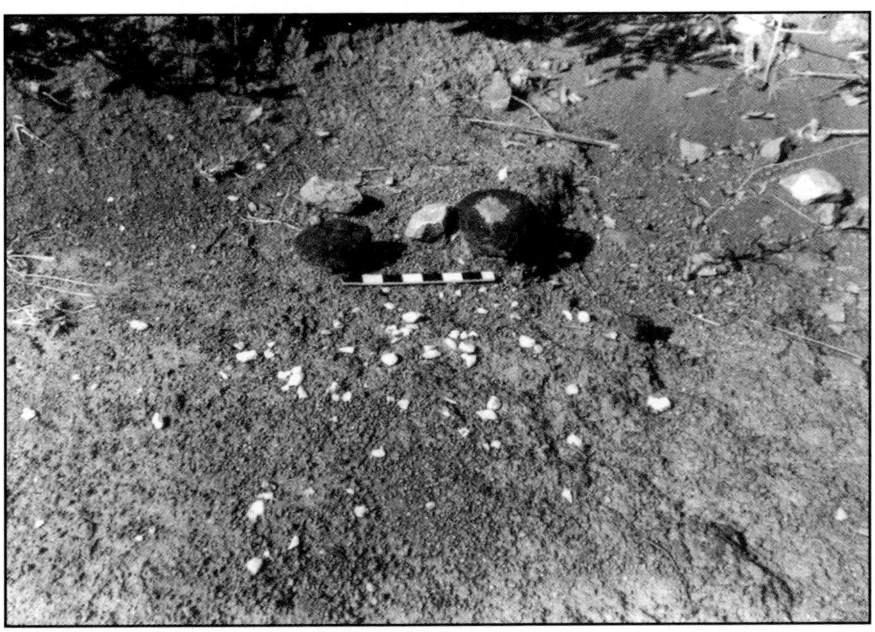

Pl. II. A cluster of Mesolithic artefacts lying exposed on the erosional surface at Burla.

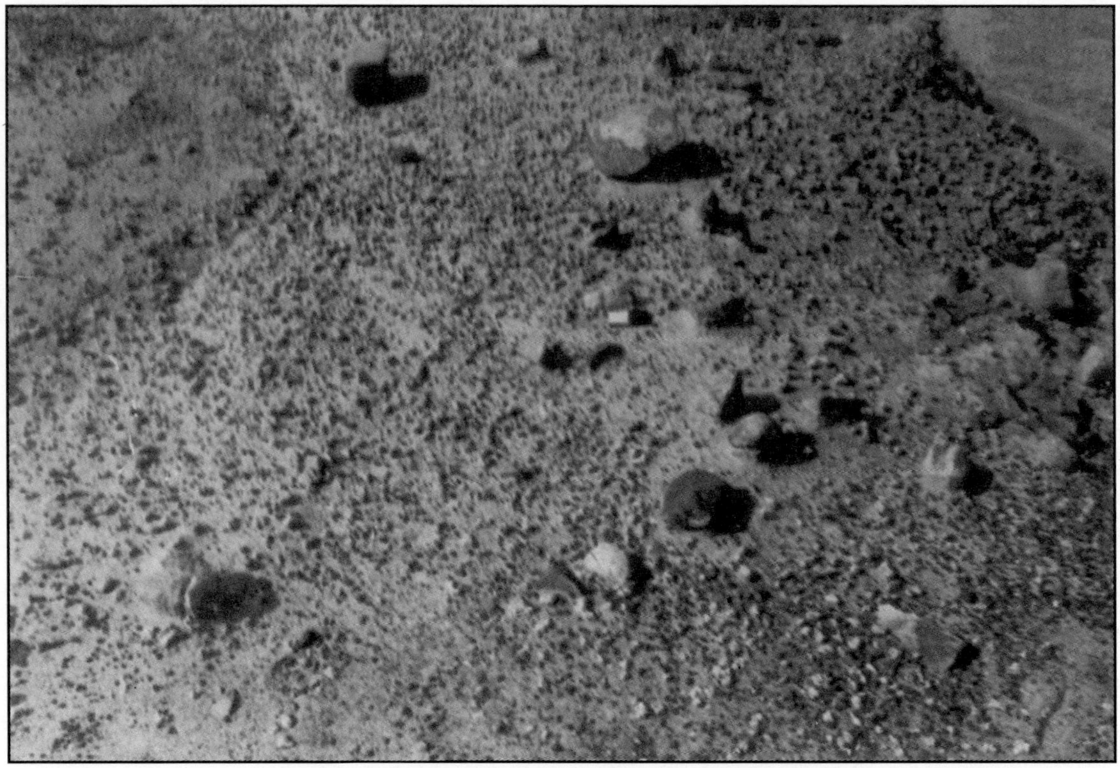

Pl. III. A chopper knapping spot, lying exposed on the erosional surface at Burla.

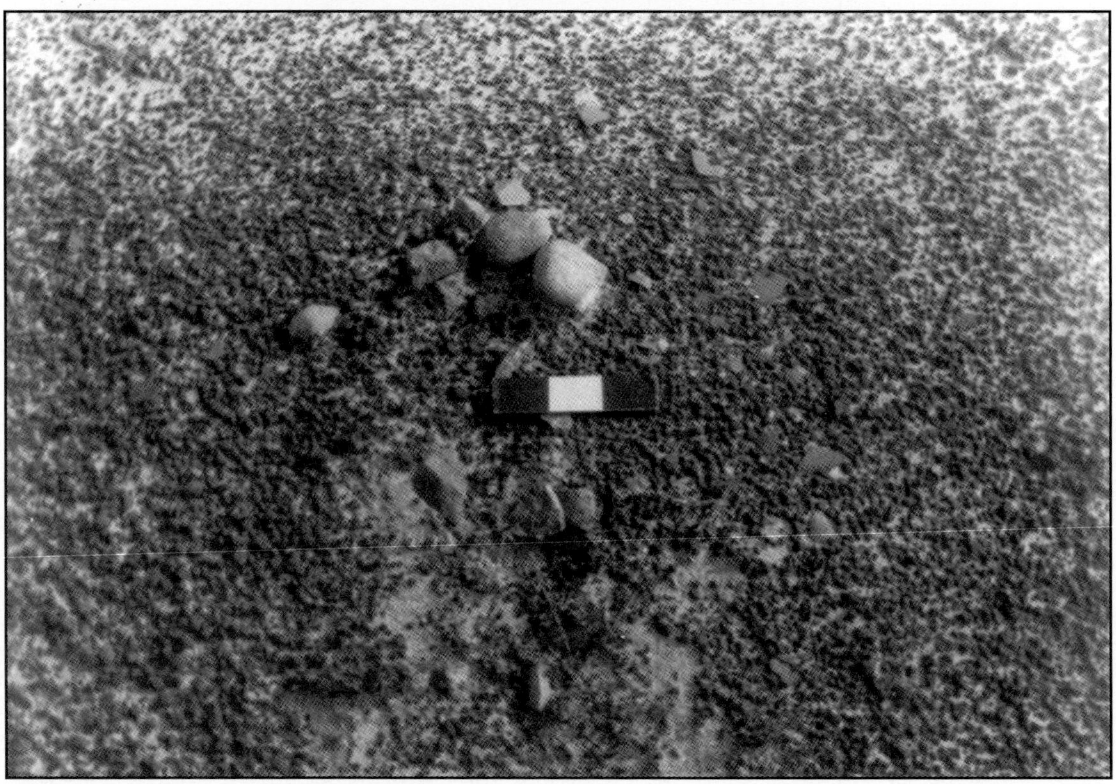

Pl. IV. A chopper knapping spot, lying exposed on the erosional surface at Burla.

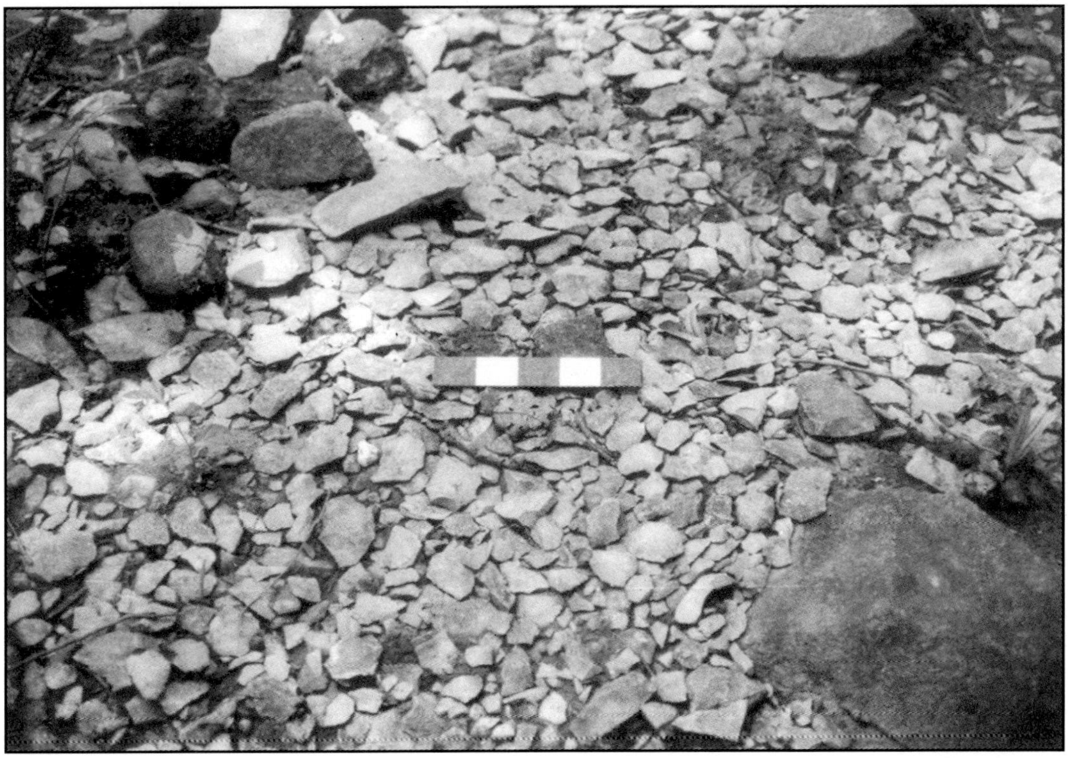

Pl. V. Showing a dense cluster of celt-dressing waste and semi-finished celts near a dolerite dyke at Lahanda site.

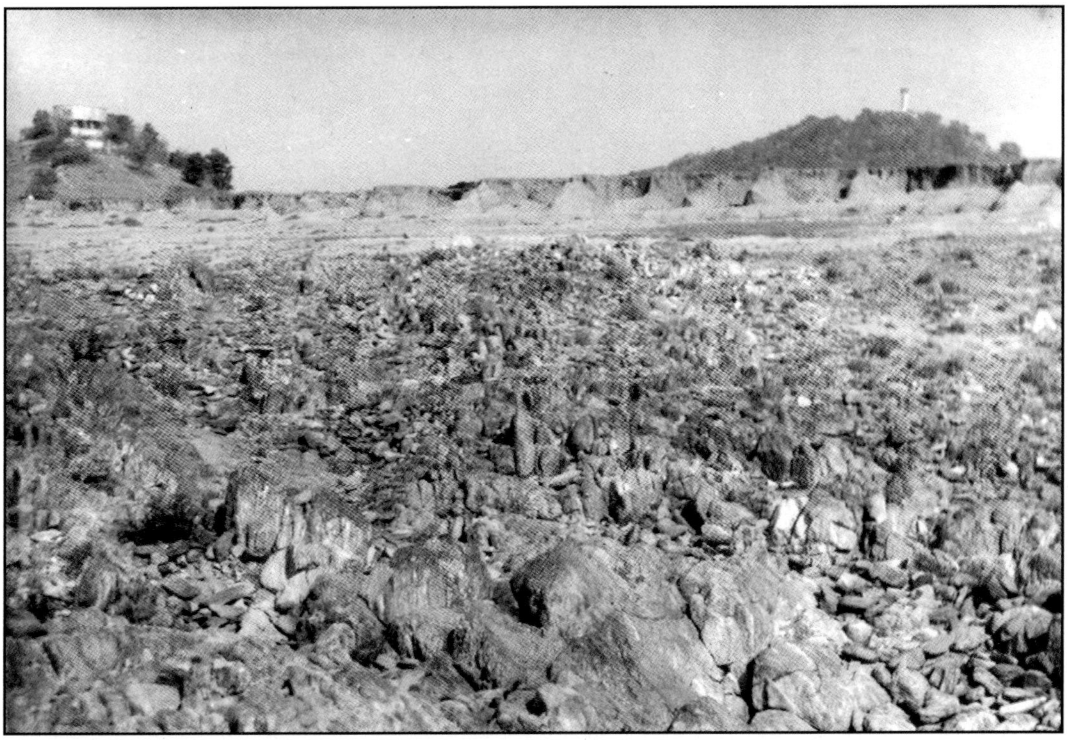

Pl. VI. A general view of the exposed granodiorite rock at the Neolithic quarry-based celt production site of Hirakud.

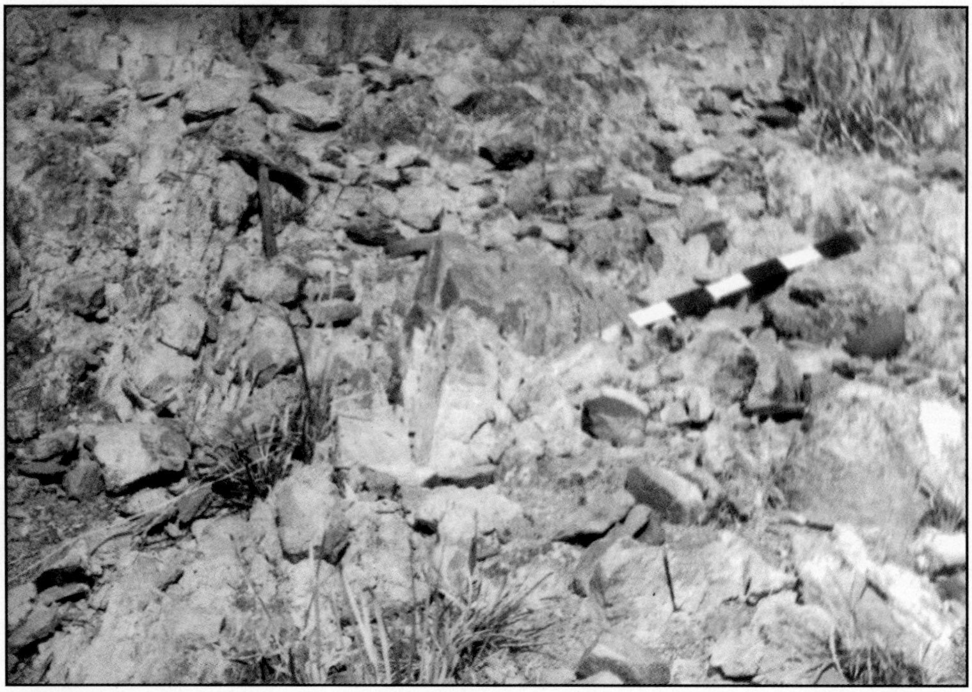

Pl. VII. A closer view of the quarry area of milonitic rocks for celt production at Hirakud.

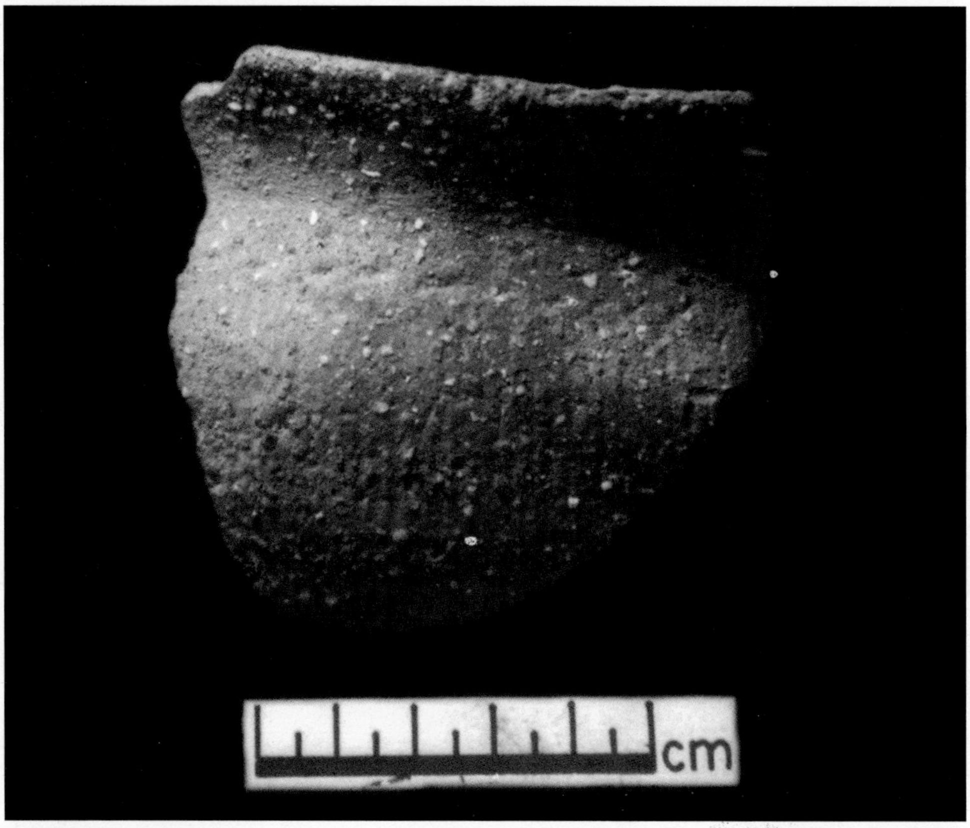

Pl. VIII. A Neolithic pottery from Hikudi, showing vertical cording pattern on its outer surface.

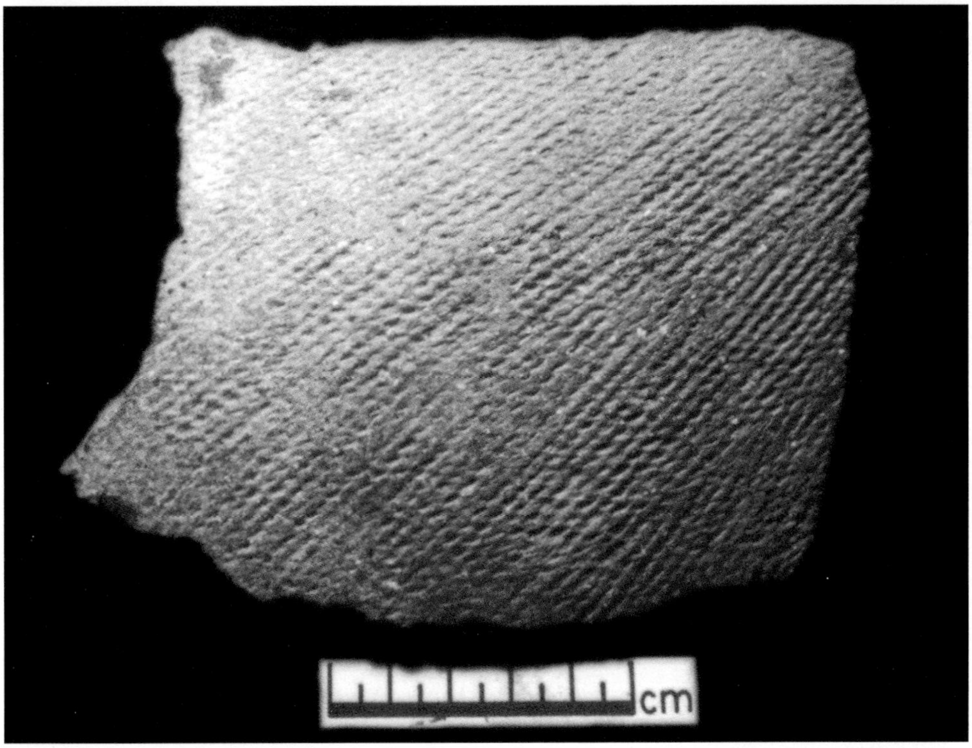

Pl. IX. A Neolithic pottery from Hikudi, showing slanting cord marks on its outer surface.

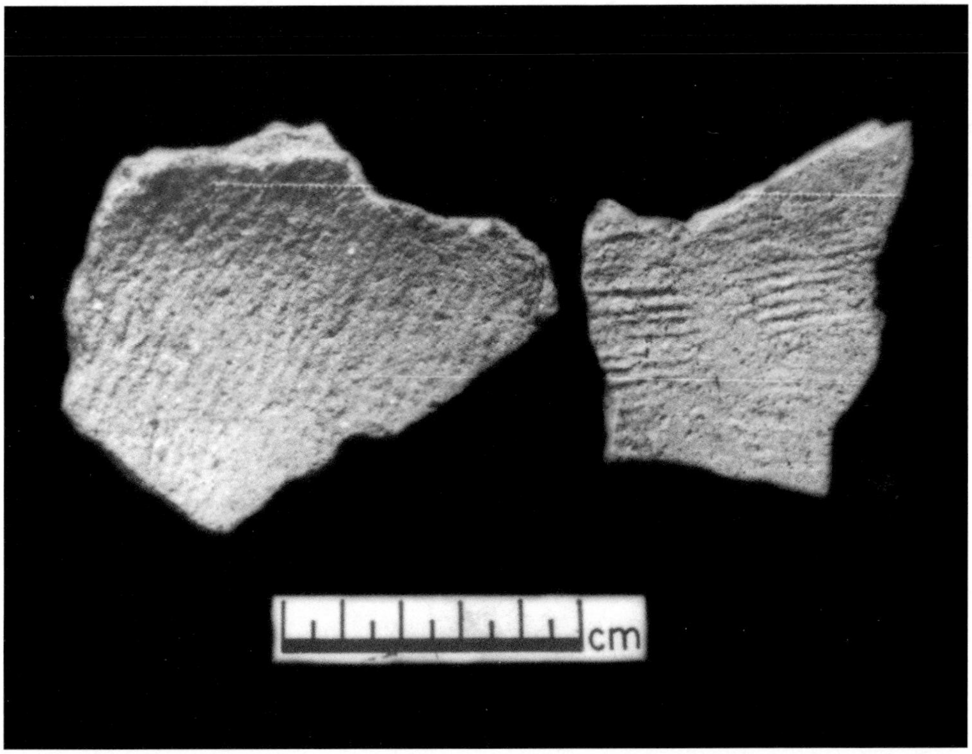

Pl. X. Neolithic sherds from Hikudi, showing cord impressions on the inner surface.

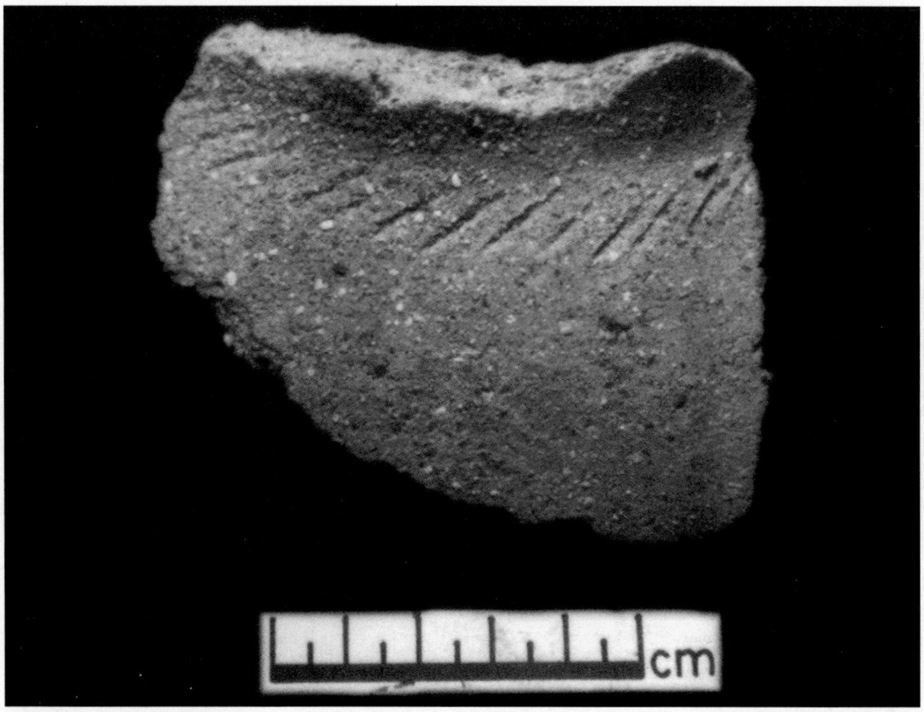

Pl. XI.

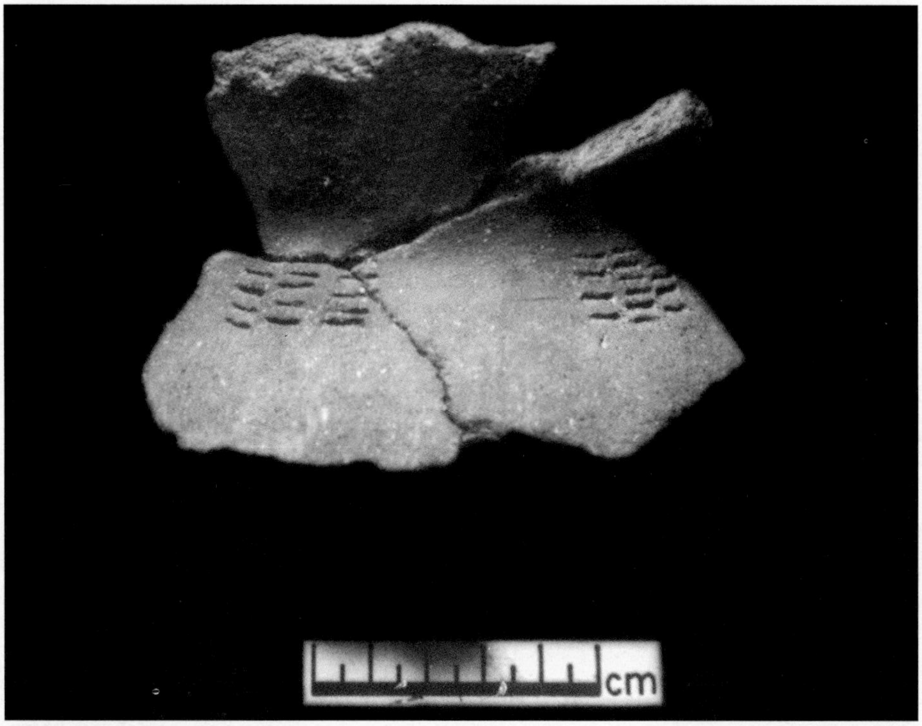

Pl. XII.

Pl. XI to XVI. Neolithic cord-impressed potteries from Hikudi, showing various types of decorative patterns on their shoulder part.

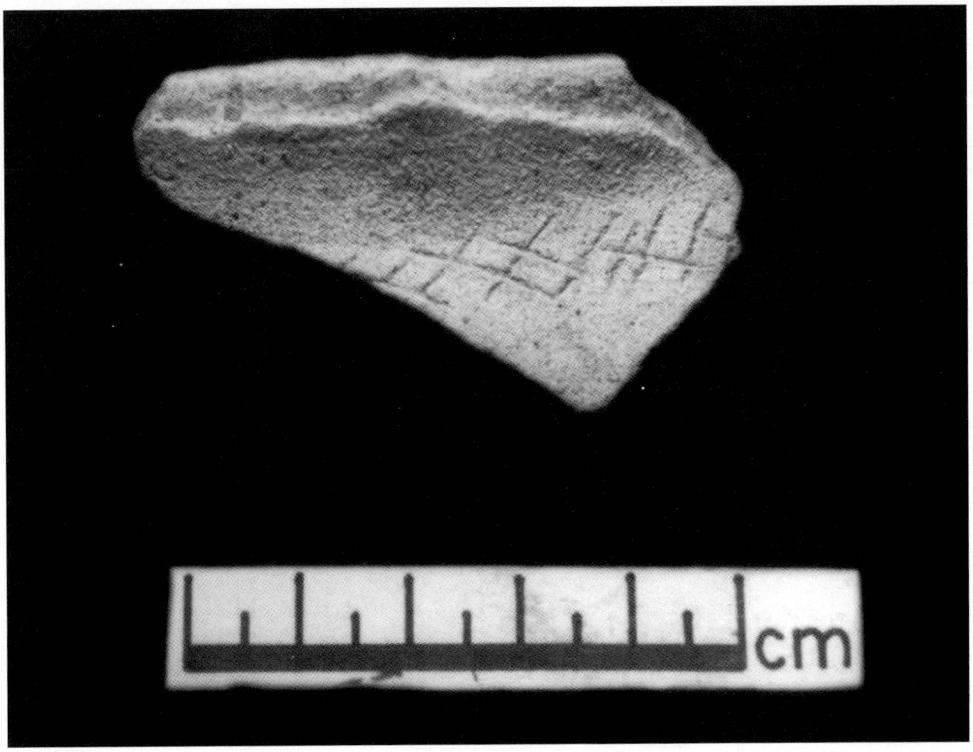

Pl. XIII.

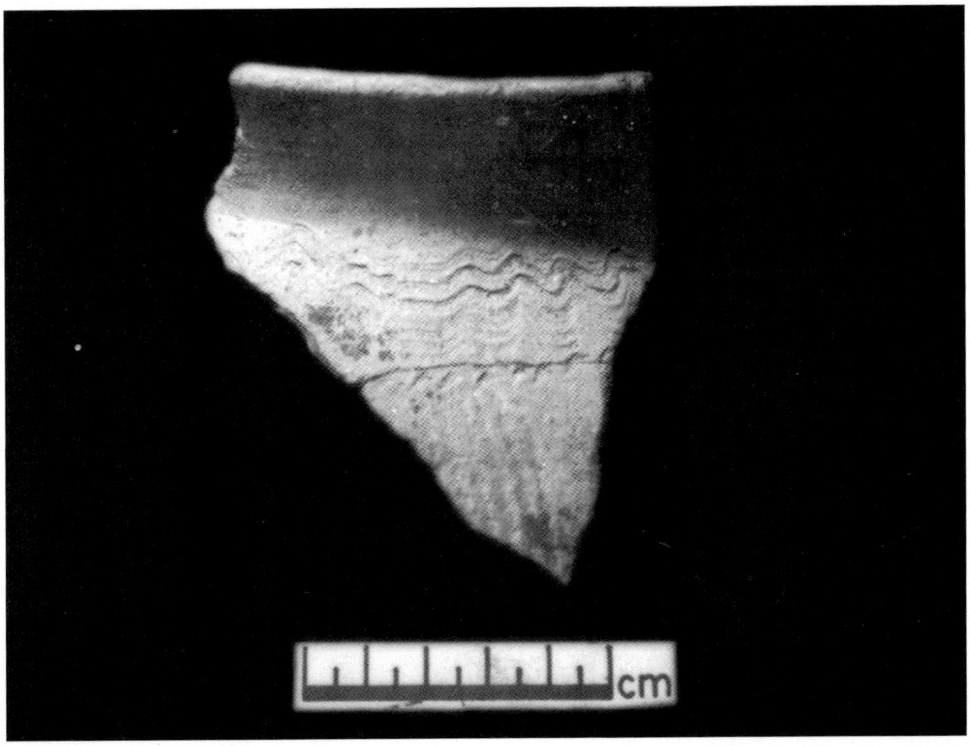

Pl. XIV.

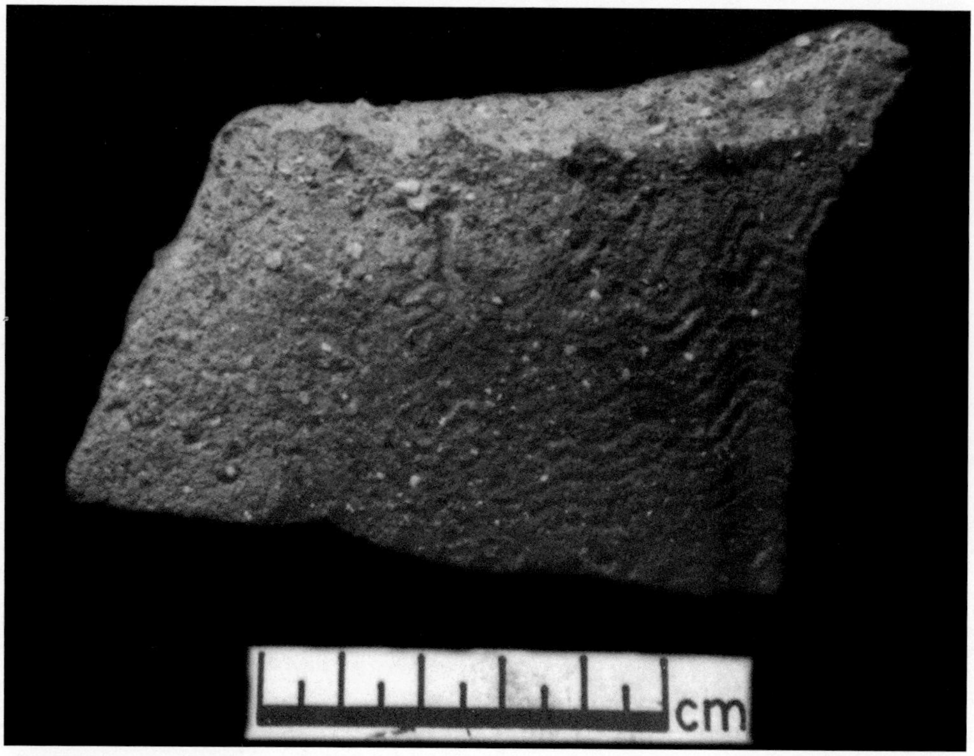

Pl. XV.

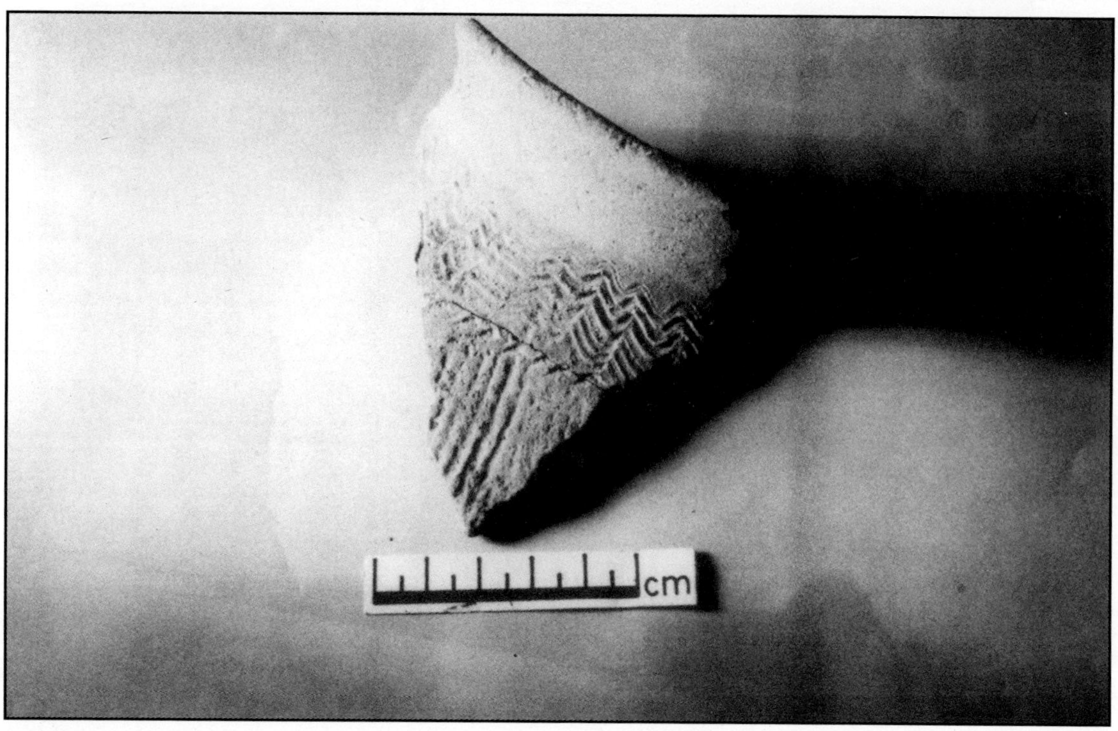

Pl. XVI.

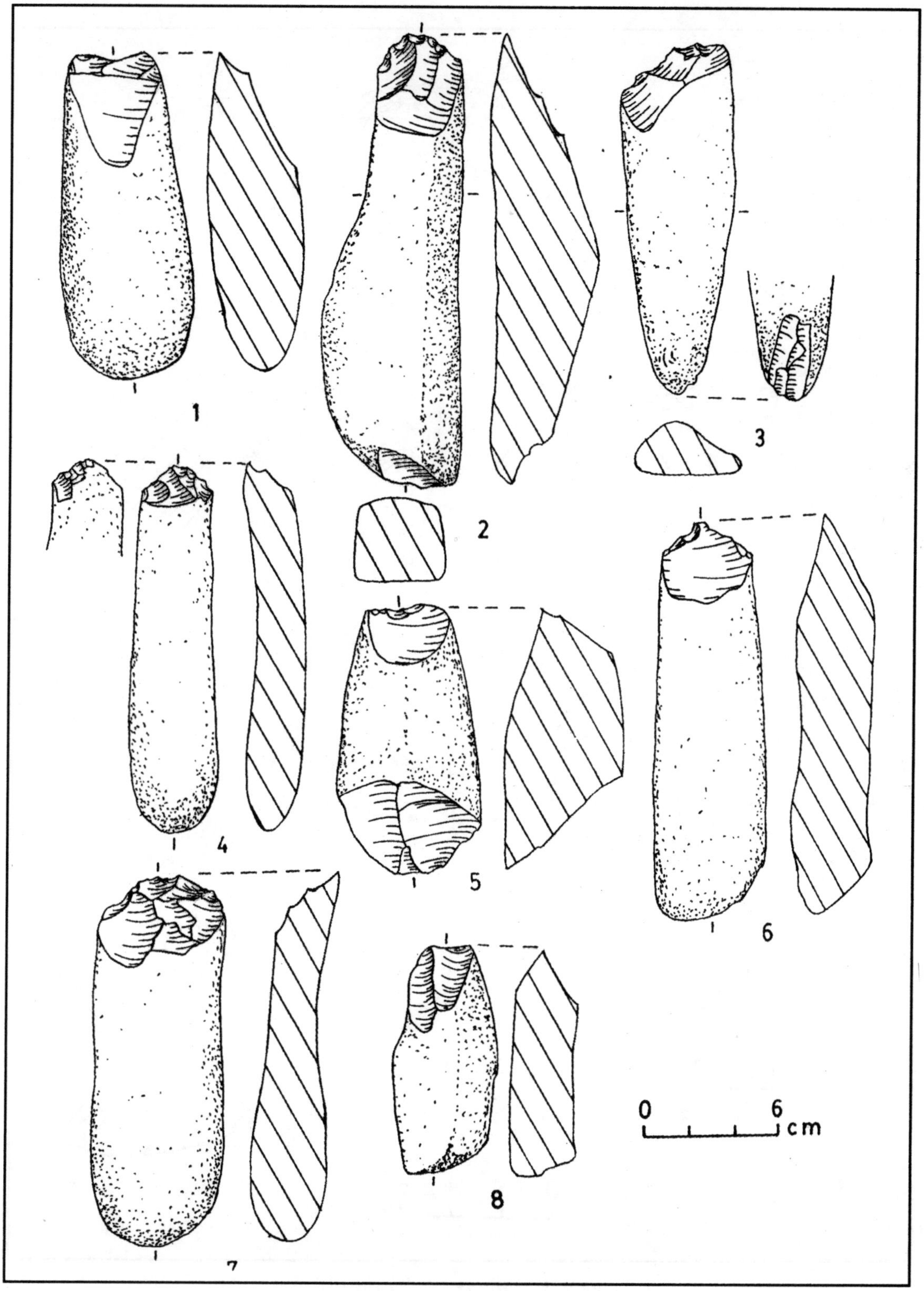

Fig. 8. Narrow, elongated choppers of "Group-A".

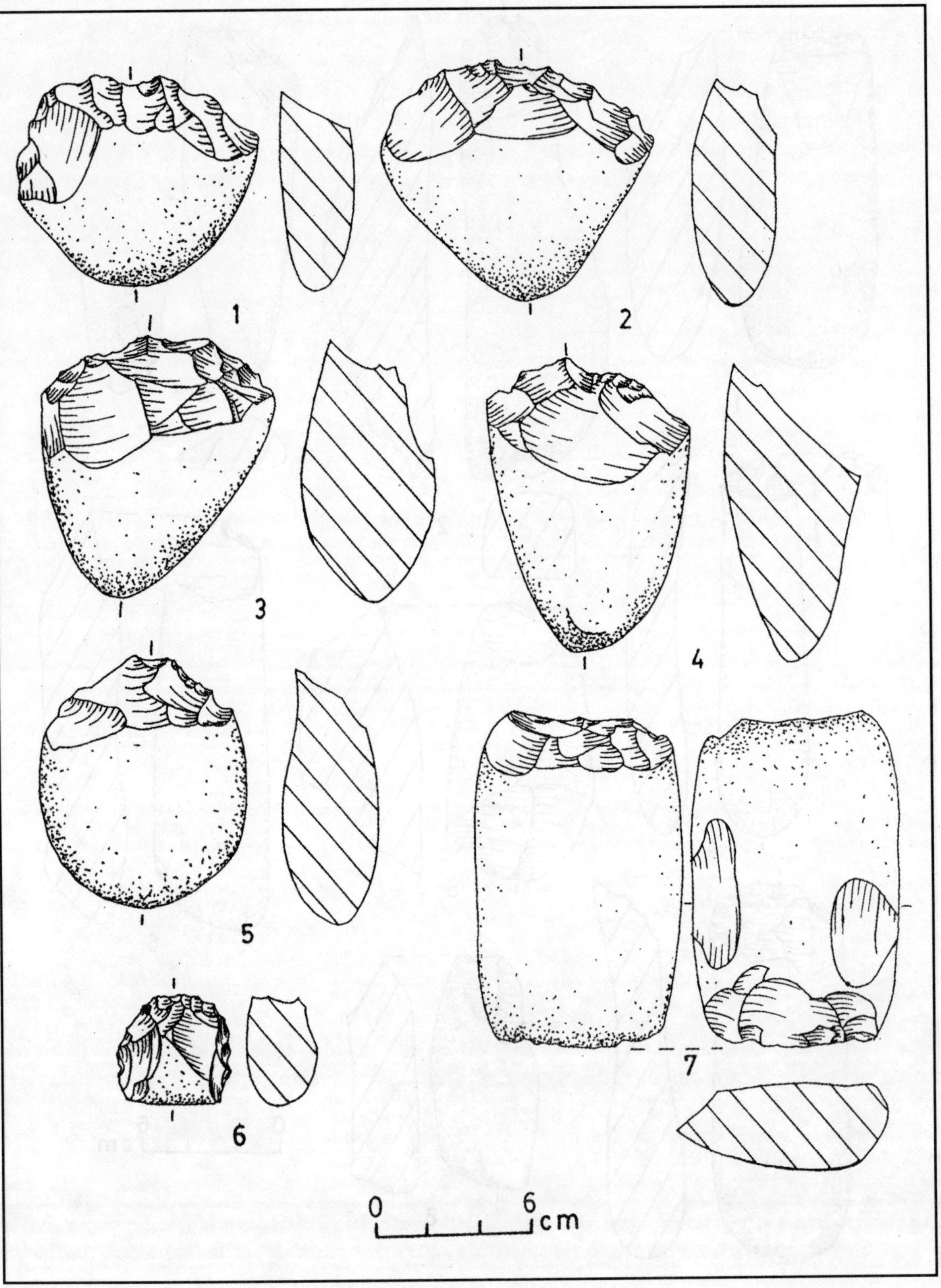

Fig. 9. Choppers of "Group-B".

The choppers of Group-C are generally broad in shape and the cord of the working-edge is almost parallel to the longer axis of the cobble (Fig. 10). These are variously termed as side or lateral choppers in various literatures. Out of the 21 specimens of this group, 14 are made of argillite and the remaining 7 of quartzite material. Their B/L ratio ranges between 1.31 and 1.70, with the length, breadth and thickness measuring 55-79 mm (mean 67.5), 72-118 mm (mean 97.00) and 26-57 mm (mean 41.05), respectively. Their weight falls between 200 gm and 1030 gm (mean 388.33) and the angle of the working-edge between 43° and 85° (mean 69.86).

The Group-D comprises only seven choppers, the B/L ratio of which lies between 1.71 and 2.84. In comparison to their length, the working-edge is too wide. Of the seven samples, four are made of quartzite and the remaining three of argillite. Their length, width and thickness vary from 41-93 mm, 80-173 mm and 32-61 mm, respectively. The working-edge angle lies between 35° and 78° and weight between 135 gm and 885 gm.

The foregoing accounts clearly demonstrate the intensity and range of manufacturing activities with regard to the production of pebble-cobble choppers at the Mesolithic site of Burla. These are also fairly well represented in almost all the discussed assemblages of the Middle Mahanadi Valley. Outside Orissa, several Pre-Neolithic or Mesolithic horizons of peninsular India are reported to have yielded heavy-duty pebble tools in association with microliths, of which particular mention may be made of Sangankallu[14] and Kupgal in Karnataka,[15] sites in Dharmapuri and North Arcot districts[16] as well as several Teri sites[17] in Tamil Nadu, and the Mesolithic sites in northern Kerala.[18] Outside India, pebble tools occur in the Pre-Neolithic Hoabinhian cultures of Indo China, Malaya and Burma[19] and also in Nepal.[20] Such implements also occur in Mesolithic context in Africa[21] Russia,[22] Australia,[23] China[24] and in the Asturian industries of Europe.[25]

On the probable role of heavy-duty pebble-cobble tools in the Mesolithic culture system of the region, Ota, in the context of Phulbani, has tried to explain the occurrence by drawing parallels from several ethnographic observations as well as archaeological records.[26] Experimental and ethnographic evidence have demonstrated that while querns and hand-stones/pestles are well suited for processing wild cereals and nuts,[27] tools like choppers and horse-hoof cores could serve as excellent wood working implements.[28] The post-holes exposed during the trial digging at Burla are significant in this context, as the evidence corroborate wood working operation. It also seems likely that during the time of Mesolithic occupation the area around the Mahanadi was fairly well vegetated. This view is further supported by the *in situ* occurrence of loose ferricrete guttings in the Mesolithic horizons at all the investigated sites. It is generally claimed that ferricrete guttings are formed in a humid, tropical climate (supported by luxuriant growth of vegetation with an abundant supply of bacterial life and organic compounds) through residual concentration process.[29] Even today the natural landscape around the Mahanadi holds a wide range of non-subsistence related plants besides wild edible plant products, including seeds of grasses, roots, tubers, rice, etc.[30] Presumably, the heavy-duty pebble-cobble tools were produced in a large number to exploit the plant resources for the subsistence and/or non-subsistence related requirements of the Mesolithic population of the region. However, given the lack of proper data-base on the Post-Pleistocene environment and ecology of the region, no conclusive explanation can be given on the specific role played by the heavy-duty tools in the activity patterns of the Mesolithic people.

Similarly, the predominance of non-geometric and non-microlithic tools as well as blanks with evidence for sickle gloss (?), in majority of the discussed assemblages appear to suggest a greater emphasis on the plant processing activities at these sites. However, there is a great deal of controversy as to whether this represents gathering and processing of wild cereals or non-subsistence related plant materials.[31] Besides, there are also a variety of interpretations advocated regarding the function of tools such as scrapers, notches and denticulates.[32] The available geometric and backed points were probably used for making composite tools and/or hunting projectiles.[33] It should be mentioned here that the Mahanadi and its surrounding landscape are equally rich in aquatic, avian as well as large and small game animal resources.[34] Very likely, some of the microlithic tools might have been intensively used for the procurement and processing of such resources. Thus, the secondary evidence suggests patterned intra-site variation in activities and subsistence endeavours.

The foregoing results of our investigations merely represent a stage in the continuing research process dealing with the Post-Pleistocene adaptation in highland Orissa. A proper understanding of the Mesolithic subsistence and settlement systems in the area can be achieved through more detailed examination of inter- and intra-regional variation and quantitative analyses of site structural features, material culture and primary subsistence data in the form of floral and faunal remains. The area is still highly variable in terms of potential resource distribution and we expect a complex mosaic of adaptations during the Mesolithic Phase.

BEGINNING OF SEDENTISM: THE NEOLITHIC EVIDENCE

Although a well-defined Mesolithic Phase did exist in the Middle Mahanadi Valley, no picture is yet available of the dynamics of the transition from the Mesolithic to the Neolithic stage, as has been identified in the Vindhyan region where there is a continuous sequence of transition from the stage of intensified food gathering and selective hunting through incipient food producing to settled village farming.[35] Till recently, the existence of a Neolithic Phase in this part of Orissa has been largely attested to by stray occurrences of ground stone implements with or without the association of pottery.[36] In view of this the recent discovery of a couple of quarry-based celt production sites and Neolithic habitation site in the Middle Mahanadi Valley becomes significant. The discovery adds a new dimension to the Neolithic researches in highland Orissa. The results of our investigation are briefly mentioned below.

Quarry-based celt production sites

Our investigation has brought to light two sites, viz, Lahanda and Hirakud in the Middle Mahanadi Valley with evidence for quarry-based celt production activities. The village Lahanda is situated on the western flank of an elongated hill named Chandli Dungri, which rises to a height of about 393 m above mean sea level. The village is located about six kilometers south-west of Burla township as crow flies. The Kuliari stream, a minor seasonal tributary of the Mahanadi, flows in almost north-south alignment between Lahanda and the Chandli Dungri. The basic rock formation of the area is characterized by a medium grained granodiorite, which is intruded at places by dolerite dykes and quartz veins.[37] About one kilometer east of Lahanda, dolerite dykes are found exposed along the bed of the Kuliari stream. The dykes formed the major source of raw materials for manufacturing celts in the area. The celt production site spreads over little less than half a square kilometer area and littered with innumerable celt dressing wases (Pl. V), specially struck large-sized flake/blade blanks, dolerite boulder

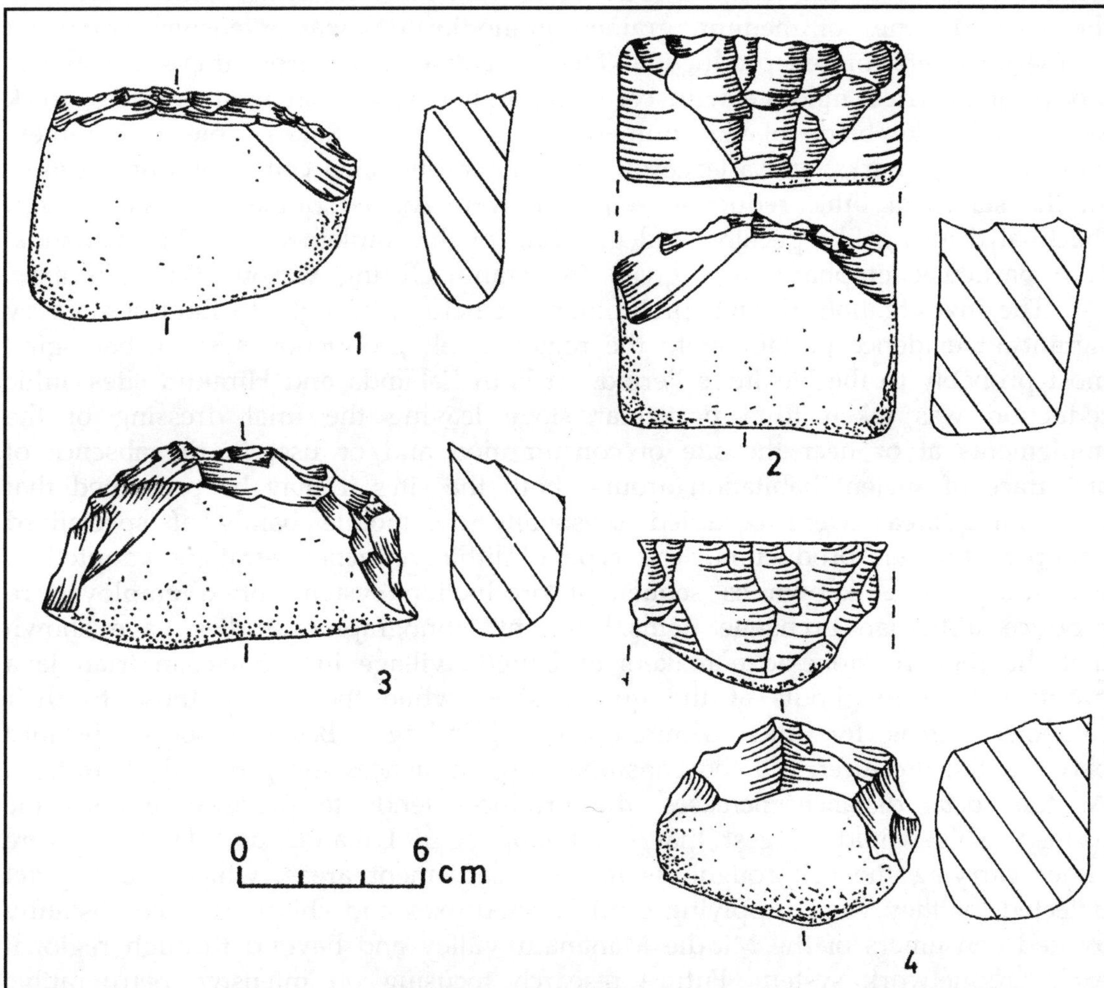

Fig. 10. Choppers of "Group-C".

blocks with marks of core preparation on their surfaces, prepared elongated and ovaloid hammers, and a large number of broken as well as complete specimens of unfinished and semi-finished celts or celt preforms. From the study of the available celts it appears that the site was used mainly for manufacturing semi-finished celts, viz, axes and chisels, leaving final stages, like micro-chippjng, pecking and grinding of the implements to the people who used them in their habitations and/or areas of activities. The typical specimens produced at Lahanda are thick, elongated semi-finished celts (chisels?) with rectangular to roughly trapezoidal medial cross-section, plano-convex long-section and bevelled working edge. Majority of the celts were fashioned through bilateral and/or quadrilateral flaking methods. Comparable celt production sites have been reported from the Bonaigarh[38] and Pallahara[39] area in the Brahmani Valley of Orissa.

Another locality which has yielded evidence for celt production activities is situated just half a kilometer west of the Hirakud township, on the left bank of the Mahanadi (Fig. 11). The site is located around an outcrop of granodiorite, lying very close to the riverbed (Pls. VI & VII). Here milonite, which occurs in the sheared zones of medium grained granodiorite,[40] was intensively quarried by the knappers for celt production. The lithic assemblage from this site includes blocks of quarried milonite with core preparation marks on their surfaces, thick large-sized flake/blade blanks, numerous celt dressing flakes, dolerite hammers with battering marks, and a large number of semi-finished celt roughouts. Almost all the stages of lithic reduction sequence were carried out at this site, except the final dressing like pecking and grinding of the implements. Unlike Lahanda, here particular emphasis was given for manufacturing various types of axes.

The investigation, though preliminary in nature, brought to light some very significant evidence pertaining to the regional celt production system, belonging most probably to the Neolithic Period. At both Lahanda and Hirakud sites, lithic reduction was taken to a particular stage leaving the final dressing of the implements at or near the site of consumption and/or use. In the absence of any trace of ancient habitation around both the sites it may be presumed that the source areas were occupied seasonally by mobile bands of specialized knappers for celt production. The type of lithic reduction strategy adopted at both the sites is known as sequential production system, often employed to produce utilitarian exchange items.[41] Recent ethnographic studies have shown that the modern stone-adze makers of Langda village in Indonesian Irian Jaya produce adze roughouts at the quarry sites, while they carry those to their settlement areas for micro-trimming and grinding.[42] Besides, social distance between the producer and the consumer also influences the production strategy. As the social distance increases, the producer tends to produce less specific forms.[43] This would suggest that the knappers of Lahanda and Hirakud were either carrying the celt roughouts to their settlement areas, which are not yet detected, or they were supplying semi-finished axes and chisels to their distantly located consumers of the Middle Mahanadi Valley and beyond through regional exchange network system. Future research focusing on intensive petrographic analysis alongside chemical characterization of artefacts from the quarry-based production sites and contemporary habitation areas would definitely provide

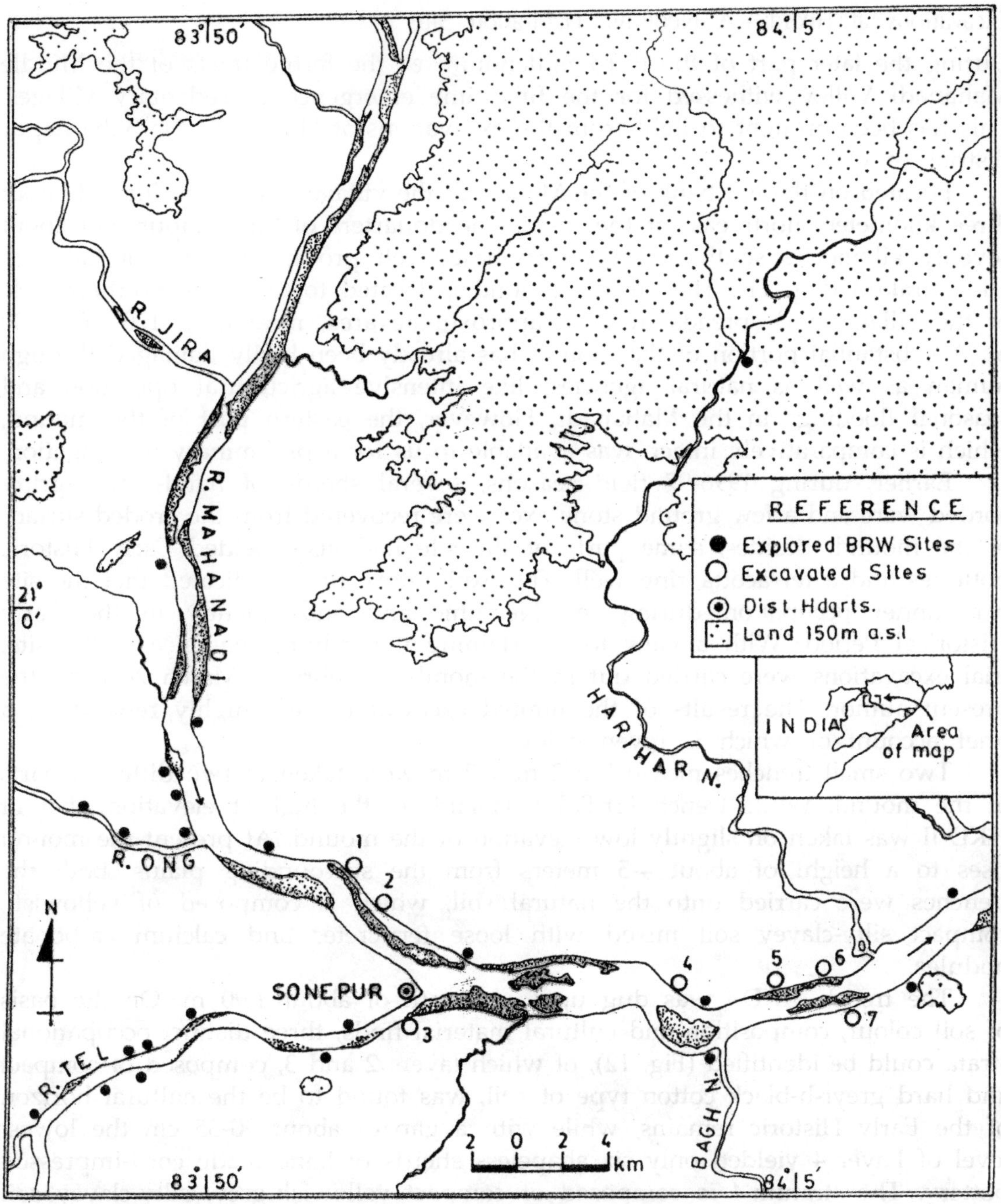

Fig. 11. Distribution of Black-and-red ware settlements and excavated sites in the central part of the Middle Mahanadi Valley. The excavated sites are 1-Khajeriapali, 2-Hikudi, 3-Manamunda, 4-Khameswaripali, 5-Kumersingha, 8-Nuagarh, and 7-Kurumpadar.

further information of significance. Since celt production is a skilled labour-intensive process, it is inextricably interwoven with the broader socio-economic context in which the entire activity takes place. Hence, future investigation must try to address the socio-economic contexts of the archaeological evidence as encountered at Hirakud and Lahanda.

Excavations at Hikudi – A Neolithic Habitation Site

During the later part of the third millennium BC the fertile tracts of the Middle Mahanadi Valley witnessed for the first time emergence of sedentary villages. This has been brought to light from the excavations at Hikudi in the Subarnapur district of Orissa.

Located on the left bank of the Mahanadi the village Hikudi is situated about three kilometers north-east of the district headquarters of Subarnapur and about seventy kilometers south of the quarry-based celt production sites of Lahanda and Hirakud (Fig. 11). The ancient mound is located towards the northern side of the village, and spreads over an approximate area, measuring 170 m x 130 m. A substantial portion of the mound has already been badly damaged through human as well as natural agencies, like intensive agricultural operation and seasonal floodings in the Mahanadi. However, the eastern part of the mound, which is comparatively intact, was available to us for a preliminary investigation.

Earlier, during 1996-97 field seasons, several sherds of hand-made, gritty corded ware and a few ground stone axes were recovered from the eroded surface of the mound. Besides, some parts of the site had also yielded Early Historic potteries and a terracotta ring well. The exploratory finds indicated that the site was under occupation during the Neolithic and subsequently in the Early Historical Period. With a view to ascertaining the culture sequence at the site, trial excavations were carried out in the month of February-March 2000 by the present author. The results of the limited excavation were highly rewarding, a brief account of which is given below.

Two small trenches measuring 2 m x 2 m were taken in two different parts of the mound. While trench HKD-I was laid on the highest elevation, that of HKD-II was taken on slightly low elevation of the mound. At present the mound rises to a height of about 4-5 meters from the surrounding plains. Both the trenches were carried onto the natural soil, which is composed of yellowish, compact silty-clayey soil mixed with loose ferricretes and calcium carbonate nodules.

The trench HKD-I was dug up to a depth of about 1.90 m. On the basis of soil colour, composition and cultural material finds, three distinct occupational strata could be identified (Fig. 12), of which layers 2 and 3, composed of compact and hard greyish-black cotton type of soil, was found to be the cultural horizon of the Early Historic remains, while with a gap of about 30-35 cm the lowest level of Layer 4 yielded only six shapeless sherds of hand-made cord-impressed pottery. The stratum-4 is composed of compact yellowish-grey, silty-clayey soil with sparse distribution of loose ferricretes. The top-most deposit (Layer 1) of light-brown, sandy-silt soil did not yield any artefactual remains. The trench HKD-II was laid some 20 meters north-east of HKD-I, and dug up to a depth of about 85 cm. Of the three layers identified in this trench (Fig. 13), the Layer 2, composed of yellowish-grey, silty-clayey soil with loose ferricretes, yielded a large number of shapes as well as shapeless sherds of corded ware potteries, ground celts, terracotta animal figurines, terracotta ball, broken part of a saddle quern and a few faunal material, besides a portion of a burnt floor and charcoal.

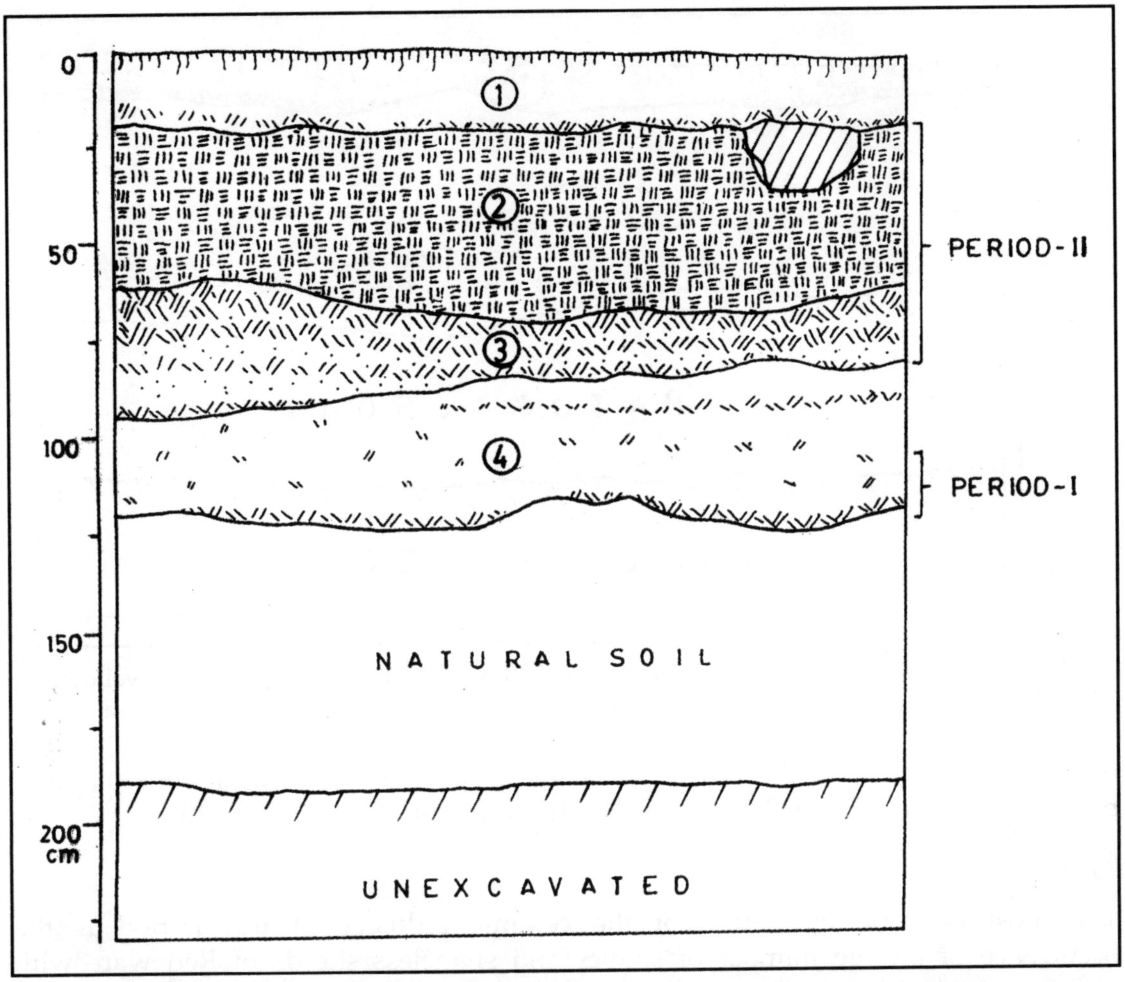

Fig. 12. Excavated section (facing south) in Trench-I at Hikudi, *Layer-1:* light-brown, loose sandy-silty; *Layer-2:* compact, greyish-black, silty-clayey soil; *Layer-3:* same as above; *Layer-4:* compact, yellowish-grey, silty-clayey soil with sparse distribution of ferricrete pellets.

The combined testimony of the excavated trenches HKD-I and HKD-II brought to light archaeological evidence for two distinct phases of human habitation, Period-I (Neolithic) and Period-II (Early Historic), with an occupational gap between them. However, considering the limited scope of the present investigation, the possibility of the existence of Post-Neolithic horizons in other parts of the mound cannot be ruled out.

The main features of the cultural phases identified during the 1999-2000 excavations are briefly mentioned below.

Period-I (Neolithic)

As mentioned earlier, stratum 2 of HKD-II and the bottom level of stratum 4 of HKD-I represent the Neolithic horizon of the site. The thickness of the habitation deposit of this period in HKD-II varies between 35 cm and 50 cm. The earliest settlers lived in wattle-and-daub huts as revealed from the occurrence

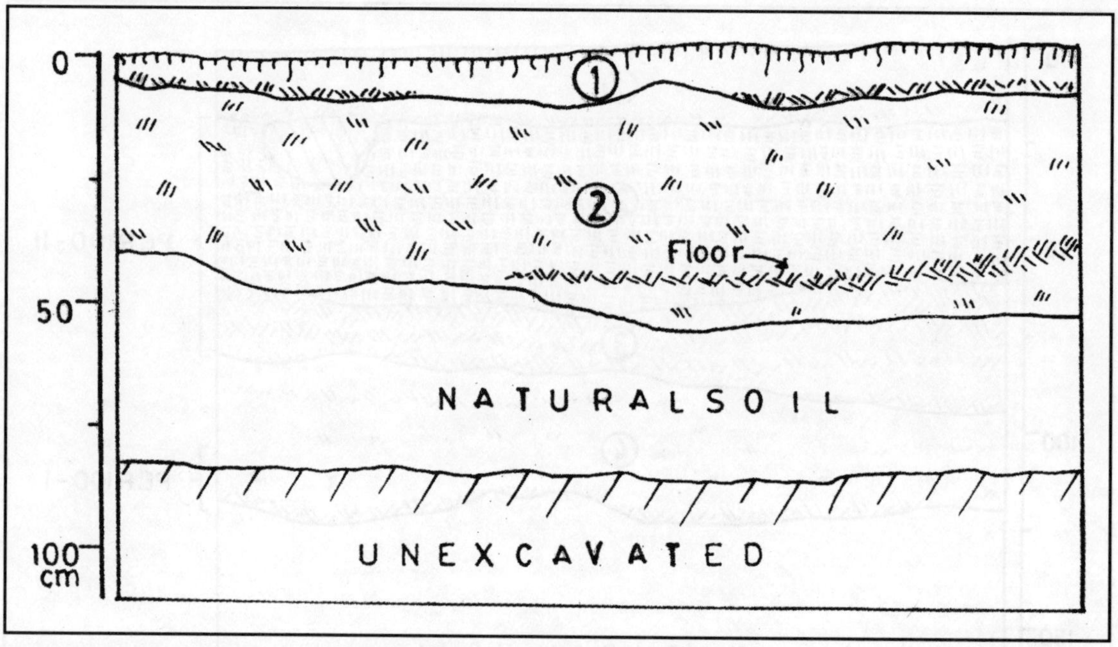

Fig. 13. Excavated section (facing east) in Trench-II at Hikudi. *Layer-1*: compact, yellowish–grey, silty-clayey soil with loose ferricretes; *Layer-2:* same as above but more dark in colour.

of burnt clay lumps with reed impressions. A portion of a burnt floor has also been encountered in HKD-II at a depth of about 45 cm (Fig. 13).

Ceramics

The most outstanding feature of the ceramic industry of this period is the occurrence of a large number of shapes and shapeless sherds of Red ware with a variety of cord impressions on their surfaces. Barring a few specimens of simple Red ware and those with thick drab reddish slip, the large majority of the pots are cord impressed. The potteries are generally hand-made as is evident from the uneven outer surface and finger impressions on the inner side of the pots. However, in case of some of the vases, the rim portion was separately produced probably on a slow wheel and luted to the body during the manufacturing process. This feature continued to exist even during the Chalcolithic Phase in the Middle Mahanadi Valley.[44] The clay used for potting the corded ware, particularly the larger ones, are found to be heavily tempered with aplastic inclusions like crushed quartz/sand particles and lime. This was done probably to ensure greater durability and to avoid breakage due to thermal stresses. The colour of the pots varies from orange-red, dull-red to brownish, reddish-grey and grey. In some cases, the upper half of the vases are chocolate slipped and burnished, though they constitute a negligible percentage. The general fabric of the pots varies from medium to coarse.

The thickness of the individual cord mark varies from 1 mm to 3 mm and the impressions are very often deep. The cording strokes are generally vertical (Pl. VIII), oblique or slanting (Pl. IX). Interestingly, a large number of pots, particularly the wide-mouthed jars and elliptical *handis*, bear cord impressions on both inner as well as outer surfaces (Pl. X). This can be achieved by using both dabber and beater wrapped with corded fabric/cords while shaping the pots in leather hard condition. It should be mentioned here that except Hikudi, no other Neolithic site of India has produced evidence for such type of cord impressed potteries so far.

Another significant characteristic feature of the potteries of this period is the occurrence of a variety of decorative patterns. Potteries are decorated by incision, appliqué, puncture and impressed methods, which occur invariably on the shoulder part of the potteries, while in some cases all the above methods have been integrated to create certain design patterns (Pls. XI-XVI). These are indicative of the rich aesthetic sense of the potters and that of the contemporary society as well. The tradition of incised and impressed methods of decoration almost ceased to exist during the subsequent Chalcolithic Phase in the region and were replaced by exotic painted design patterns executed mostly in white/off-white colour.[45] However, some of the vases in Red ware, Red slipped ware and burnished Black ware potteries of the Chalcolithic culture of this area bear oblique incised slashes on the rim edges only.

The functional shapes represented in the ceramic assemblage of this period include medium to large-sized vases/jars with flaring/splayed out featureless rim, carinated/concave neck and expanding/bulbous body; vases/jars with vertical featureless rim, carinated/short concave neck and expanding body; wide-mouthed *handi* with flaring/splayed out featureless rim and almost elliptical body; bowls with featureless rim; basins with flared internally thickened rim; and lastly, lids with vertical rounded/flat handles (Figs. 14 & 15). Thus, shapes are few in number and mostly utilitarian in nature. Significantly, most of these shapes continued to exist in the early Chalcolithic levels of the Middle Mahanadi Valley.[46] This and other similar factors prompt us to believe that the Chalcolithic culture of this region developed out of its antecedent cultural phase/phases.

Other Finds

The miscellaneous finds from the excavations consist of two small stylized terracotta animal figurines (bull/goat?); one terracotta sling ball; one broken part of a bone point; few skeletal and dental remains of ungulates (?); stone objects, viz, two chert blades, one broken part of a saddle quern, two circular discs, and eight ground axes; and lastly, a large number of burnt clay lumps with reed and other vegetative impressions. Besides the above, a broken head of a terracotta bull was also recovered from the surface nearby the trench HKD-II. The terracotta figurines, representing perhaps objects of worship, are reported for the first time in Orissa from Neolithic context. It appears that cattle as a whole occupied a significant position in the subsistence economy of the Neolithic settlers of Hikudi. It should also be noted here that even today the peasant communities of this part of Orissa worship locally manufactured terracotta toy carts of bulls/oxen once in a year. The basic idea behind this cult is to preserve the cattle wealth, which plays a prominent role in the subsistence economy of the local peasantry.

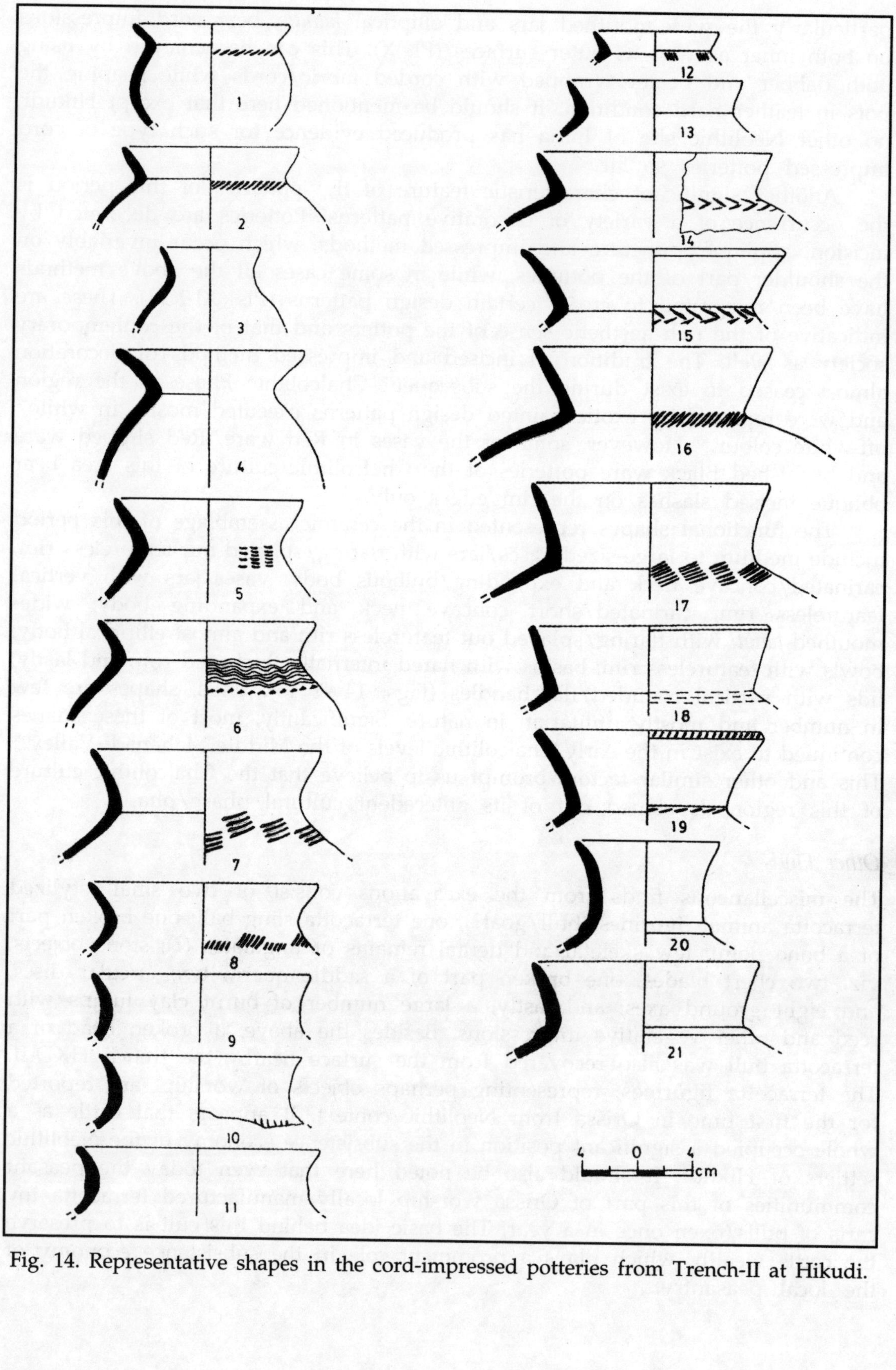

Fig. 14. Representative shapes in the cord-impressed potteries from Trench-II at Hikudi.

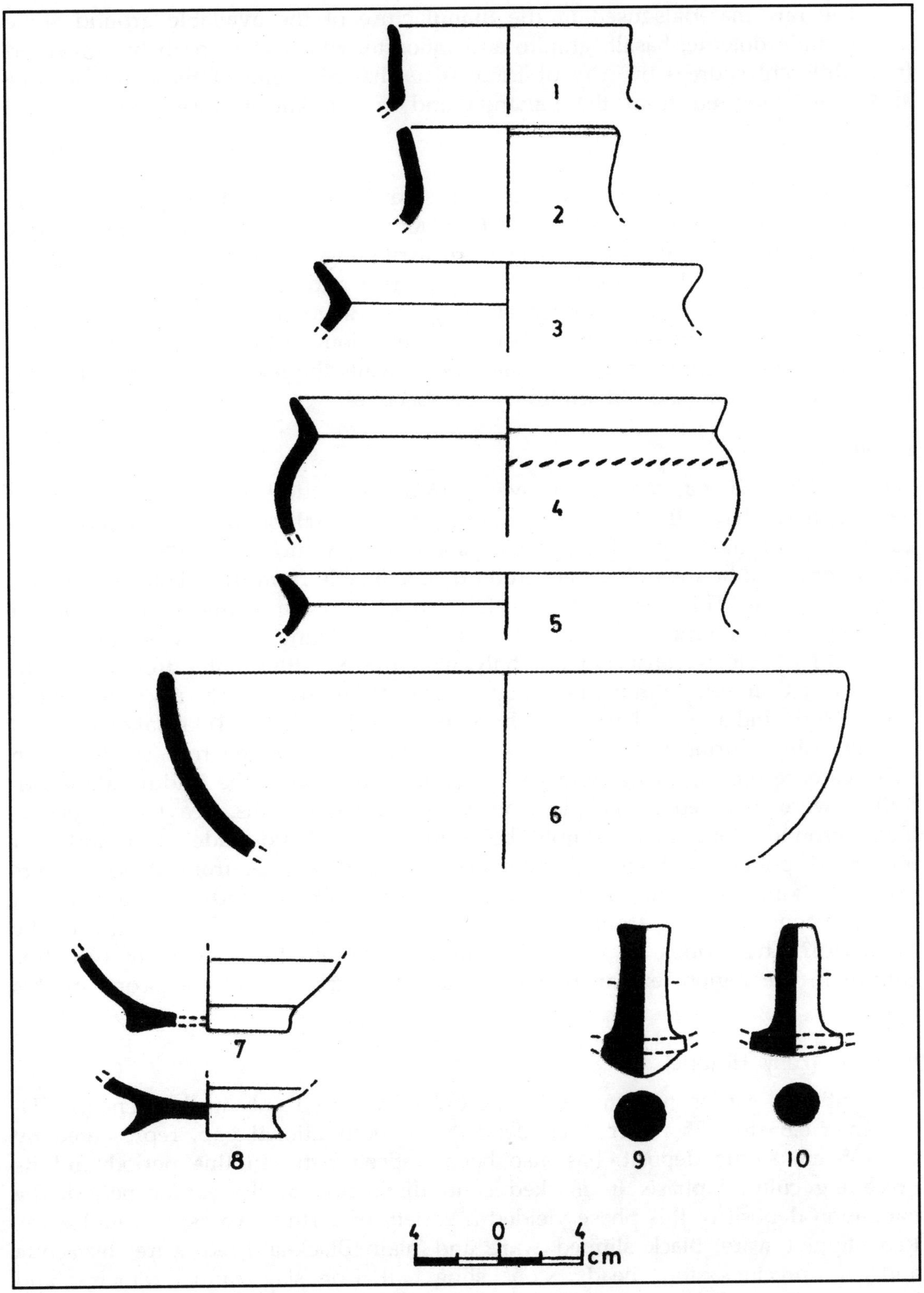

Fig. 15. Cord-impressed potteries from Trench-II at Hikudi.

The raw materials used in the manufacture of the available ground stone axes include dolerite, basalt, granite and milonite, which were probably procured from different sources by way of trade or exchange. Some of these might have also been imported from the Lahanda and/or Hirakud factory sites.

Subsistence economy

The available evidence from the limited excavations seem to suggest that the Neolithic inhabitants practised a mixed economy based on limited farming, stock raising, hunting and fishing. People were exploiting the local resource base for their subsistence endeavours. Impressions of rice and millets were recorded on several burnt clay lumps. However, at the present state of our knowledge nothing conclusive can be said about the subsistence behaviour of the Neolithic population at Hikudi and a clearer picture on this aspect awaits the results of further detailed investigations from multi-disciplinary perspectives.

Chronology

Significantly, charcoal samples recovered from the middle level of the Neolithic deposit from HKD–II have been dated to 3800±100 BP by the Radiocarbon Laboratory of the Physical Research Laboratory, Ahmedabad (PRL No. 2139). This happens to be the only radiocarbon date available from the Neolithic deposits of Orissa so far. This has given us a fair scope to assign a time period of about late third millennium BC, tentatively, for the beginning of early settlement at Hikudi. The date is consistent not only with the Neolithic dates from Northern India, viz, Chirand,[47] Vindhyan group of sites,[48] Senuwar,[49] but also with those from South India, viz, Utnur,[50] ash mound of Kodekal,[51] Tekkalakota,[52] etc.

Probably, during this phase most of the naturally formed rock shelters with rich evidence for engravings and paintings, located close to the Middle Mahanadi Valley, were occupied by people who were using microliths, heavy-duty pebble tools, ground stone tools, simple bone tools, and hand-made cord and mat impressed potteries.[53] Some of the cord impressed sherds from these shelters exhibit striking similarities with those from Hikudi. Does it indicate mere contact or movement of people from the rock shelter habitats to the fertile tracts of the Mahanadi? This brings us to the problem relating to the genesis of Neolithic culture in the region, explanation of which is clearly out of the scope of this paper.

Period-II (Early Historic)

As mentioned earlier, remains of this period were traced only in the trench HKD-I from a 0.65 to 0.75 meter thick deposit. An occupational gap, represented by a 30-35 cm sterile deposit, has also been noticed between this period and its preceding cultural phase. In marked contradistinction to the earlier period, the habitation deposit of this phase yielded a variety of earthen wares, viz, Red ware, Red slipped ware, black slipped ware and plain Black-and-red ware; terracotta and semi-precious stone beads; stone sling ball; iron slag; faunal remains; and lumps of burnt clay with reed impressions. There is total absence of earlier ceramic tradition. The representative shapes in the black slipped and Black-and-red ware included bowls, dishes, vases, basins, storage jars and dishes with central knob on the inner side of the base. The overall nature of the ceramic assemblage closely resembles with that of Period-I of the excavated site of Manamunda, located about four kilometers south-west of Hikudi.[54] A terracotta ring-well located in the north-eastern part of the mound appears to belong to this period.

THE CHALCOLITHIC SETTLEMENTS

Existence of a Chalcolithic Phase in the Middle Mahanadi Valley has now been confirmed from the excavations at Khameswaripali, located about 12 km east of the district headquarters of Subarnapur.[55] The excavations were conducted during February-March 1997, which brought to light three developmental stages within the Chalcolithic Period at the site. In the subsequent years cognate assemblages were brought to light from different parts of the Middle Mahanadi Valley.[56] Among these, the site of Khajeriapali was subjected to initial probing during February-March 2000 by the present author. The material assemblages recovered from this excavation revealed close affinity with those from the middle-late levels of the Chalcolithic deposit at Khameswaripali. Main characteristic features of the Chalcolithic culture represented at the excavated sites of Khameswaripali and Khajeripali are briefly outlined below.

Khameswaripali

The ancient habitation of Khameswaripali is situated about four kilometers south-west of Birmaharajpur town (20° 46′ N. latitude and 83° 50′ E. longitude) and oriented SE-NW along the left bank of the river Mahanadi in Subarnapur district (Fig. 11). The mound, partly eroded by the seasonal flooding in the Mahanadi and partly occupied by the present-day village of Khameswaripali, measures about 130 m in length, 80 m in width and rises to a height of about 7 meters from the surrounding plains. Vertical excavations at two places revealed a 2.20-1.40 meters thick habitational deposit relating to three cultural periods with two sub-phases, in Period-I. Of these, Period-I and II belonged to Chalcolithic Phase, while Period-III to the Iron Age.

The early settlers of Khameswaripali lived in wattle-and-daub houses, as revealed from the occurrence of a large number of reed-impressed burnt clay lumps in the habitation deposit. Besides, a portion of a circular rubble-laid foundation has also been encountered in one of the trenches.

Ceramics

The ceramic industry of the Chalcolithic period is predominantly wheel-made and the vast majority is slipped and burnished. On the basis of surface treatment and nature of firing, four major ceramic types with a number of sub-variants have been identified, viz, plain and painted Black-and-red ware, burnished black/dark-grey ware, plain and painted red slipped were, plain Red ware and corded ware (Figs. 16, 17 & 18). Among these, Black-and-red ware constitutes the most

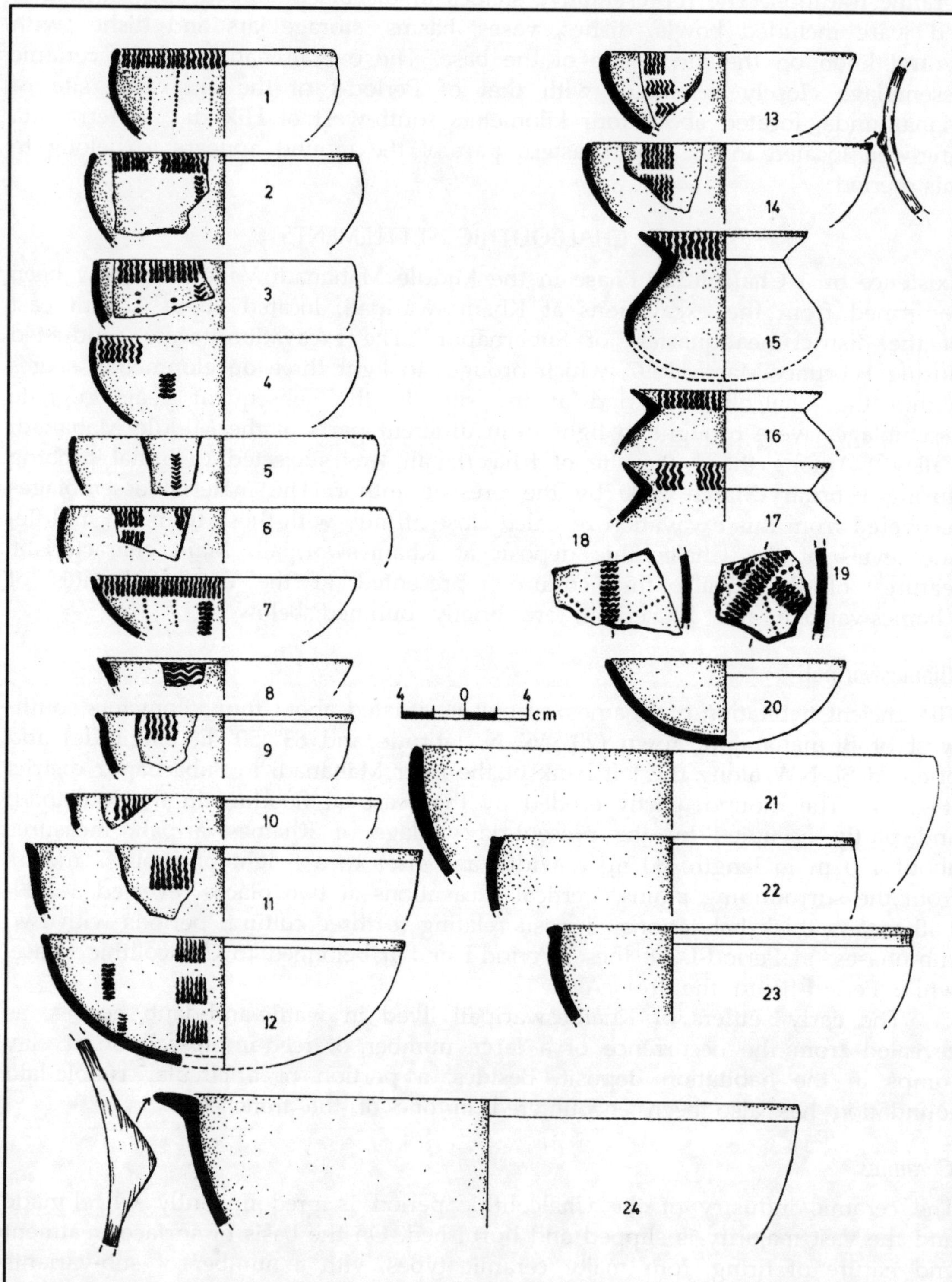

Fig. 16. Representative shapes in the white-painted (1-19) and plain (20-24) Black-and-red ware potteries of *Period-IA* (Chalcolithic) from Khameswaripali.

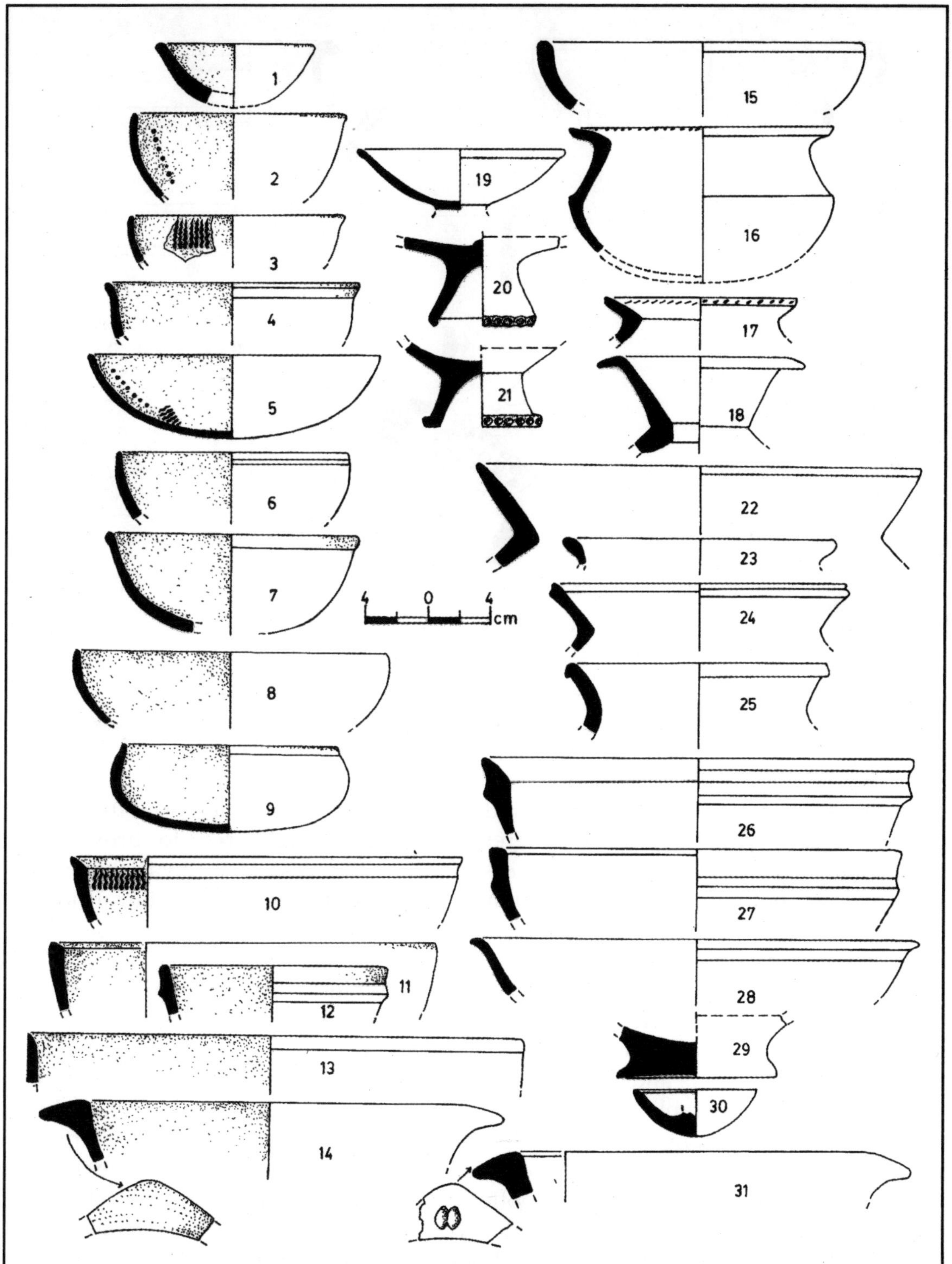

Fig. 17. Ceramic types of *Period-IB* (Chalcolithic) from Khameswaripali. Black-and-red ware (1-14), black slipped ware (15), burnished Black ware (16 and 17), Red slipped ware (18-27) and plain Red ware (28-31).

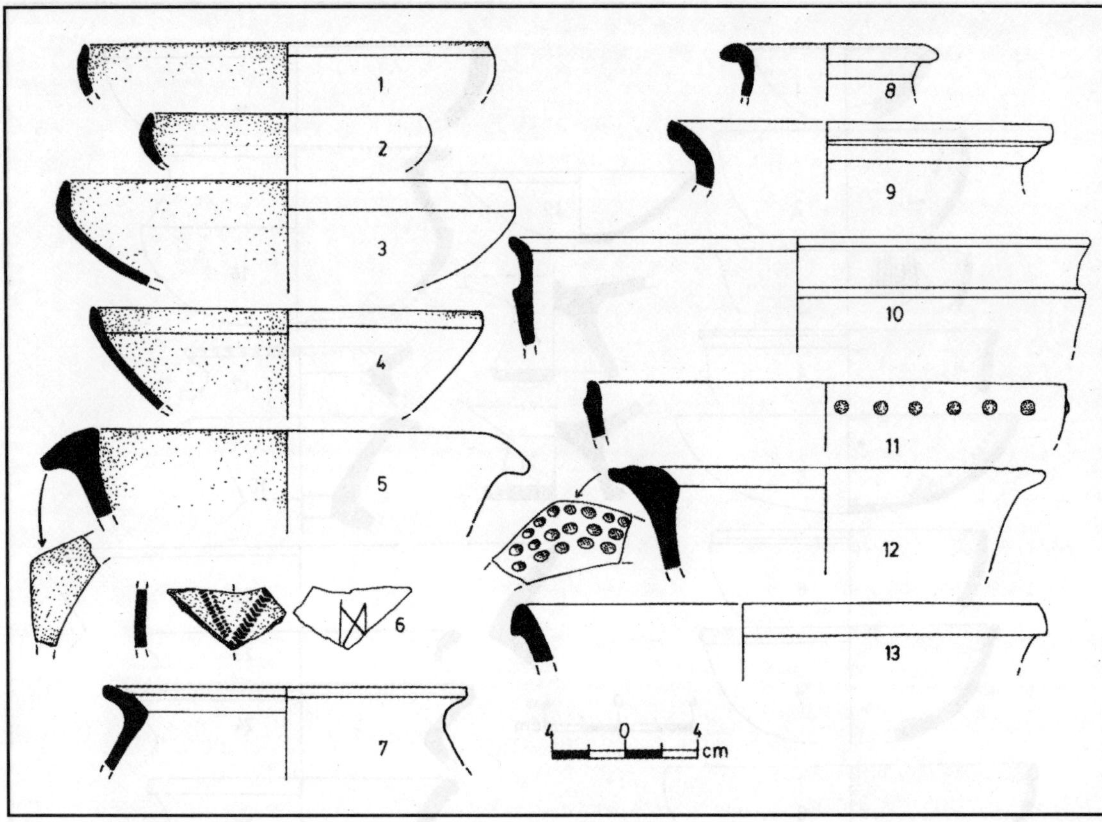

Fig. 18. Shapes from *Period-II* (Late Chalcolithic) at Khameswaripali. Black-and-red ware (1-6), burnished Black ware (7), Red slipped ware (8-11), and plain Red ware (12-13).

characteristic ceramic type of this period. While the outer surface exhibits a good deal of colour variation, from different shades of bright red to brown and occasionally creamish-white, the inner surface of the vessels is invariably of jet black colour. Both the surfaces are treated with a slip and highly burnished to achieve a glossy effect. The vessel forms in this variety mainly comprise wide-mouthed, convex-sided bowls of varying sizes, basins and small-sized vases. Most of the bowls and vases are profusely painted in white/off-white pigments, which occur only on the black interior surface. The motifs comprise groups of horizontal/vertical rows/columns of short strokes, wavy and zig-zag lines, herring bones, zigmas, and small solid dots. As regards methods of placement and designs, comparable patterns have been noticed on the black-and-red potteries from Lothal,[57] Rangpur,[58] Eran,[59] Pandu Rajar Dhibi,[60] Chirand,[61] Senuwar,[62] and Prakash.[63] Besides the above, the rim portion of some of the bowls and basins of black-and-red potteries and vases of burnished Black ware, exhibits post-firing application of red ochre pigment, instances of which have been found in Orissa,[64] Bihar[65] and South India.[66]

The vessel forms in the burnished Black ware, Red slipped ware and Red ware comprise vases with flaring/splayed out rims and sometimes with a ring at the base, bowls and those with multiple perforations on the base, *handis*, shallow bowls-on-stand, four-legged miniature vases, and lids with flat handles. Decoration on these vessels consists of incised and punctured designs, which occur only on the rim portion, and simple appliqué bands on the shoulder of the pots. However, some of the shallow bowls in Red slipped ware are decorated with white painted designs on the inner surface. Although there are a few corded ware potteries, these are mostly shapeless sherds.

Technology

The tools and implements of the Chalcolithic communities of Khameswaripali were mainly made of bone and/or antler. They include bone points of single and double-ended types, tanged bone points of various sizes and a bone spear-head. In addition, small ground stone axes, and microliths were also used by the people. Unlike most of the Neolithic and Chalcolithic sites of India where microliths constitute a significant class of artefacts, they form a negligible percentage at Khameswaripali. This clearly indicates that the use of this component declined after the Mesolithic Phase in the Middle Mahanadi Valley. Besides the above, the late level of Period-II has yielded a tiny fragment of a copper object. Probably, copper was not yet popular in this part of Orissa during the Chalcolithic Period.

Miscellaneous objects

The Chalcolithic deposit at the site has yielded a variety of small objects of daily use, viz, terracotta beads of areca nut type, pottery discs with or without a central hole, barrel-shaped beads of carnelian and quartz, mollusc shell pendant, stone pestles and charred ivory bangles of various sizes (Fig. 19). Except pottery discs, the proportional occurrence of other objects is too small.

Subsistence economy

The food economy of the early settlers of Khameswaripali is known mainly from a large collection of charred as well as uncharred skeletal remains of a variety of animals and botanical remains in the form of impressions on burnt clay lumps and potteries. A preliminary examination of the skeletal remains has attested to the presence of both wild and domesticated animals in the collection. The bones which have been identified so far included *Bos indicus* (cattle), *Bubalus bubalis* (buffalo), *Ovis orientallis vignei/Capra hircus* (sheep/goat), bones of rodents, *Antilope cervicapra* (black buck), *Tetraceros quadricornis* (four-horned deer), *Cervus* and a number of fresh water molluscs of bi-valve variety[67].

Many of these bones are charred, giving evidence of being roasted on fire for consumption. Besides, some of these also exhibit marks of chopping on their surfaces. Thus, it appears that animal food constituted a significant part in the dietary requirements of the early farming communities of Khameswaripali.

A cursory examination of the impressions on burnt clay lumps revealed existence of rice and millets. However, a detailed report on the faunal and botanical remains is awaited.

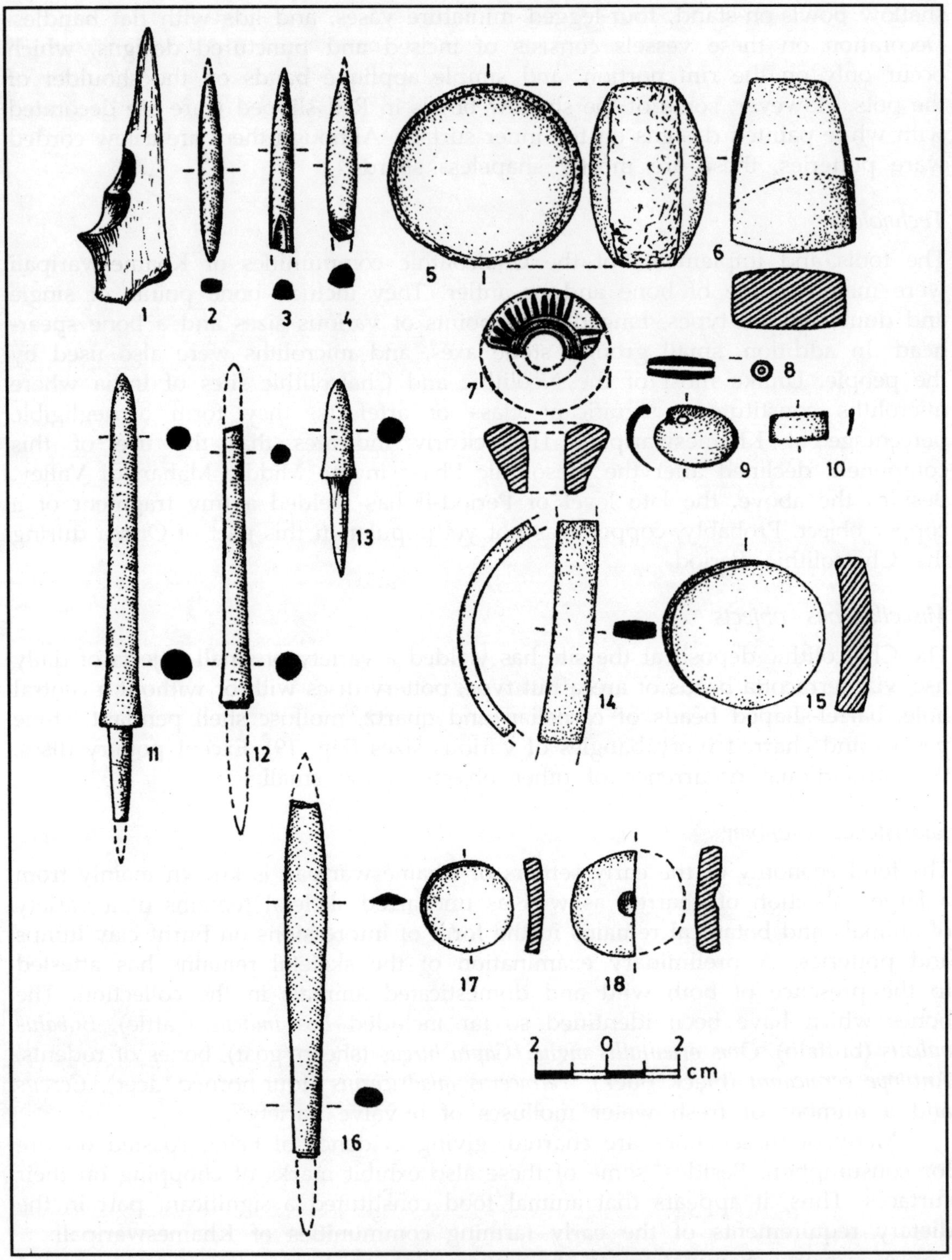

Fig. 19. Various small finds from the Chalcolithic levels at Khameswaripali. *Period-IA:* bone points (1-4), stone disc (5), ground axe (6), terracotta spindle whorl (7), stone bead (8), shell pendant (9), shell blade (10); *Period-IB*: tanged bone points (11-13), ivory bangle (14), pottery disc (15); *Period-II:* bone spear-head (16) and pottery discs (17 and 18).

Khajeriapali

The ancient mound of Khajeriapali is located on the left bank of the Mahanadi and situated about five kilometers north of the district headquarters of Subarnapur (Fig. 11). The mound, located about half a kilometer west of the village Khajeriapali, measures approximately 150 m in length, 130 m in width and rises to a height of about 4 meters from the surrounding plains. The surface of the mound has already been badly disturbed by agricultural activities of the present villagers. A megalithic structure, represented by some horizontally laid stone slabs encircled by six upright stones, is noticed on the eastern foot of the mound.

The mound was subjected to small-scale excavations during February-March 2000. The primary objective of the excavations was to trace the extension of the Chalcolithic culture as represented at Khameswaripali. Of the two small trenches, measuring 2 m X 2 m, trench KJP-I was laid on the top of the mound and excavated up to a depth of 1.10 m, while KJP-II was laid on the peripheral slope and dug up to a depth of 1.05 m. Both the trenches were carried into the natural soil, which is composed of yellowish, compact, sandy-silty-clayey soil mixed with loose ferricretes and calcium carbonate nodules (Fig. 20).

The excavations revealed that it is a single period site with the thickness of the habitation deposit varying from 50 cm to 70 cm. The Layer 1, composed of dark-grey coloured, compact, sandy-silty-clayey soil, and the uppermost part of Layer 2, which is composed of compact sandy-silty-clayey soil of greyish-yellow

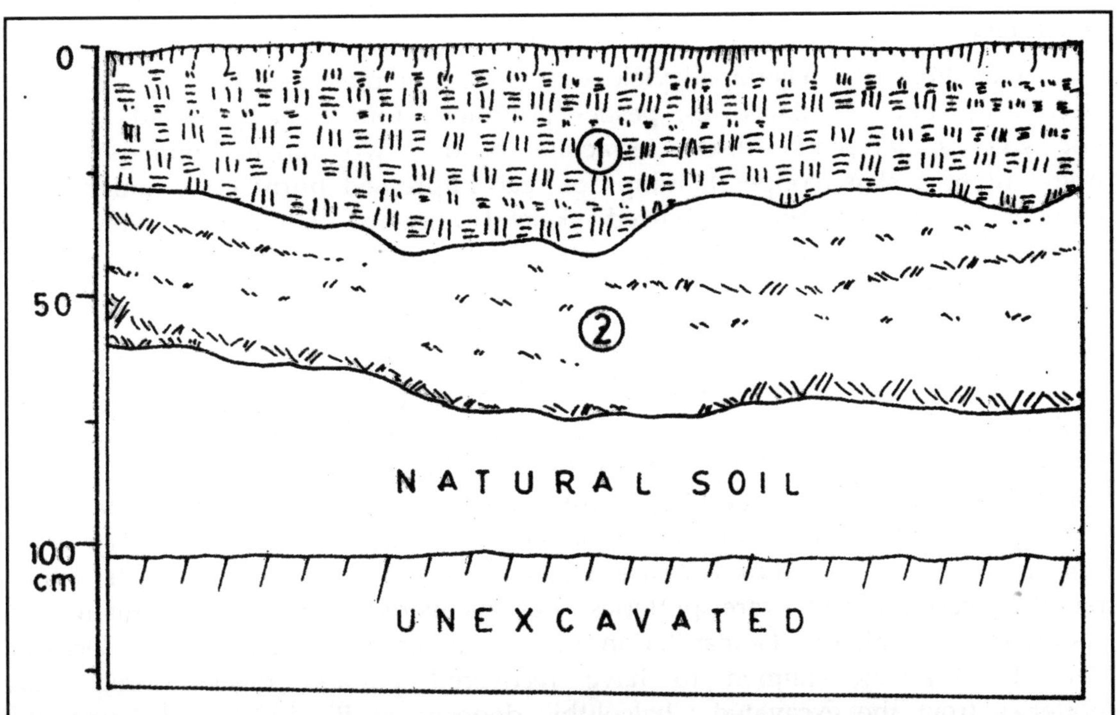

Fig. 20. Excavated section (facing west) in Trench-II at Khajeriapali. *Layer-1:* dark-grey, compact, sandy-silty-clayey soil; *Layer-2*: greyish-yellow, sandy-silty-clayey soil.

colour, in both KJP-I and KJP-II, have yielded a wide range of earthen wares and other material finds, a brief description of which is given below.

Ceramics

The potteries of this site are predominantly wheel-made, though there are also instances of hand-made specimens. Most of these are slipped and burnished ware, and their fabric varies from thick to medium, while fine fabric pot is a rare occurrence. The clay used in the manufacture of the pots is not well levigated and contains aplastic inclusions and organic matters. On the basis of surface treatment and nature of firing six major ceramic types have been recognized. They are simple Red ware; Red slipped ware, plain and white painted Black-and-red ware, burnished black/grey ware, a few black slipped ware and lastly cord-impressed ware. As regards general technology, forms and decorative patterns, the potteries of Khajeriapali, demonstrate striking resemblance with those from Period-II of Khameswaripali. The representative shapes in Black-and-red ware and black slipped ware include bowls with convex sides, featureless rims and round base, basins, medium-sized vase with flaring rims and a few dishes, while those in the Red ware and Red slipped ware comprise bowls and those with multiple perforation at the base, vases, jars, basins, platters, shallow bowls-on-stand, *handis* and lids with vertical round as well as flat handles. The available cord-impressed ware is represented by shapeless sherds only. In fabric as well as texture these are different from the Hikudi specimens.

Small finds

The excavations at Khajeriapali yielded a variety of material remains, viz, a few microliths, stone circular discs, pestles/pounders, four carnelian beads, pottery hop-scotches, terracotta discs, terracotta beads, two tanged bone-points, a fragment of a slag (copper?), lumps of reed-impressed burnt clay, and a large number of charred and uncharred skeletal remains of animals, which also included some specimens of fresh water mollusc shells of bivalve variety. The small finds indicate that people at Khajeriapali lived in wattle-and-daub houses and their subsistence economy was based on hunting, fishing, cattle herding/breeding, besides agriculture.

The foregoing brief description of the material remains from the limited probings at Khameswaripali and Khajeriapali clearly demonstrate that with the continuation of some trait elements of the preceding Neolithic Phase, several new features emerged during the Chalcolithic Period in the Middle Mahanadi Valley region. The noteworthy contribution of these excavations is the discovery of an iron-free antecedent cultural phase characterized by the profusion of white-painted Black-and-red ware potteries, not recovered hitherto at Manamunda, Asurgarh, Sisupalgarh, Golbai Sasan or any other excavated sites of Orissa.[68] Recently, Pradhan claimed to have recovered painted Black-and-red ware potteries from the excavated Chalcolithic deposits at Bhejidih[69] and Nuagarh,[70] located in the Middle Mahanadi Valley. It should be mentioned, however, that in terms of general vessel forms and fabric the potteries from the above two sites do not show any resemblance either with those from Khameswaripali or from Khajeriapali sites. Rather, they demonstrate close similarities with the early Iron Age potteries from the excavated sites of Kumersingha and Kurumpadar, which will be discussed in the next section.

The fact that the area witnessed Pre-Iron Age village establishment in a major way is now almost clear. This is particularly evident from the horizontal exposure of sites with comparable Chalcolithic material remains not only in the lower half of the Middle Mahanadi Valley[71] but also its major tributary like the Tel.[72] In terms of technology and other aspects, the ceramic industries and other concomitants of the culture from the early levels of Khameswaripali and Khajeriapali share many common characteristic features with those from several excavated Chalcolithic settlements of northern, western and central India.[73] Significantly, the early Chalcolithic Phase (Period-IA) at Golbai Sasan, located in coastal Orissa, which shares some characteristic features with the corresponding levels at Khameswaripali and Khajeriapali, has been dated by radiocarbon method to 4100±100 BP. In the absence of absolute date, but keeping in view the radiocarbon date from Hikudi and that of Golbai Sasan, a tentative time-bracket of early middle second millennium BC may be proposed for the beginning of Chalcolithic settlements in the Middle Mahanadi Valley of Orissa. The Chalcolithic settlements of this area gradually developed into full-fledged Iron Age villages with several new trait elements.

IRON AGE AND EARLY HISTORIC SETTLEMENTS

Till recently, scholars were sceptical about the existence of an Iron Age phase in the archaeological culture sequence of Orissa.[74] Despite the fact that a number of important Early Historic sites, in both hinterland and coastal Orissa, were subjected to excavations, viz, Sisupalgarh,[75] Jaugarh,[76] Manikpatna,[77] Lalitagiri,[78] Asurgarh,[79] and Manamunda,[80] no clear-cut Iron Age horizon was successfully encountered as has been the case of Pre-NBPW Phase in the Gangetic Valley.[81] For the first time excavations at Golbai Sasan brought to light an early Iron Age horizon, which the excavator has labelled as 'Ferro-Chalcolithic' in view of the association of a lone iron object and continuation of most of the earlier Chalcolithic features.[82] Similarly, Basa[83] has brought to light an Iron Age level in the trial excavations at Sankerjang, a Chalcolithic site[84] in Central Orissa. However, our knowledge of these recent discoveries is limited to a few brief notices. This insufficient data rendered no help in working out the extent and stages of development of this culture in space and time. In view of this, the recent discovery of a large number of Early Historic settlements with antecedent cultural phases in the Middle Mahanadi Valley becomes extremely significant.

In comparison to the Neolithic and Chalcolithic settlements, sites belonging to the Iron Age and Early Historic periods are fairly widespread in the region. They are not only found along the level tracts of the Mahanadi, but also in its several perennial tributaries, like the Ong, the Tel, the Harihar and the Karandi. Largest number of sites have been brought to light in the Tel and its tributaries, viz, the Suktel, the Raul, the Udanti, the Under, the Utai, etc.[85] It appears that due to population pressure, techno-economic factors and increased social complexity, settlements during the Iron Age and Early Historical periods expanded to the tributaries of the Mahanadi. Occurrence of some Early Historic fortified settlements in the area indicates not only expansion of settlements, but also the emergence of urbanization with its concomitant trait elements.[86]

With a view to understanding the nature of the Post-Chalcolithic settlements in the Middle Mahanadi Valley, two sites, viz, Kumersingha and Kurumpadar, were selected for trial excavations by the present author, during February-March 2001. The excavations revealed continuous occupation of the sites right from the Late Chalcolithic/Early Iron Age Phase to the Early Historical Period. A brief account of the results of the excavations is presented below.

Excavations at Kumersingha

Located on the left bank of the Mahanadi, the village Kumersingha (20° 51′ 54.0″ N and 84° 05′ 00.0″ E) is situated about six kilometers east of the Chalcolithic site of Khameswaripali and about four kilometers south-east of the tahsil headquarters of Birmaharajpur in Subarnapur district (Fig. 11). Earlier, a copper plate charter issued by Jajati II of Somakula was recovered from near this village.[87]

The ancient mound, measuring roughly 175 m in length and 100 m in width with a height of about 4-5 m from the surrounding plains, is located on the eastern outskirt of the village Kumersingha. Approximately 150 m further east of this mound, there is another ancient habitation lying very close to the village Nuagarh.[88] Excavations at the Nuagarh mound revealed Chalcolithic as well as Iron Age/Early Historic remains.[89]

While a major portion of the southern side of the Kumersingha mound has been badly damaged by the recent flooding in the Mahanadi, the northern side is presently under active cultivation. There is a gradual slope from the top of the mound receding towards the bank of the Mahanadi. In order to know the culture sequence and potentialities of this site, two test trenches, measuring 3 m x 2.5 m (KMS-I) and 2.5 m x 2.5 m (KMS-II), were excavated in different parts of this mound. While trench KMS-I was laid on the top of the mound, trench KMS-II was located some 25 meters south of KMS-I. Both the trenches were excavated up to the natural soil, which is composed of compact yellowish coloured silty-clayey soil mixed with calcium carbonate nodules and loose ferricretes. A total of seven occupational layers were identified and the thickness of the entire habitation deposit varies from 2.30 m in KMS-I to 1.70 m in KMS-II (Fig. 21). Our limited excavations have brought to light a two-fold culture sequence with two sub-phases in Period-I. Details regarding each period are as follows.

Period-IA

The thickness of the habitation deposit of this sub-period in both KMS-I and KMS-II varies between 65 cm and 55 cm. The first settlers lived in wattle-and-daub houses, as revealed from reed marks in burnt clay lumps. It is marked by the occurrence of black-and-red were, black slipped ware, Red slipped ware (colour varies from deep red to orange red, brown and chocolate), and plain

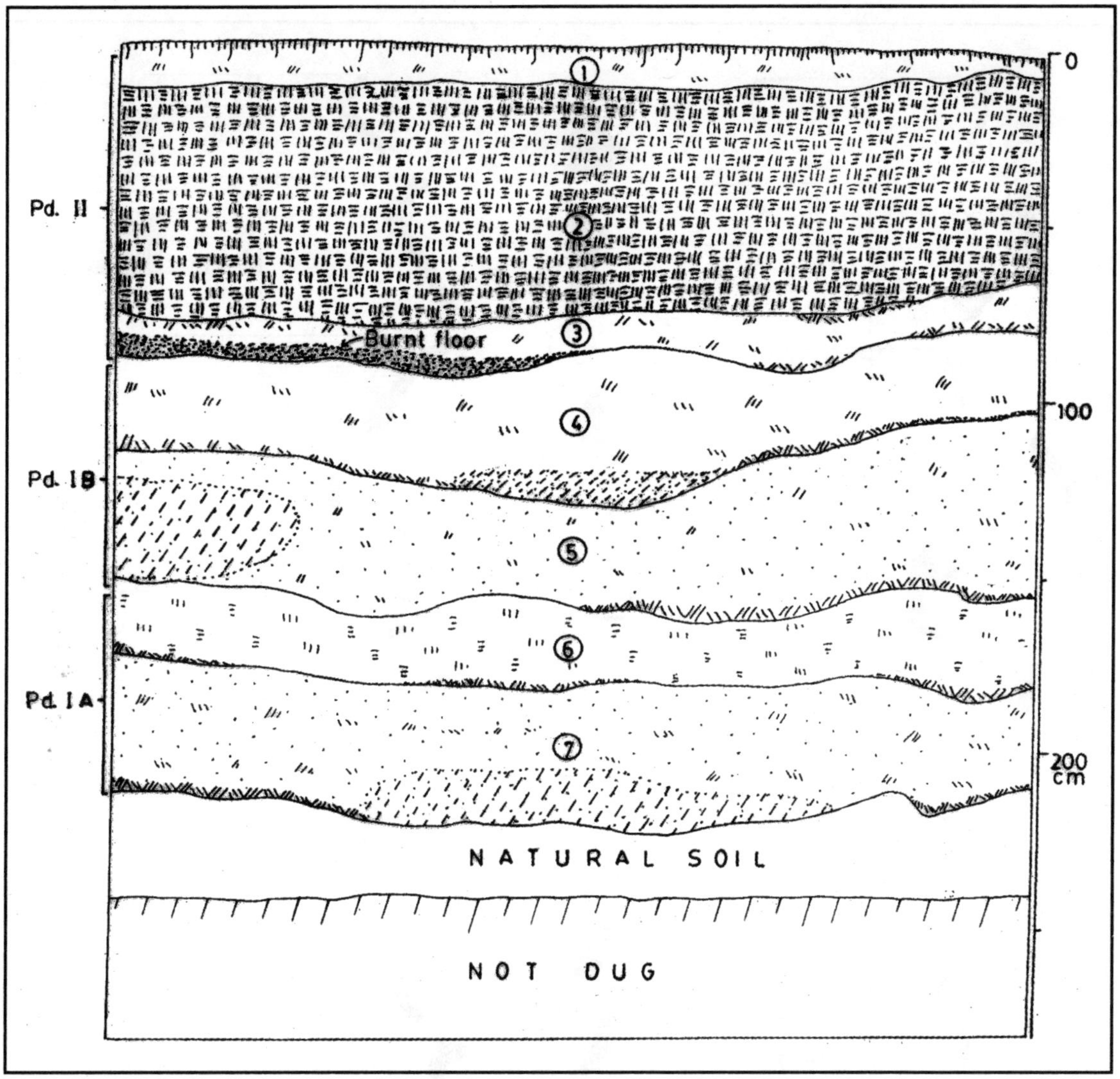

Fig. 21. Excavated section (facing north) in Trench-II at Kumersingha. *Layer-1*: greyish-brown, loose, sandy-silty soil; *Layer-2*: compact, dark grey, sandy-silty-clayey; *Layer-3*: same as above; *Layer-4*: slightly compact, greyish-yellow, sandy-silty-clayey soil with patches of ash and charcoal; *Layer-5*: same as above; *Layer-6*: loose, yellowish-brown, sandy silty soil with patches of ash and charcoal; *Layer-7*: same as above but very loose in texture.

Red ware. Potteries are wheel-turned and generally medium to thick in fabric and medium textured, though there are some fine fabric pots in Black-and-red ware and black slipped ware from the late level of this sub-period. Except plain Red ware, almost all the available pots are slipped and finely burnished.

Some of the pots in Black-and-red ware, black slipped ware, burnished Black ware and chocolate slipped ware, are decorated with painted designs (mostly groups of wavy and zig-zag lines) in white colour, which occur on the inner as well as outer surface of the pots (Fig. 22). This is in marked contrast with the Chalcolithic potteries from Khameswaripali and Khajeriapali, where only the

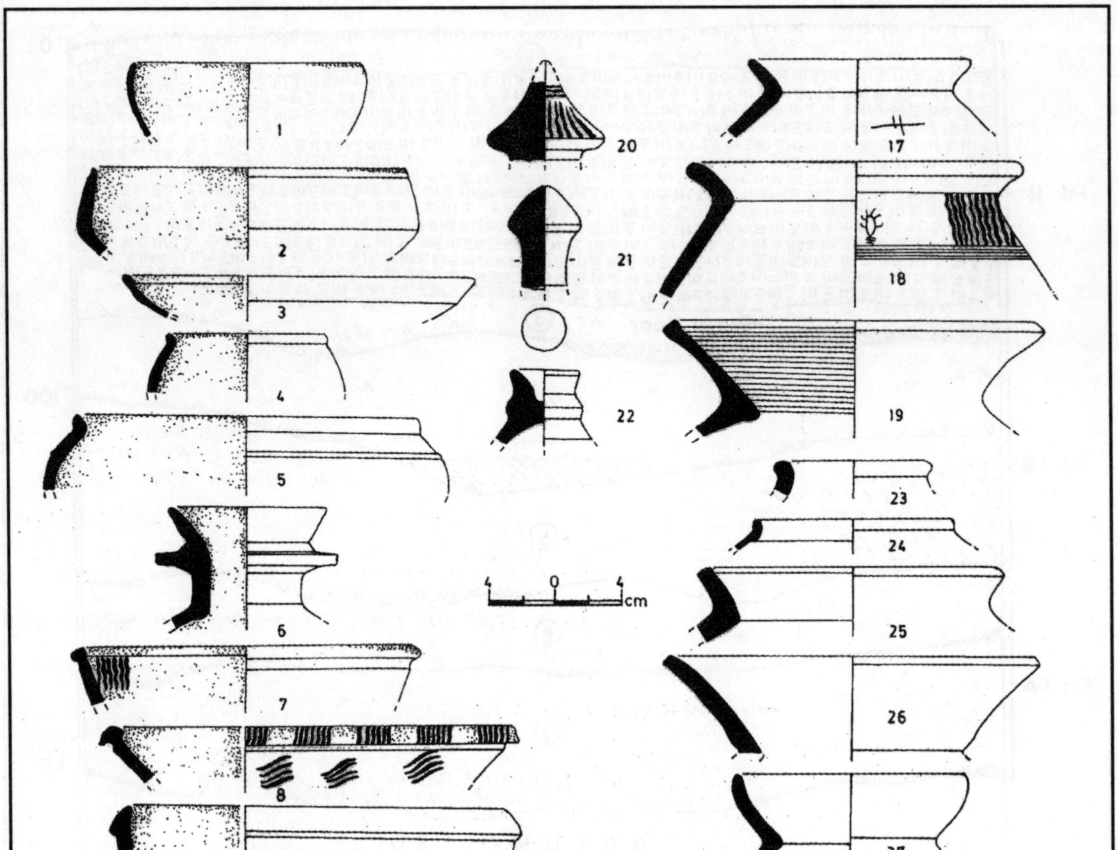

Fig. 22. Important pottery shapes of *Period-IA* from Kumersingha. Black-and-red ware (1-9), black slipped ware (10-22), Red slipped ware (23-32), and plain Red ware (33 and 34).

black inner surface of the Black-and-red ware and the inner surface of some bowls in Red slipped ware, are painted in white design patterns.[90] Besides paintings, pots are also decorated with appliqué and incised designs as well as grooved concentric circles and spirals, which occur on the inner surface of the flat base of bowls and dishes in Black-and-red ware and black slipped ware. Sometimes bands of such parallel grooved lines also occur on the outer surface of the body of bowls in Black-and-red ware and black slipped ware as well as on the inner surface of the flaring rims of vases/jars (Fig. 22).

Interestingly, two shapes and one sherd in black slipped ware contain post-firing graffiti marks on the outer surface (Fig. 23). Two of these depict probably some sort of insect and one oblique line.

The principal shapes in Black-and-red ware are bowls, dishes with carinated body, vases and jars; those in black slipped ware include bowls, dishes, vases,

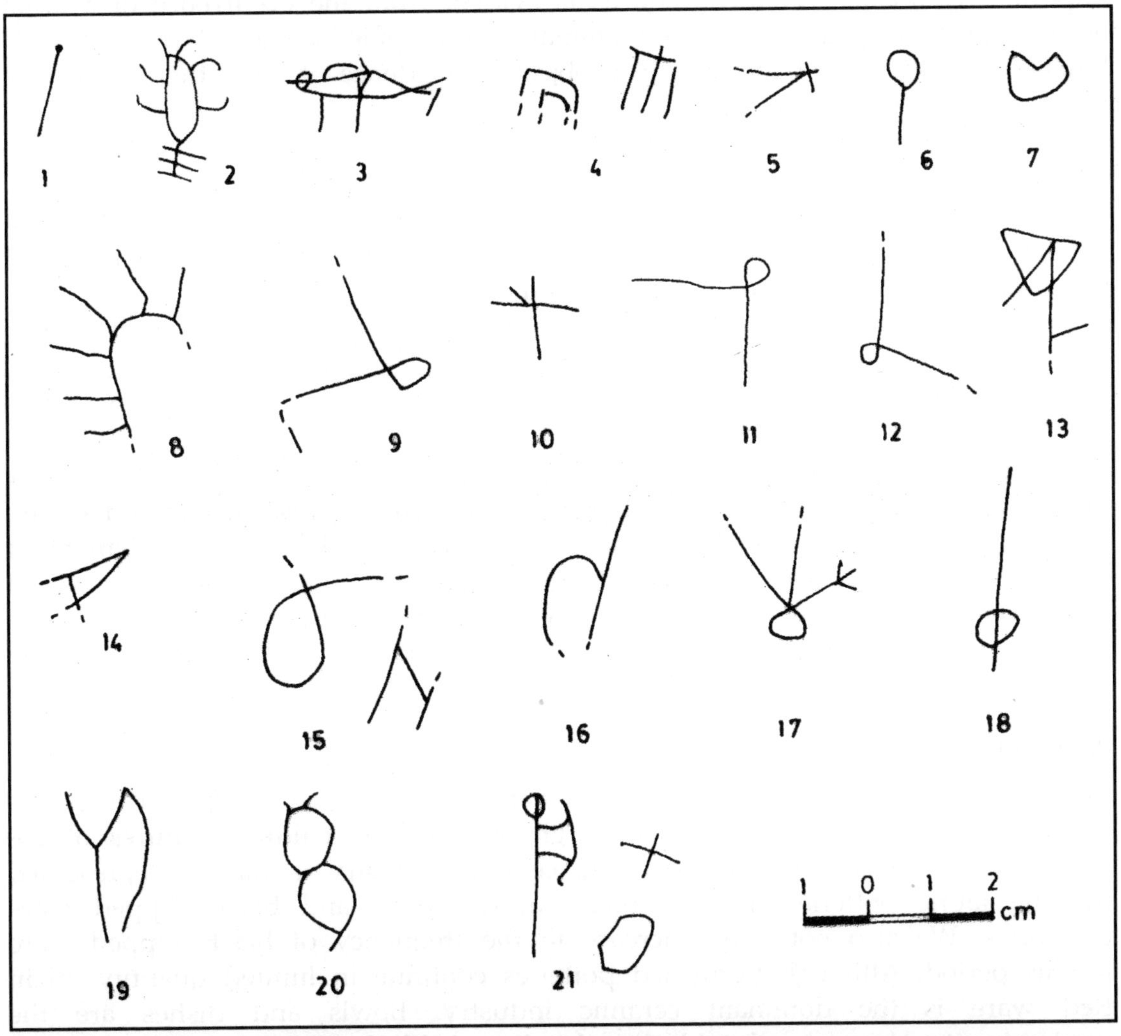

Fig. 23. Graffiti marks on potteries from Kumersingha. *Period-IA*: 1-3 on black slipped ware; *Period-IB:* 4 and 5 on black slipped ware, 6 on Red slipped ware and 7-15 on Black-and-red ware; *Period-II*: 16-21 on Black-and-red ware.

handis, platters, and lids with mostly vertical phallic-shaped handle; those in red slipped include basins, bowls, miniature vases, platters, lids and pot stand; those in simple Red ware include storage jars, basins, vases, *handis*, bowls with multiple perforation on the base, platters, *handis* with ring base, and lids (Fig. 22). Interestingly, the rim portion of some of the bowls and vases in Black-and-red ware and Red slipped ware potteries contains post-firing application of red ochre pigments, a feature already noticed in the Chalcolithic potteries of the Middle Mahanadi Valley.

The most significant discovery of this sub-period is an iron object (nail?) from a depth of 2.20 m. This indicates that the early settlers of this site were acquainted with the use of iron. Other small finds include pottery discs in large number, triangular sherds with ground edges and a fragment of a stone pestle. Although the first settlers practised agriculture, animal food constituted an important component of their diet, as is evident from the occurrence of a large number of charred and uncharred animal bones, some of them having distinct butchery marks. Except the lone iron object no evidence of any other metal was reported from the limited dig.

Chronology

Fortunately, some charcoal samples were collected from the bottom level of the habitation deposit of this sub-period (2.30 m from the top), which has been dated by radiocarbon method following AMS method as follows.

Site	Sample no.	Calib. Date	Layer
Kumersingha Period-IA	KIA 20156	762BCE	7 (230 cm b.s.)

Thus, the beginning of human habitation in this part of the site goes back to about the early 8th century BC. However, keeping in view the limited nature of the probing, more early date for the beginning of Iron Age settlement at Kumersingha is expected. Had the site been excavated in large scale, we would have been in a position to encounter antecedent phase/phases of Period-IA. The available date, however, is consistent with most of the dated Early Iron Age deposits of eastern India.[91]

Period-IB

This period is represented by an average habitation deposit of 70-75 cm thickness in both the excavated trenches. Although most of the cultural features of the preceding phase continue to exist, the ceramic industry is mainly represented by fine fabric potteries in both Black-and-red ware and black slipped ware categories. We also notice an increase in the frequency of black slipped ware in this period. Although burnished potteries continue in limited quantity, plain Red ware is the dominant ceramic industry. Bowls and dishes are the predominant shapes in the black-and-red and black slipped ware potteries. Several new shapes were also introduced, of which particular mention may be made of dishes-on-stand in black slipped ware (Fig. 24). The inner surface of

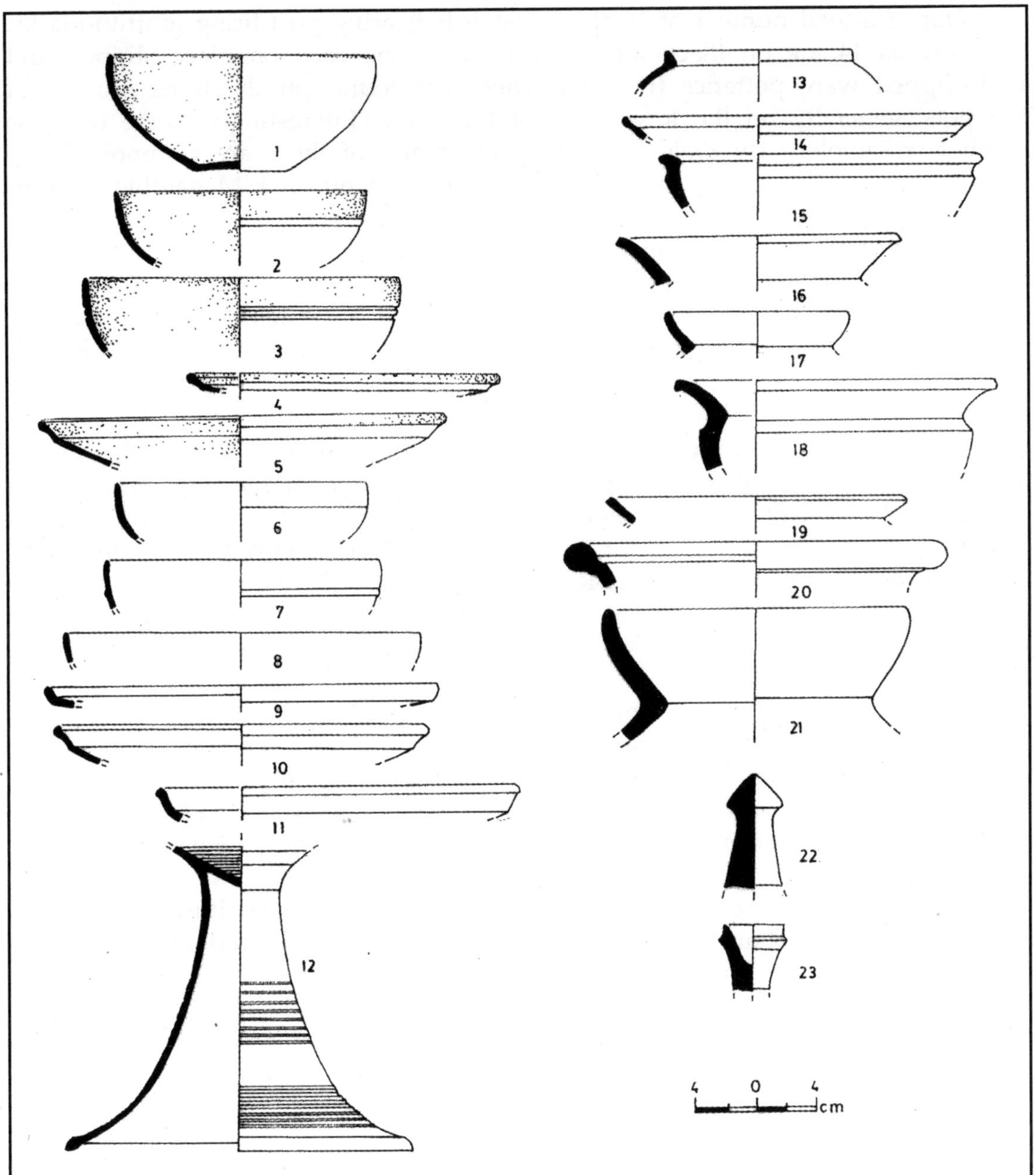

Fig. 24. Representative potteries of *Period-IB* from Kumersingha. Black-and-red ware (1-5), black slipped ware (6-16), Red slipped ware (17 and 18), and plain Red ware (19-23).

the dishes in these cases bears fine concentric grooves, which are confined to the shallow base portion only. Similar dishes-on-stand have been found widely distributed in the Iron Age deposits of the Middle Mahanadi Valley area. The continuity of most of the earlier shapes are seen with further technical progress. Most of the flat-based, fine fabric, Black-and-red ware bowls exhibit highly lusturous polished surfaces.

Out of a total number of 16 shapes/sherds bearing post-firing graffito-marks, as many as 14 are on Black-and-red ware and one each on black slipped and Red slipped ware potteries (Fig. 23). These are found on the outer surface of the pots, generally on the lower half of the body. Interestingly, some of these symbols resemble early *Brahmi* letters, while many of them are common to the Post-Harappan Chalcolithic and the more familiar peninsular Megalithic cultures of India.[92]

Among the small finds mention may be made of two iron objects (a chisel and a flat bar-celt type axe), one stone muller, two stone beads of carnelian and a number of pottery discs. Besides, the deposit also yielded a large number of charred and uncharred faunal remains and reed impressed burnt clay lumps.

Period-II

The Period-II, which in its earlier level was overlapped with Period-IB, did not augment any revolutionary change in the cultural material remains. Most of the ceramic industries of the preceding phase continued with further modifications (Fig. 25). However, the frequent occurrence of Black-and-red ware decreased considerably and plain Red ware, Red slipped ware and fine black slipped ware potteries predominate the ceramic assemblage. Painted sherds are conspicuous by their absence. Graffiti marks occur only on three Black-and-red ware sherds (Fig. 23).

The use of iron became more common, though the excavation did not yield any trace of on-site manufacturing activities. The iron objects comprise two nails, one nail parer, one drill-bit, one clamp, two chisels and one spear head. Among the other objects recovered from this period, mention may be made of two blue coloured transluscent bangle fragments, four stone beads of carnelian and quartz, one stone sling ball and a few pottery discs.

Although no house plans were recovered, reed impressed burnt clay lumps and a portion of a burnt floor, were duly met with. Uncharred faunal remains were also recovered from the deposit of this period.

The available evidence indicates that as far as this settlement was concerned, towards the close of Period-II the light appeared to be flickering out. The site was abandoned after this period.

Excavations at Kurumpadar

Situated on the right bank of the Mahanadi, opposite Kumersingha on the southern bank, the extensive mound of Kurumpadar (as locally called) lies in the district of Boudh (Fig. 11). The site can be approached from Kumersingha by crossing the Mahanadi by ferry operating in fair weather.

The ancient site is located about one kilometer west of the present village of Tentulipali (20° 51′ 10.1″ N and 84° 07′ 03.9″ E) and measures nearly 415 m in length and 95 m in width; the longer axis, in nearly east-west orientation, runs along the Mahanadi and exhibits a prominent vertical section of about 8 meters high, severely eroded by the river. In the cliff facing the riverside, distinct structures of rubble masonry are noticed. The mound is cut into almost two halves

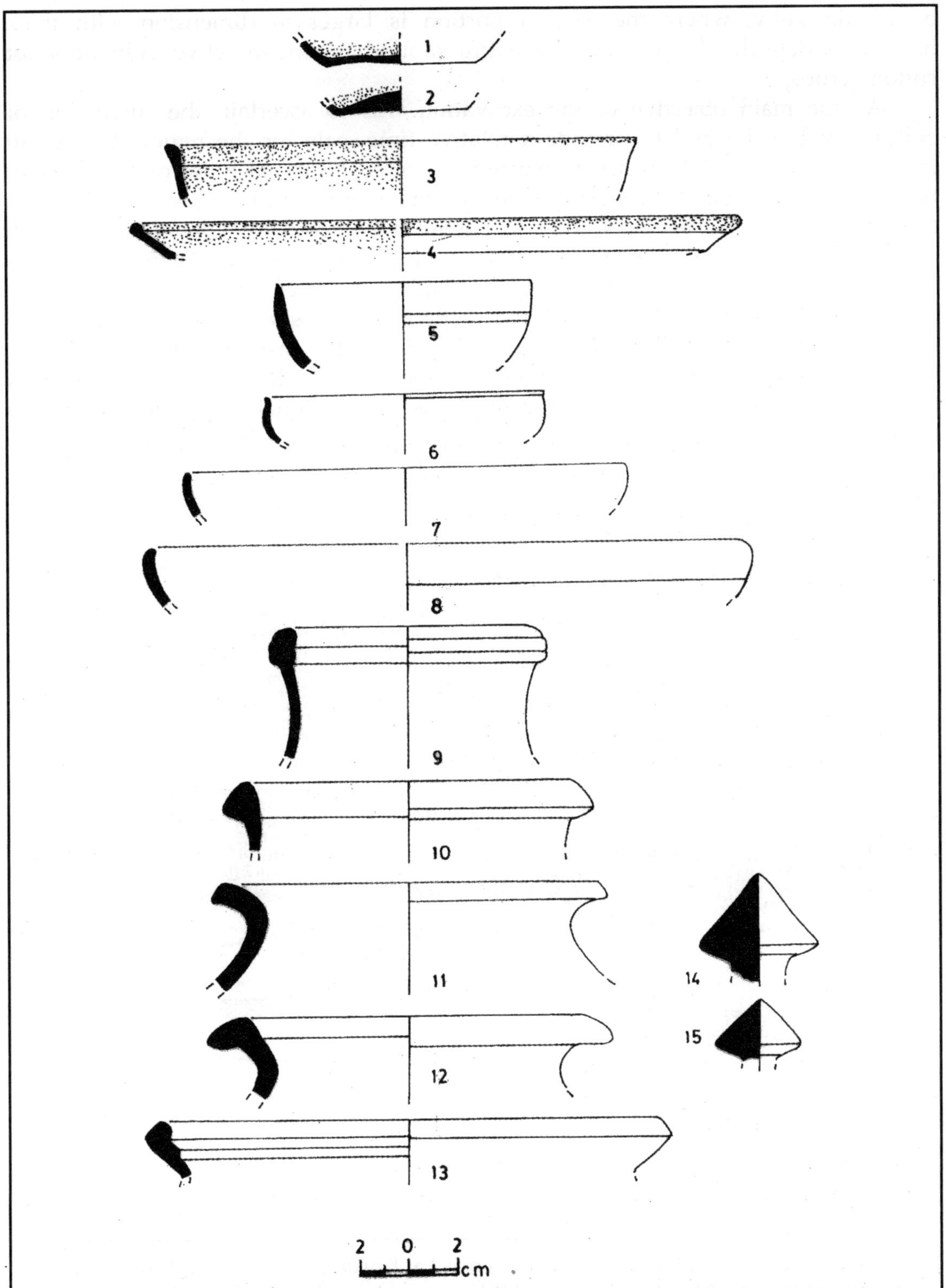

Fig. 25. Select shapes of *Period-II* from Kumersingha. Black-and-red ware (1-4), black slipped ware (5-8), Red slipped ware (9-11) and plain Red ware (12-15).

by a rain gully, where the eastern portion is larger in dimension with thick habitation deposit. At present, the entire mound is under active cultivation of cotton crops.

As the main objective of the excavation was to ascertain the succession of cultures at the site and to provide a relative time-scale for the region, two small cuttings (KMP-I and KMP-II) measuring 2.5 m x 2.5 m each, were trenched in both eastern as well as western portion of the mound and dug vertically down to the natural soil. This was done to ensure a complete section of the mound. The total cultural deposit of the mound was found to vary from 1.75 m in KMP-I (Fig. 26) to 0.90 m in KMP-II, which was laid on the western side of the mound. The excavations revealed that the first settlers of this site initially occupied the western half of the mound and then moved to the eastern portion, probably to avoid repeated seasonal floodings in the Mahanadi. From the combined testimony of both the cuttings, a continuous occupational sequence relating to three cultural periods have been identified. The main characteristics of each period are outlined below beginning with the earliest.

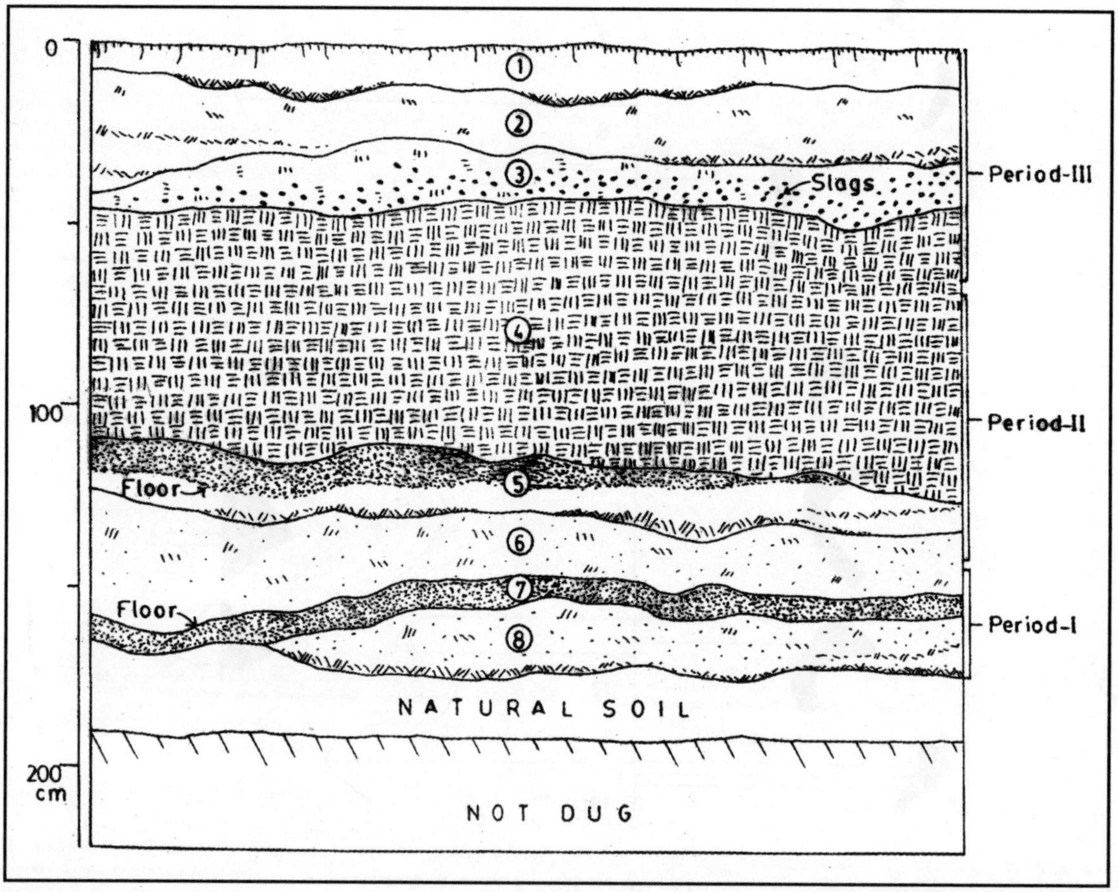

Fig. 26. Excavated section (facing south) in Trench-I at Kurumpadar. *Layer-1:* brownish, loose, sandy-silty soil; *Layer-2*: brownish-grey, slightly compact, sandy-silty; *Layer-3*: same as above; *Layer-4:* dark-grey, compact, silty-clayey soil; *Layer-5:* same as above; *Layer-7:* yellowish-grey, slightly compact, sandy-silty; *Layer-8:* ashy-grey, loose, sandy-silty soil.

Period-I (Late Chalcolithic)

The habitation deposit of this period extending to an average depth of 30 cm in KMP-I and 90 cm in KMP-II, above the natural soil, was found to be Late Chalcolithic in cultural content. Although no trace of any metal was encountered, the ceramic industry of this period, represented by a large number of Black-and-red ware, Red slipped ware (including brownish and chocolate slipped varieties), burnished black/dark-grey ware, a few black slipped ware and plain Red ware, demonstrates close resemblance with those from Khameswaripali Period-II and late levels of Khajeriapali. Except plain Red ware, all the other potteries are thick slipped and thoroughly burnished. Their fabric varies from medium to thick, while the large majority is medium textured. Barring a solitary specimen of white painted Red slipped ware shape, decoration of the potteries are mostly restricted to appliqué, incised and punctured design patterns. The vessel forms in the Black-and-red ware included convex-sided bowls, basins, and medium-sized vases or *handis;* those in Red slipped ware comprised *handis*, vases, basins, platters and a variety of lids with mostly vertical flat handles; those in plain Red ware include storage jars, vases, basins, bowls and those with multiple perforations on the base, platters and lids; and in burnished black/dark-grey ware and black slipped ware comprise *handis*, medium-sized vases, platters, bowls and lids (Fig. 27). Dishes are conspicuous by their absence. Interestingly, two potsherds, one each in Black-and-red ware and burnished Black ware, contain post-firing graffiti marks (Fig. 28). The rim portion of some of the pots in Black-and-red ware, burnished Black ware and Red slipped ware, bears marks of post-firing red ochre application.

Among the miscellany of less abundant finds were reed-impressed burnt clay lumps, pottery hop-scotches and a large quantity of heavily calcretised faunal remains.

Period-II (Iron Age)

This period marks the beginning of Iron Age at the site. The systematic use of iron was known right from the early level of this period. Significantly, in trench KMP-I, at a depth of 1.05 m from the top, was encountered evidence for iron smelting activities. A shallow pit of 65 cm diameter was found to contain lumps of iron slags, charcoal, ash and a complete specimen of vitrified tuyere at the bottom.[93] This clearly demonstrates iron smelting operations at the site. Similar bowl-furnaces have also been reported from Pandu-Rajar-Dhibi and Jodhpura[94] in Early Iron Age contexts. However, it remains to be investigated whether iron smelters of Kurumpadar, belonging to Period-I, had exploited the locally available lateritic deposit or they imported regular iron ores from distantly located sources, like Bonaigarh-Keonjhar complex, located some 200 km north-west of the site. Of the three iron objects recovered from this period, two belonged to the category of chisels and one unidentifiable object. Other finds of the period included one *cowri* shell of marine origin, one bladelet core, pottery hop-scotches, reed impressed burnt clay lumps and faunal remains.

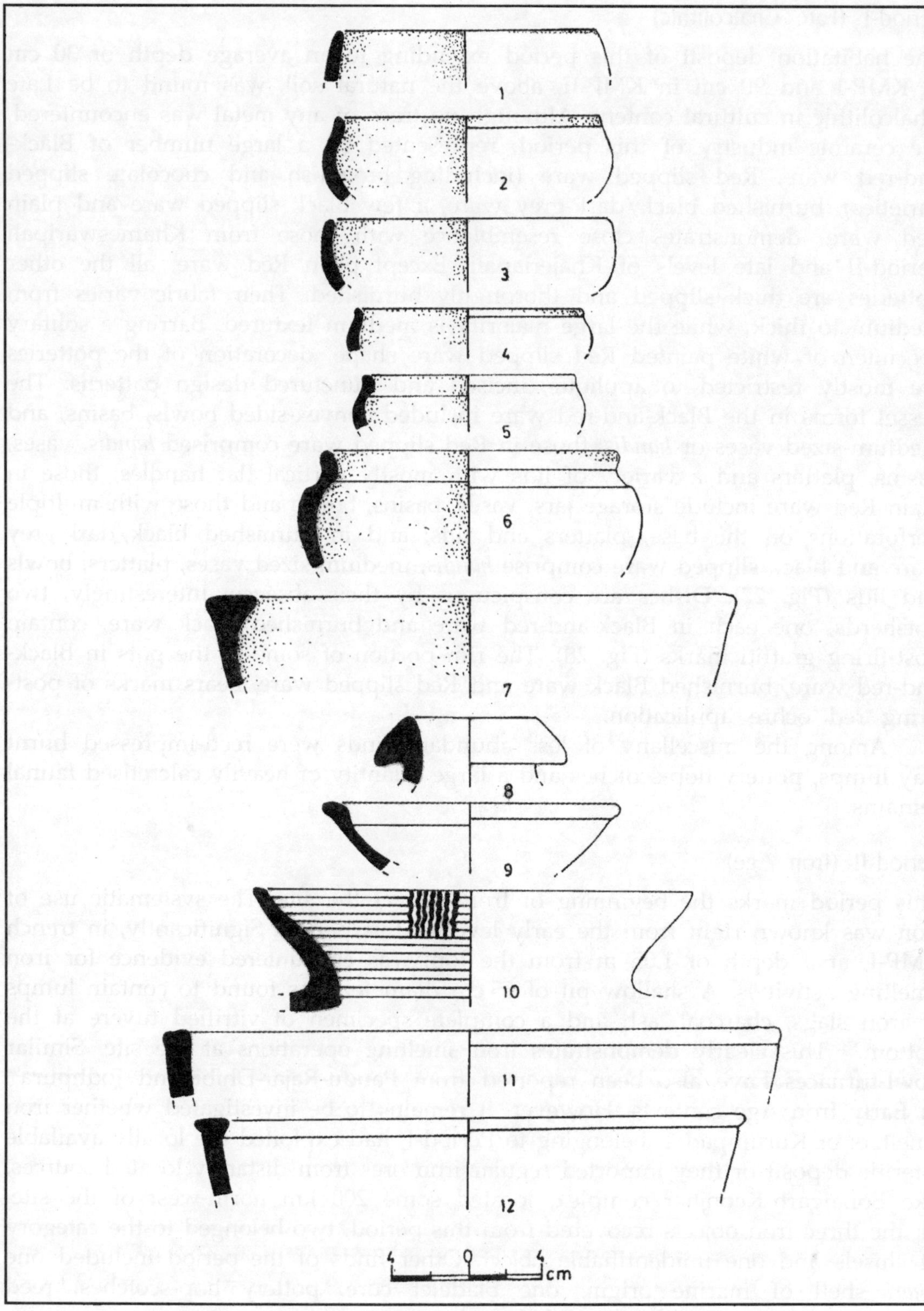

Fig. 27. Representative shapes of *Period-I* from Kurumpadar. Black-and-red ware (1-7), Red slipped ware (8-10) and plain Red ware (11 and 12).

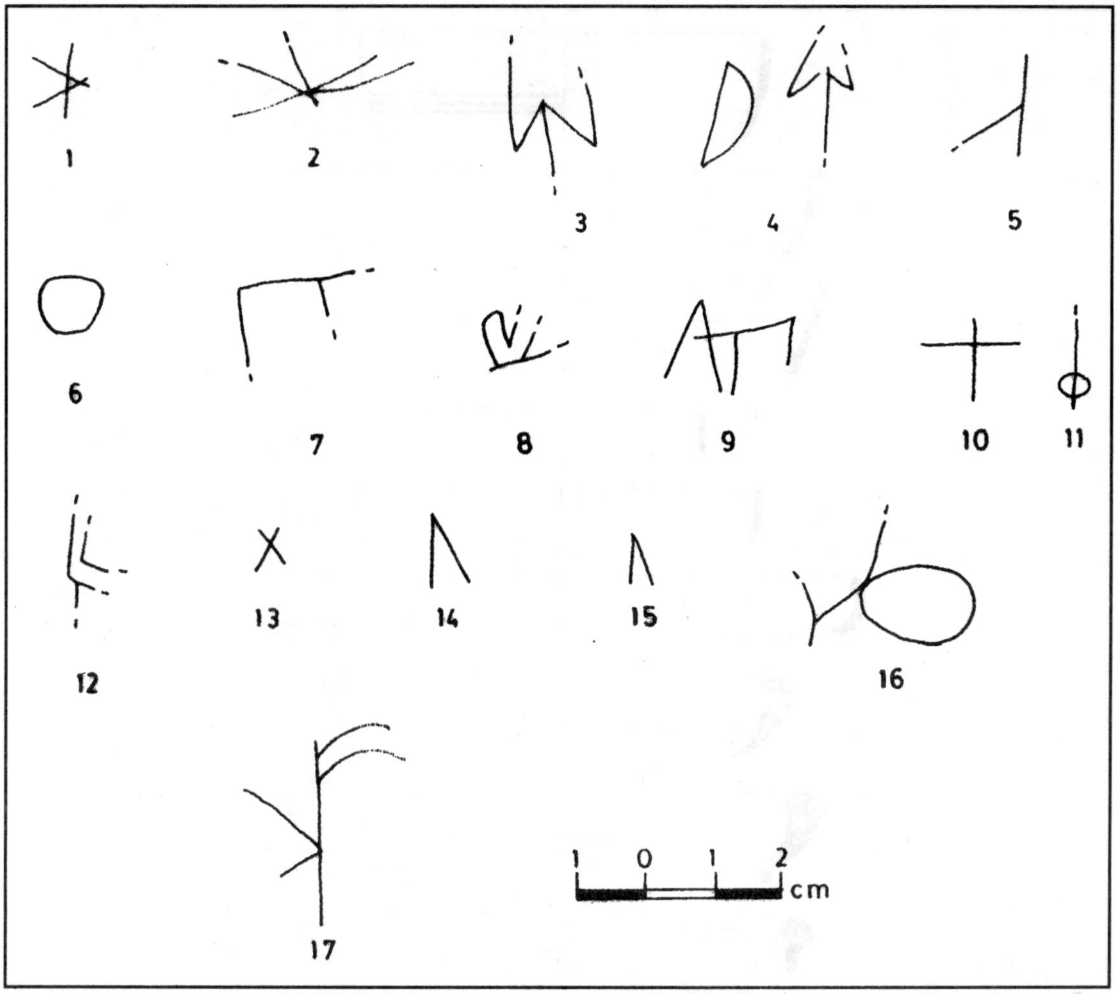

Fig. 28. Graffiti marks on potteries from Kurumpadar. *Period-I:* 1 on burnished Black ware, 2 on Black-and-red ware; *Period-II*: 3-12 on Black-and-red ware, 13-16 on black slipped ware; *Period-III:* 17 on plain Red ware.

The characteristic ceramic industries of the preceding period went into disuse and were replaced by fine fabric pots in Black-and-red ware, black slipped ware and Red slipped ware. In terms of vessel forms and manufacturing techniques, the potteries in general show striking similarities with those from Period-IB of Kumersingha site (Fig. 29). The differing ceramic industries, being quite distinctive and developed, while emphasizing the stability in economy, also indicate inter-relationship with other contemporary sites in the region. Interestingly, as many as 11 Black-and-red ware and 3 black slipped ware sherds bear a variety of post-firing graffito marks, some of which are strikingly similar to those from Kumersingha (Fig 28).

Period-III (Early Historic)

The period is distinguished principally by the occurrence of a silver-plated punch-marked coin and evidence for large-scale glass manufacturing activities.

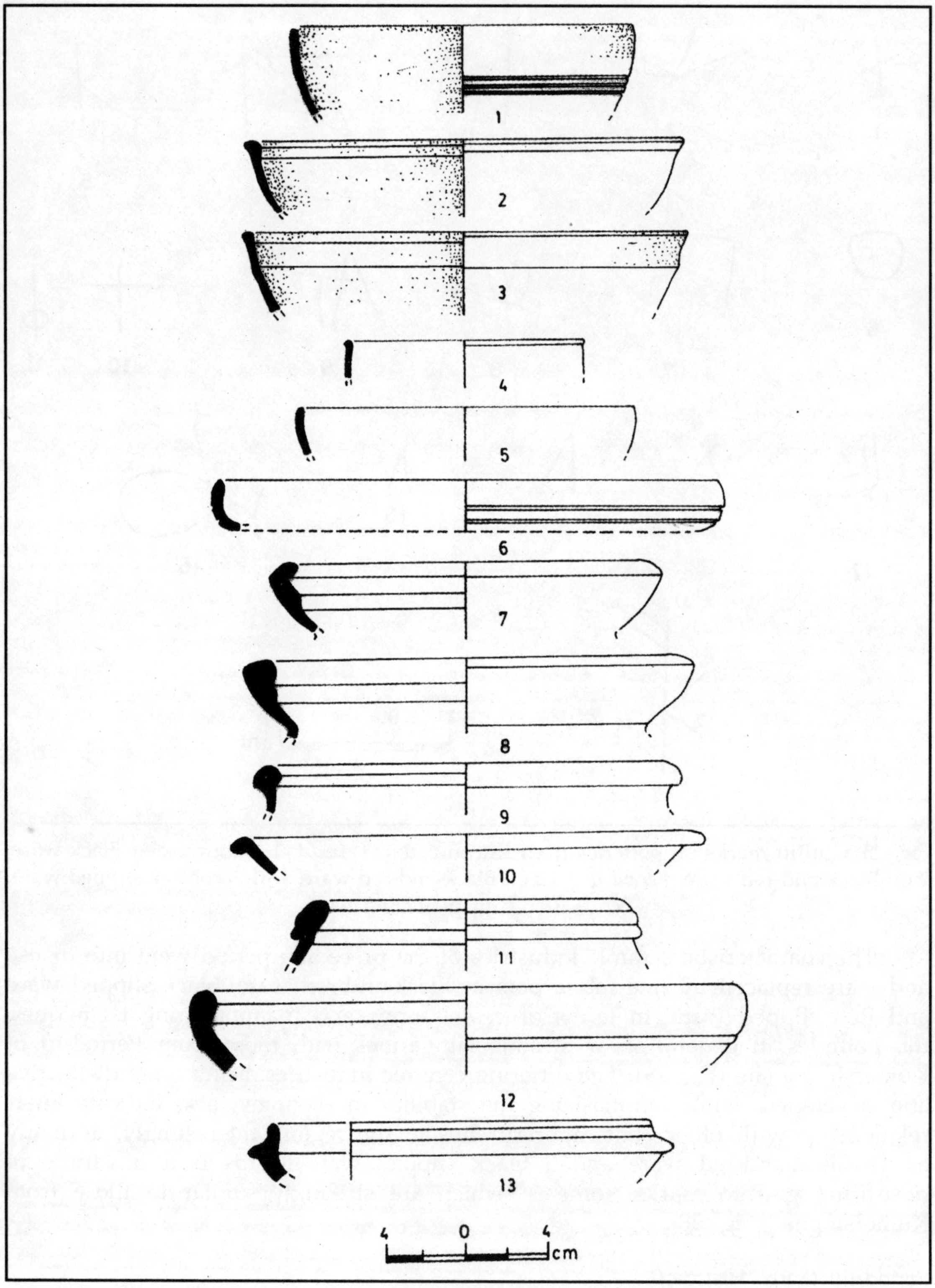

Fig. 29. Representative potteries of *Period-II* from Kurumpadar. Black-and-red ware (1-3), black slipped ware (4-6), Red slipped ware (7-10) and plain Red ware (11-13).

The coin was encountered in the second layer at a depth of 44 cm from trench KMP-I. After a thorough chemical treatment of the heavily patinated coin, it was found that the specimen was made of silver-plated copper, having five distinct symbols on the obverse and two lightly punched identical minute symbols on the reverse side.[95] Most of the symbols registered on the coin occur frequently on the typical imperial variety of silver punch-marked coins of the earlier series, reported from different parts of Orissa.[96] Similar coins dated to about 4th-3rd century BC have also been reported from the excavations at Sonpur in Bihar.[97]

From a depth of 35 cm in trench KMP-I, were recovered 35 kg of slags, several blue coloured glass ingots, drawn tubes, several fragments of semi-finished glass bangles, broken parts of burnt tuyeres and one each of monochrome (blue) and bi-chrome (blue and deep orange) glass bangle fragments. The evidence clearly suggests large-scale manufacturing of glass objects, mainly bangles. It appears that by this time glass industry as a specialized craft emerged in the Middle Mahanadi Valley region of Orissa. A preliminary chemical and spectroscopic analyses of some glass ingots and bangles clearly suggest Kurumpadar as an important trading centre, which was probably supplying glass ingots to the neighbouring areas for manufacturing different objects.[98] Interestingly, the chemical composition of glass objects from Kurumpadar also exhibit close resemblance with those from the Sisupalgarh site,[99] except the colouring agents, viz, copper, manganese and cobalt, which were added during the manufacture of different objects.

Amongst the metal objects, mention may be made of three iron nails and a copper bangle fragment. Other small finds included two *cowri* shells of marine origin, four spherical stone beads of carnelian and quartz and a number of pottery hop-scotches.

The ceramic industry is mainly represented by Red ware and black slipped ware. Although Red slipped ware and Black-and-red ware continued to exist, they constituted a negligible percentage in the collection (Fig. 30). The ceramic industries, though for the most part utilitarian and of little aesthetic value, exhibited widespread inter-relationship.

As noted earlier, near the trench KMP-I, a portion of a rubble structure was found exposed on the cliff section facing the Mahanadi. Although no such structures were encountered inside the trench KMP-I, on circumstantial grounds the rubble masonry may be assigned to Period-III.

The period was marked by occupational specialization, which emerged with the impact of the iron-using traits. The economic and social development no longer remained local but was influenced by other trait elements diffused through inter- as well as intra-regional trade and exchange network. Here particular mention may be made of the marine *cowri* shells, which were brought to the site from the coastal Orissa, probably by way of trade. Similarly, the nearest source of iron ore lies some 200 km north-west of the present sites. The system of coinage, concomitant of urbanization, came into being towards the later part of the period. The excavated assemblages appear to suggest a gradual transformation from reciprocity economy of the preceding phases to the conscious choice of economic activity centred around coinage with the adoption of

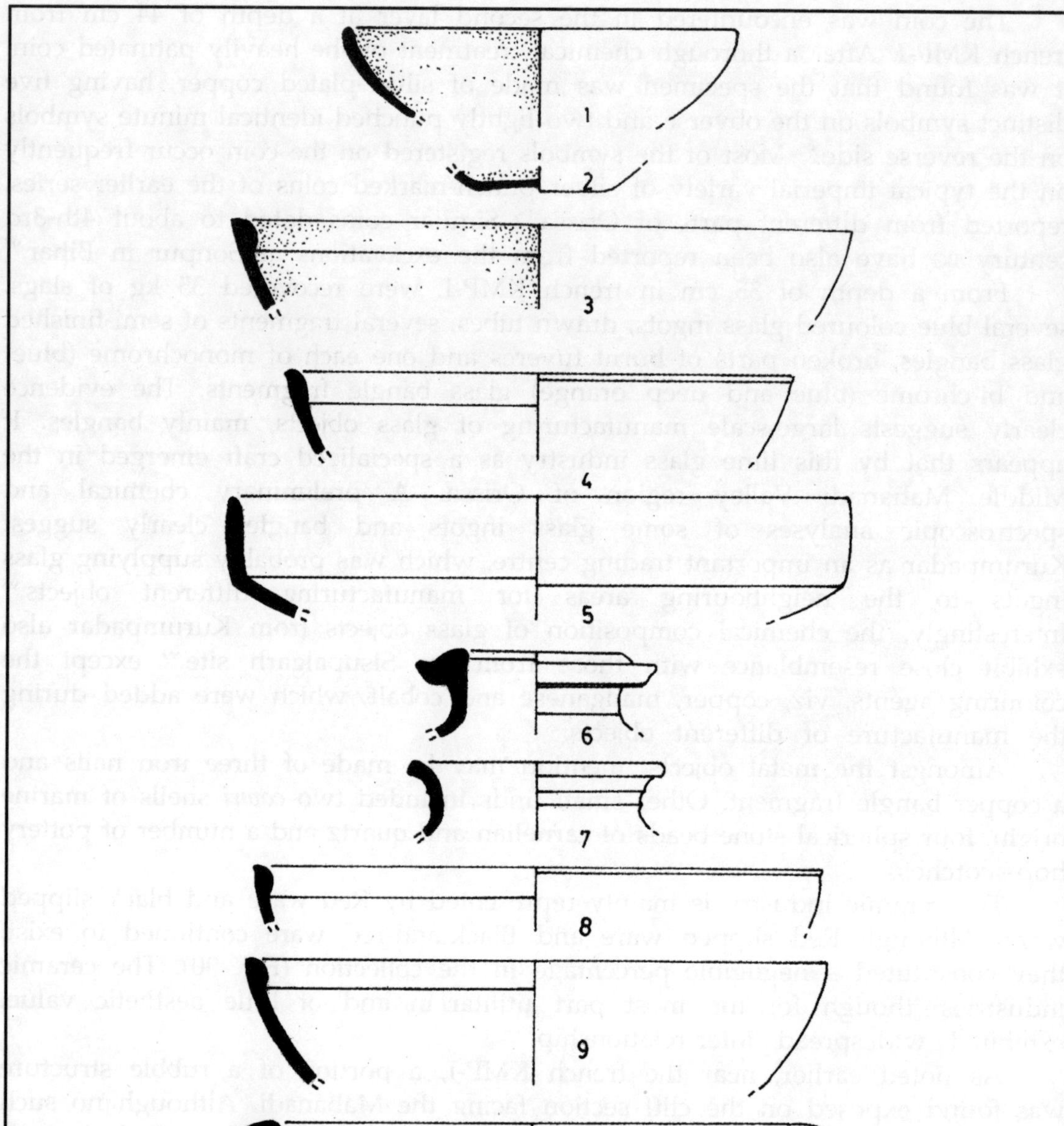

Fig. 30. Select shapes of *Period-III* from Kurumpadar. Black-and-red ware (1-3), black slipped ware (4 and 5), Red slipped ware (6-9) and plain Red ware (10 and 11).

specialized crafts during the Early Historical Period. On circumstantial grounds the beginning of Iron Age at Kumersingha and Kurumpadar may tentatively be assigned a time period of early first millennium BC and that of Early Historical Phase, 5th-4th century BC.

The fact that the Middle Mahanadi Valley of Orissa witnessed burgeoning of settlements during the Iron Age and Early Historical phases, is now sufficiently attested to by the wide geographical distribution of rural as well as fortified settlement sites, characterized by the occurrence of a variety of homogeneous ceramic industries, evidence for craft specialization in the manufacture of metal tools and implements, glass objects and semi-precious and precious stone beads, punch-marked and cast coins of copper and silver, evidence for inter- as well as intra-regional trade and exchange network, etc. Similar trend of development has also been traced in the middle Ganga plains[100] and West Bengal.[101] However, we believe that the process of early state formation in this part of Orissa highlands, which form the potential natural resource zone of the state, has to be looked for in its proto-historic root.

CONCLUDING REMARKS

The foregoing accounts of the recent archaeological investigation in the Middle Mahanadi Valley of Orissa clearly reveal the tremendous potential of the region for furnishing insights into how the egalitarian hunter-gatherer adaptations gradually shifted towards permanent settlement and food production and finally to complex urbanization. Obviously, a considerable amount of work still remains to be done in the Middle Mahanadi Valley before more scientific observations about the history of human settlement can be presented. However, the author is fully aware of the limitations of the present investigation as it is based on the study of surface sites as well as restricted vertical excavations. Nevertheless, it is also observed that human occupation of the valley and its contiguous areas saw no major periods of abandonment right from the Mesolithic to the Early Historical Period.

REFERENCES

1. R.L. Singh, *India: A Regional Geography,* Varanasi, NGSI, 1971, pp. 754-75.
2. P. Mohanty, "Stone Age Research in Orissa, An Overview", *Man in India,* Vol. 72 (2), 1992, pp. 207-32.
   K.K. Basa, *Problems and Perspectives on Archaeology of Orissa, India,* Bhubaneswar, D.S.A. Department of Anthropology, Utkal University, 1994.
3. S.B. Ota, "Mesolithic Cultures of the Phulbani District of Orissa: With Special Reference to the Heavy Tool Components", *Bulletin of the Deccan College Post-Graduate and Research Institute,* Vol. 45, 1986, pp. 79-85.
4. S.B. Ota, "New Research Designs in the Prehistoric Research in Orissa with special reference to Pebble industry of North Boudh–Khandhamal District", *Manav,* Vol. 1 (1), 1982-83, pp. 166-80.
   P. Mohanty, "Mesolithic Hunter Gatherers of Keonjhar, Orissa, India", *Asian Perspectives,* Vol. 32(1), 1993, pp. 87-104.

P. Mohanty, *et al.*, "Stone Age Cultures of Mayurbhanj District, Orissa", *Men in India*, Vol. 77 (2 & 3), 1997, pp. 159-77.

5. S. Panda, "A survey of Archaeological sites in the Ong Valley, Orissa with special reference to the Mesolithic industries", *Unpublished M.Phil Thesis*, Sambalpur University, 1995-96.
6. P. Mohanty, "Mesolithic Culture and Ethnography of Keonjhar District, Orissa", in K.K. Basa and P. Mohanty (eds.), *Archaeology of Orissa*, New Delhi, Pratibha Prakashan, 2000, pp. 114-52.
7. F. Bordes, "Considerations sur la typologies et les Techniques dans le paleolithique", *Quarter Band*, 18, 1967, pp. 25-55.
8. D.J. Mulvaney, *The Prehisotry of Australia*, London, Thames & Hudson, 1969.
9. J. Kamminga, "Journey into the Microcosmos: A functional analysis of certain classes of prehistoric Australian stone tools", *Unpublished Ph.D. Thesis*, University of Sydney, 1978.
10. G.J. Bartstra, *Contributions to the study of the Paleolithic Patjitan Culture, Java, Indonesia*, Leiden, Rijkus Universities, 1976.
11. C.G. Sampson, *The Stone Age Archaeology of South Africa*, New York Academic Press, 1974.
12. P. Mohanty, *op. cit.*, 1993.
13. S.B. Ota, *op. cit.*, 1982-83,
14. H.D. Sankalia, *Mesolithic and Premesolithic industries form the Excavation at Sangankallu, Bellary*, Poona, Deccan College, 1969.
15. C.G. Majumdar, and S.N. Rajguru, *Ash Mound Excavations at Kupgal*, Poona, Deccan College, 1966.
16. B. Narasimhaiah, *Neolithic and Megalithic Cultures in Tamil Nadu*, New Delhi, Sandeep Prakashan, 1980.
17. P. Rajendran, "The Coastal Mesolithic Industries of South India and their Chronology", *Bulletin of the Indo Pacific Prehistory Association*, Vol. 4, 1983, pp. 18-31.
18. P. Rajendran, "Environment and Stone Age Cultures of North Kerala", *Unpublished Ph.D. Thesis*, University of Poona, 1979.
19. A.H. Dani, *Prehistory and Protohistory of Eastern India*, Calcutta, 1960.
20. G. Corvinus, "Quarternary Stratigraphy of Intermontane Dun Valley of Dang Deokhuri and Associated Prehistoric Settlements in Western Nepal", in S. Wadia *et al.* (eds.), *Quaternary Environment and Geoarchaeology of India*, Bangalore, GSI, Memo no. 32, 1995, pp. 124-49.
21. J.D. Clark, *The Prehistory of Africa*, New York, Praeger, 1970.
22. A.A. Formozov, "Microlithic sits in the Asiatic USSR", *American Antiquity*, Vol. 27 (1), 1961, pp. 82-92.
23. D.J. Mulvaney, *op. cit.*, 1969.
24. C. Chun, "The Microlithic in China", *Journal of Anthropological Archaeology*, Vol. 3 (2), 1984, pp. 79-115.
25. G.A. Clark, *The Asturian of Cantabria: Early Holocene Hunter – Gatherers in Northern Spain*, Tucson, University of Arizona Press, 1983.
26. S.B. Ota, "Mesolithic Culture of Phulbani District, Orissa with special reference to heavy tool component", *Bulletin of the Deccan College, Post-graduate and Research Institute*, Vol. 45, 1986, pp. 79-85.
27. D. Kraybill, "Pre-Agricultural tools for the preparation of foods, in the Old Worlds", in C.A. Reed (eds.), *Origins of Agriculture*, The Hague Mouton, 1977, pp. 485-521.
28. J. Kamminga, *op. cit.*, 1978.

   B. Heyden, *Paleolithic Reflections Lithic Technology and Ethnographic Excavations Among the Australian Aborigines, Atlantic Highlands*, N.J. Humanities Press, 1979.

W.C. Ferguson, "Edge Angle Classification of the Quninup Brooks Implements Testing the Ethnographic Analogy", *Oceania,* Vol. 15, 1980, pp. 58-72.

E.N. Wilmsen, "Functional Analysis of Flaked Stone Artefacts", *American Antiquity,* Vol. 33, 1968, pp. 155-61.

T.R. Hester, *et al.,* "A Functional Analysis of Clear Fork artefacts from the Rio Grande Plain, Texas", *American Antiquity,* Vol. 33 (1), 1973, pp. 90-96.

29. A.M. Bateman, *Economic Mineral Deposits*, New York, John Wiley, 1955.
30. N. Senapati, *Orissa District Gazetteers: Sambalpur,* Cuttack, Government Press Orissa, 1971.
31. P.C. Anderson Gerfaud, "A Consideration of the Uses of Certain Backed and Lustered Stone Tools form late Mesolithic and Natufian Levels of Abu Hureyra and Mureybet (Syria)", in *Travaux de la Maixon de L' Orient Meditraneen,* 1983.

    P.C. Anderson Gerfaud, "Using Pre-historic Stone Tools to Harvest Cultivated Wild Cereals Preliminary Observations of Traces and Impact Oxford", *BAR International Series*, 1988.

    R. Unger Hamilton, "Microscopic striations on flint sickle blades as an indication of plant cultivation: preliminary results", *World Archaeology*, Vol. 17, 1985, pp. 121-126.
32. B. Heyden, "Stone tool functions in the western desert", in R.V.S. Wright (ed.), *Stone Tools as Cultural Markers: Change, Evolution, Complexity*, Canberra A.I.A.S., 1977, pp. 178-88.

    H.J. Juel Jensen, "Functional Analysis of Prehistoric flint tools by high power microscopy : A Review of West European Research", *Journal of World Prehistory*, Vol. 2 (1), 1988, pp. 53-88.

    R.A. Gould, *et al.*, The Lithic Assemblage of the Western Desert Aborigines of Australia, *American Antiquity,* Vol. 36, 1971, pp. 149-69.
33. O. Bar-Yosef, "Direct and Indirect Evidence for Hafting in the Epi-Paleolithic and Neolithic of the Southern Levant", in D. Stordeur (ed.), *Travaux De La Maison de L'Orient,* 15, Lyon Maixon De L'Orient, 1987, pp. 155-64.

    A. Fisher, *et al.,* "Macro and micro wear traces on lithic projectile points experimental results and prehistoric examples", *Journal of Danish Archaeology,* Vol. 3, 1984, pp. 13-46.
34. N. Senapati, *op. cit.,* 1971.
35. B.K. Thapar, *Recent Archaeological Discoveries in India,* Paris, The Center for East Asian Cultural Studies, UNESCO, 1985.
36. *Indian Archaeology, 1981-82: A Review,* New Delhi, Archaeological Survey of India, p. 54.

    K.C. Tripathy, "South Orissa Prehistory: The First Record of Stone Age Tools", *Asian Perspectives*, Vol. 15, 1972, pp. 47-59.

    K.C. Tripathy, "Preliminary Archaeological Survey of the Ib", *Manav*, Vol. 1 (1), 1982-83, pp. 60-66.

    S.K. Mishra, "Stone Age Antiquities of Sarsara and other sites in the Jira River Basin of Orissa : A Reappraisal", *Manav,* Vol. 1 (1), 1982-83, pp. 31-42.

    B. Tripathy, "Archaeological exploration in Boudh district, Orissa: A Preliminary Report", *BDCRI*, Vol. 56-67, 1996-97, pp. 41-54.

    P. Mohanty and B. Mishra, "Early Historic Kalahandi", in P. Pal (ed.), *Orissa Revisited,* Mumbai, Marg Publication, 2001, pp. 17-26.

    P. Mohanty, and B. Mishra, "Recent Archaeological discoveries in Kalahandi District of Orissa", (In Press).
37. A. Naik, "Structural and Geochemical Evolution of the Pre-Cambrian of Sambalpur Area in North West Orissa (India)", *Unpublished Ph.D. Thesis,* Sambalpur University, 1994.

38. P.K. Behera, "Sulbhdihi: A Neolithic Celt Manufacturing center in Orissa", *Puratattva*, Vol. 22, 1992, pp. 124-32.
    P.K. Behera, "Neolithic Culture Complex of Banaigarh, Orissa", in K.K. Basa and P. Mohanty (eds.), *Archaeology of Orissa*, New Delhi, Pratibha Prakashan, 2000, pp. 222-63.
39. K.K. Basa, *op. cit.*, in *Archaeology of Orissa*, 2000, pp. 16-61.
40. A. Naik, *op. cit.*, 1994.
41. J.E. Ericson, "Towards the analysis of lithic production systems", in J.E. Ericson and B.A. Purdy (eds.), *Prehistoric Quarries and Lithic Production*, Cambridge, Cambridge University Press, 1984, pp. 1-9.
42. D. Stout, "Skill and Cognition in Stone Tool Production", *Current Anthropology*, Vol. 43 (5), 2002, pp. 693-722.
43. J.E. Ericson, *op. cit.*, 1984, p. 6.
44. P.K. Behera, "Excavations at Khameswaripali: A Protohistoric Settlement in the Middle Mahanadi Valley, Orissa: A Preliminary Report", *Pragdhara*, Vol. 11, 2001a, pp. 13-34.
45. *Ibid.*
46. *Ibid.*, pp. 22-27.
47. G.L. Possehl (ed.), *Radiocarbon Dates for South Asian Archaeology*, Philadelphia University of Pennsylvania, 1990, pp. 11-12.
48. V.D. Misra, *et al.*, "Neolithic cultures of Northern Vindhyas with special reference to Tokwa", *Bharati*, 25 (I & II), 1998-1999, pp. 211-33.
49. B.P. Singh, "Stages of culture development in the middle Ganga plains : A case study of Senuwar", *Pragdhara*, 11, 2001, pp. 109-18.
50. G.L. Possehl (ed.), *op. cit.*, 1990, p. 60.
51. D.P. Agrawal, and S. Kusumgar, *Prehistoric Chronology and Rediocarbon Dating in India*, New Delhi, Munshiram Manoharlal, 1974.
52. G.L. Possehl (ed.), *op. cit.*, 1990, p. 56.
53. P.K. Behera, "Prehistoric rock art pertaining to fertility cult and other subjects of Orissa", *Pragdhara*, Vol. 2, 1992, pp. 7-17.
    P.K. Behera, "Investigations into the Newly Discovered Rock Art Sites of Deulga Hills, Orissa", *Pragdhara*, 11, 2001b, pp. 1-11.
    S. Pradhan, "Rock Art in Orissa", in *Archaeology of Orissa, op. cit.*, 2001, pp. 635-50.
54. *Indian Archaeology, 1989-90: A Review*, pp. 80-86.
55. P.K. Behera, *op. cit.*, 2001a.
56. *Ibid.*, pp. 14-18.
57. S.R. Rao, "Ceramics of the Indus valley in Gujarat", *Marg*, 14 (3), 1961.
58. S.R. Rao, "Excavations at Rangpur and other explorations in Gujarat", *Ancient India*, 18-19, 1963, pp. 5-207.
59. *Indian Archaeology, 1963-64: A Review*, p. 15.
    U.V. Singh, "Further Excavation at Eran", *Journal of the Madhya Pradesh Itihas Parishad*, Vol. 5, 1967.
60. T. Banerjee, "Chalcolithic Painted Pottery of Pandu Rajar Dhibi", *Pratna Samiksha*, 1, 1992, pp. 77-78.
61. B.S. Verma, "Black and Red Ware in Bihar", in B.P. Sinha (ed.), *Potteries in Ancient India*, Patna, 1969, pp. 102-11.
62. B.P. Singh, "The Chalcolithic Culture of Southern Bihar as revealed by the exploration and excavation in district Rohtas", *Puratattva*, 20, 1989-90, pp. 83-92.
63. B.K. Thapar, "Prakash 1955: A Chalcolithic site in the Tapi valley", *Ancient India*, 20-21, 1987, pp. 5-167.
64. B.K. Sinha, "Golbai: A protohistoric site on the coast of Orissa", in *Archaeology of Orissa*, *op. cit.*, 2000, pp. 322-48.

65. B.P. Singh, *op. cit.*, 1989-90, pp. 85, 88.
B.P. Singh, *op. cit.*, 1988-89, p. 9.
Indian Archaeology 1985-86: A Review, p. 7.
Indian Archaeology 1977-78: A Review, pp. 17-18.
66. F.R. Allchin, *Piklihal Excavation*, Hyderabad, Andhra Pradesh Government Archaeological Series, No. 1, 1960.
F.R. Allchin, *Utnur Excavation*, Hyderabad, Andhra Pradesh Government Archaeological Series, No. 5, 1961.
R.E.M. Wheeler, "Brahmagiri and Chandravali: 1947, Megalithic and Other Cultures in the Chitaldurg District, Mysore State", *Ancient India*, 4, 1984, pp. 100-310.
Z.D. Ansari and M.S. Nagaraja Rao, *Excavations at Sangankallu 1964-65*, 1969, Pune, Deccan College.
M.S. Nagaraja Rao and K.C. Malhotra, *The Stone Age Hill Dwellers of Tekkalkota*, 1965, Pune, Deccan College.
67. G.L. Badam, P.K. Behera and J. Mishra, "Chalcolithic Faunal Economy at Khameswaripali, Middle Mahanadi Valley, Orissa: A Bioarchaeological Perspective", *Current Science*, 80 (7), 2001, pp. 828-30.
68. P. Mohanty and B. Tripathy, "The Prehistoric, Protohistoric and the Early Historic Cultures of Orissa", *Pragdhara*, 8, 1997-98, pp. 69-90.
69. S. Pradhan, "Archaeological investigation in the Karandi Valley, Orissa", *Man and Environment*, 25 (1), 2000, pp. 99-101.
70. K. Barik, "A Study of the Ceramic Assemblage at Nuagarh: A Chalcolithic Site in the Middle Mahanadi Valley", *Unpublished M.Phil Thesis*, Sambalpur University, 2000.
71. P.K. Behera, *op. cit.*, 2001, pp. 14-18.
72. *Indian Archaeology 1984-85: A Review*, p. 58.
M. Brandtner, "Archaeology of Western Orissa, Finds from Nehena", in A. Parpola and P. Koskikallio (eds.), *South Asian Archaeology 1993*, Helsinki, Suomalainen Tiedeakatemia, 1994, pp. 101-14.
73. H.N. Singh, *History and Archaeology of Black and Red Ware*, 1982, New Delhi, Sandeep Prakashan.
B.P. Singh, *op. cit.*, 1989-90, pp. 83-92.
P. Singh, *Excavations at Narhan (1984-89)*, 1994, New Delhi, B.H.U. and B.R. Publishing Corporation.
V.N. Misra, "Balathal: A Chalcolithic settlement in Mewar, Rajasthan, India, Results of first three seasons excavation", *South Asian Studies*, 13, 1997, pp. 251-73.
74. K.K. Basa, *op. cit.*, 1994, p. 24.
Ibid., 2000, pp. 43-44.
D.K. Chakrabarti, *The issues in East Indian Archaeology*, 1998, New Delhi, Munshiram Manoharlal.
75 B.B. Lal, "Sisupalgarh 1948: Early Historic Fort in Eastern India", *Ancient India*, No. 5, 1949, pp. 60-105.
76 *Indian Archaeology 1956-57: A Review*, pp. 30-31.
77 D.R. Pradhan, *et al.*, "Manikapatna: An excavation report", *Purattattva*, 26, 1996, pp. 120-23.
78 G.C. Chauley, "Excavated Remains at Lalitagiri: A Buddhist Site in Orissa", in C. Margabandhu and K.G. Ramachandran (eds.), *Spectrum of Indian Culture*, 1996, New Delhi, Agam Kala Prakashan, pp. 216-20.
79 S.C. Behera (ed.), *Interim Excavation Reports*, Sambalpur University, 1982.
80 *Indian Archaeology 1989-90: A Review*, pp. 80-86.
81 D.K. Chakrabarti, *The Early use of Iron in India*, New Delhi, Oxford University Press, 1992.

D.K. Chakrabarti and N. Lahiri, "The Iron Age in India: The Beginning and Consequences", *Puratattva,* 24, 1994, pp. 12-32.

R. Tewari, "Antiquity of Iron in South Eastern Uttar Pradesh", *Bharati,* 25 (I & II), 1998-99, pp. 124-37.

82 B.K. Sinha, *op. cit.,* 2000, pp. 344-45.

83 K.K. Basa, *op. cit.,* 2000, p. 44.

84 P. Yule, *et al.,* "Sankerjang: A metal period burial site in the Dhenkanal uplands of Orissa", in M. Taddei (ed.), *South Asian Archaeology,* Rome, ISMEO, 1990, pp. 581-84.

85 Mohanty and Mishra, *op. cit.,* 2001, pp. 17-26.

B. Purohit, " A Survey of Early Historic and Historic Sites in the Middle Mahanadi Valley: with Special Reference to the Lower Tel Valley", *Unpublished M.Phil. Thesis,* Sambalpur University, 1993-94.

Brandtner, *op. cit.,* 1994.

Indian Archaeology, 1984-85: A Review, p. 58.

86 M. Lal, *Settlement History and the Rise of Civilization in the Ganga Yamuna Doab from 1500 BC to 300 AD,* 1984, New Delhi, B.R. Publishing Corporation.

G. Erdosy, "Urbanization and Early Historic India", *Oxford BAR International Series,* 1988.

F.R. Alchin, *The Archaeology of Early Historic South Asia,* Cambridge University Press, 1995.

D.K. Chakrabarti, *The Archaeology of Ancient Indian Cities,* New Delhi, Oxford University Press, 1995.

87 P.C. Rath, "Notes on important archaeological sites, Asurgarh in Sonepur State", *Journal of Kalinga Historical Research Society,* 1 (4), 1947, p. 308.

88 K. Barik, *op. cit.,* 2000.

89 *Ibid.* p. 37.

90 P.K. Behera, *op. cit.,* 2001.

91\. D.K. Chakrabarti, *The Early use of Iron in India,* 1992, Madras, Oxford University Press.

V. Tripathi, *The Age of Iron in South Asia,* 2001, New Delhi, Aryan Books.

92 B.B. Lal, "From the Megalithic to the Harappan. Tracing Back the Graffiti on the pottery", *Ancient India,* 16, 1986, pp. 4-24.

93 P.K. Behera, "Excavations at Kumersingha and Kurumpadar – the Iron Age settlements in the Middle Mahanadi Valley, Orissa: Results of the first season's work", *Pragdhara,* no. 13, 2002-2003, pp. 98-99.

94 R. Shrivastava, "Smelting furnances in Ancient India", *Indian Journal of History of Science,* Vol. 34(1), 1999, pp. 33-45.

95 P.K. Behera, and S. Khamari, "A Note on the Discovery of Silver Punch Marked Coin from Excavation at Kurumpadar, District Boudh (Orissa)", *Bharati,* 25 (I & II), 1998-99, pp. 205-10.

96 S. Tripathy, *Early and Medieval Coins and Currency System of Orissa,* 1986, Calcutta, Punthi Pustak.

97 B.P. Sinha and B.S. Verma, *Sonpur Excavations (1956 and 1959-1962),* 1977, Patna.

98 R. Singh and P.K. Behera, "A note on the Scientific Examination of Glass objects form Kurumpadar, District Boudh (Orissa)", *Pragdhara,* 12, 2001-2002, pp. 173-76.

99 B.B. Lal (Dr.), "Examination of some Ancient Indian glass specimens", *Ancient India,* No. 8, 1952, pp. 17-25.

100 R.S. Sharma, *The State and Varna Formation in the Middle Ganga Plains: an Ethno-Archaeological View,* 1996, New Delhi, Manohar Publisher.

101 D.K. Chakrabarti, *op. cit.,* 1998.

EXCAVATIONS AT NUAGARH-ASURGARH: A PRELIMINARY REPORT

Sadasiba Pradhan

Nuagarh-Asurgarh (20° 26' 4.87" N and 84° 0.5' 3" E) is an extensive archaeological mound situated between the twin villages of Kumersingha and Nuagarh at a distance of about 6 kilometers southeast of the *tehsil* headquarters of Birmaharajpur in Sonepur district of Orissa (Fig. 1).

The mound measures 580 meters in length (east-west), along the left bank of the Mahanadi, 300 meters in breadth (north-south) and about 7.5 meters in height above the present bed of the Mahanadi. The village Kumersingha (the site) reported the discovery of a copper plate charter of 12th century AD[1] issued by Raja Somesvara Deva of Telgu-Choda Dynasty from the capital city of Suvarnapura that recorded the donation of a village Kumarisingha to a Brahmin named Kadrapani Sarma.

The site is locally known as Asurgarh on account of the occasional discovery of human skeletal remains, iron objects and potteries of unknown antiquity in the cultivated surface and eroded sections of the mound. A series of ancient sites in Western Orissa bear the name Asurgarh for similar archaeological finds. Two such sites, namely, Narla-Asurgarh in Kalahandi district and Manamunda-Asurgarh in Boudh district (erstwhile Phulbani district) have been excavated by the Post-Graduate Department of History, Sambalpur University.

The present site was first reported by P.C. Rath in 1947.[2] In 1998, the author re-visited the site and took license from the ASI for trial excavation in 1999 in order to ascertain the culture-sequence of the site and find out its relationship with other Asurgarh sites in Western Orissa.

EXCAVATION

On account of its close proximity to the river along its left bank, much of the southern part of the mound have largely been eroded with deep cuts at several places caused by the high floods of the Mahanadi (Pl. 1). The northern portion of the mound that stands about four meters high above the adjoining plains

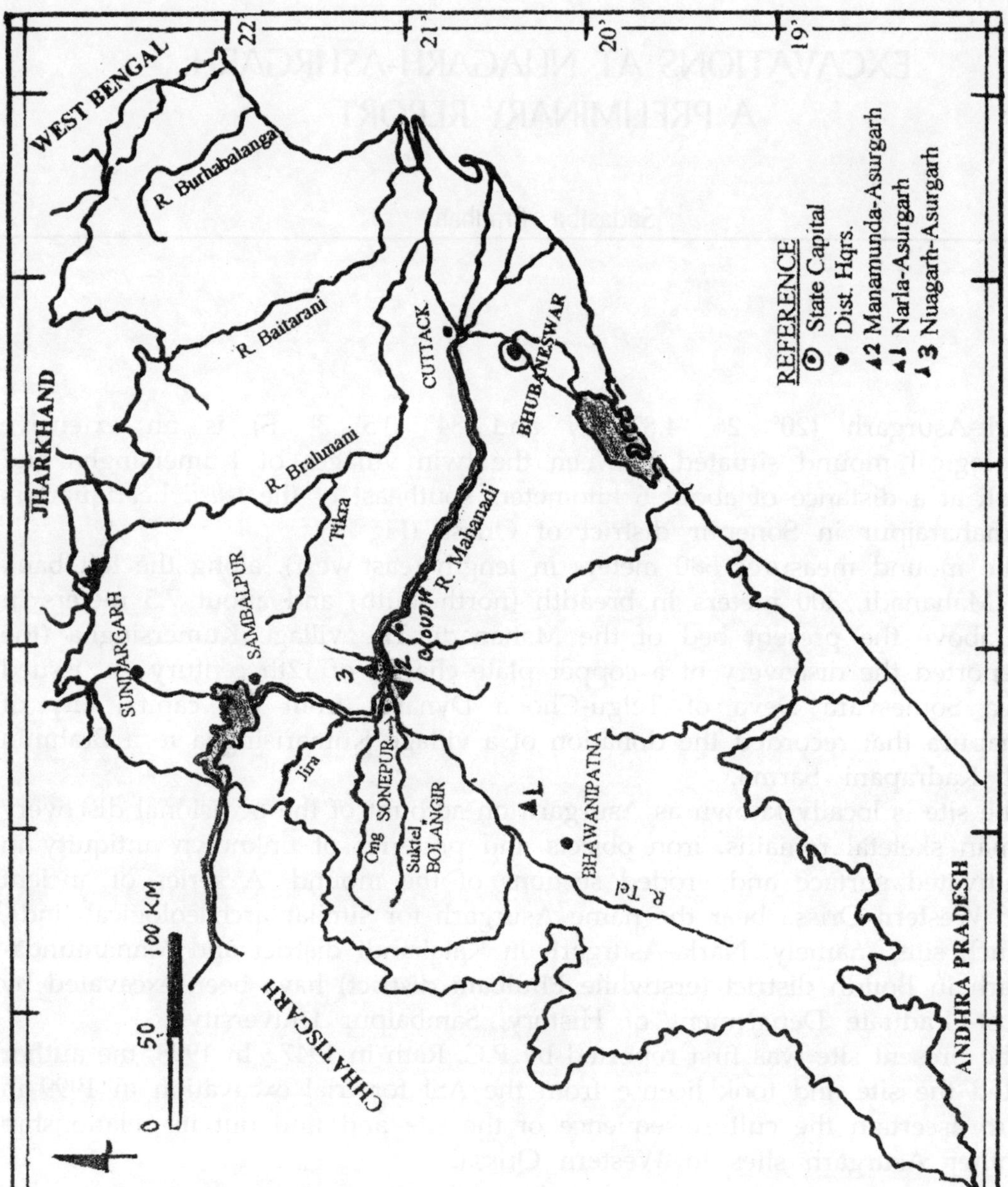

Fig. 1. Map of Orissa showing excavated Asurgarh sites.

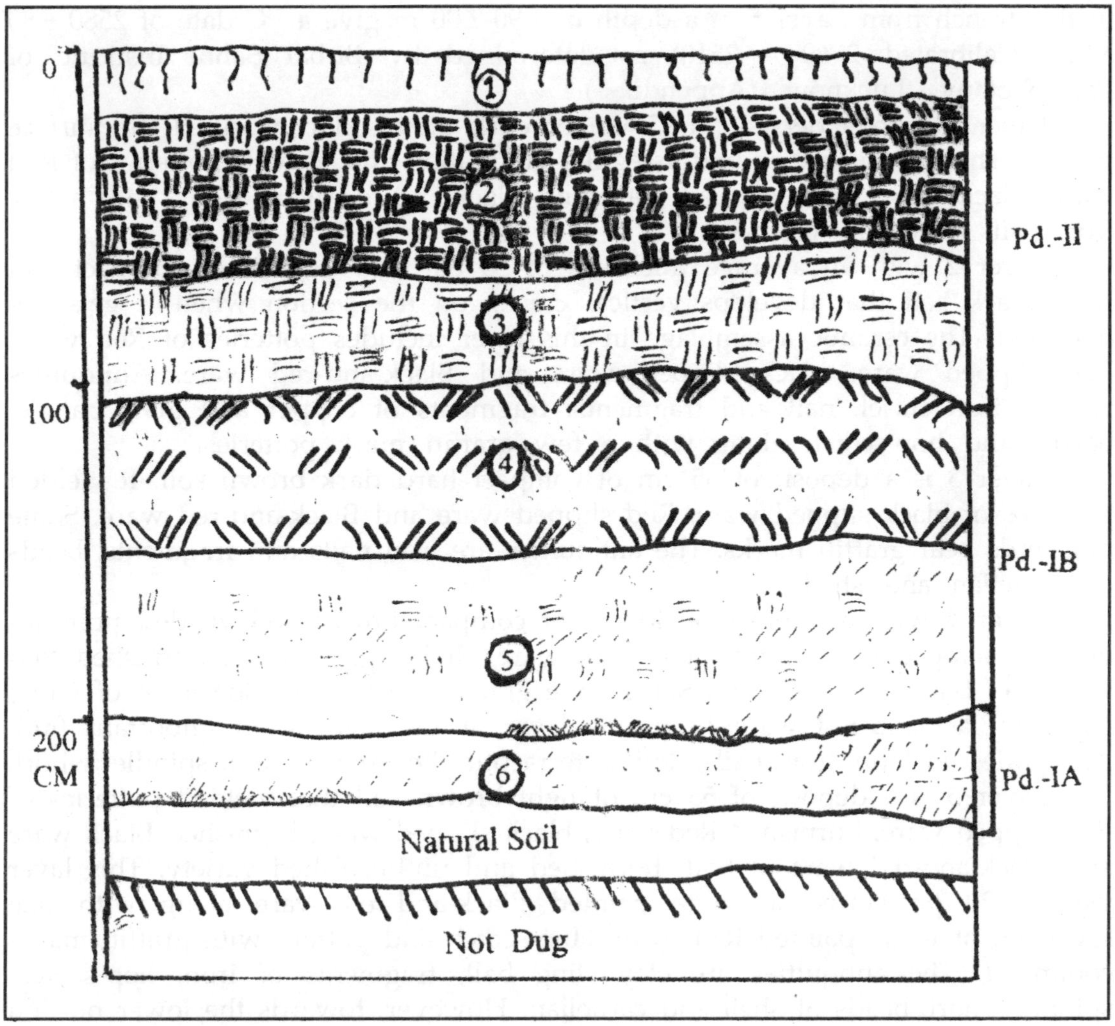

Fig. 2. Excavated section facing west to trench NGH-I.

and appears least affected is under active cultivation by the villagers, who own different portions of the mound. Three trial trenches (NGH-I, NGH-II & NGH-III) measuring 3 x 3 m each were laid in different locations of the mound taking into account its elevation, frequency of pottery and other artefacts from the surface find. While NGH-I and NGH-III were laid on the top of the mound that appeared to have been least affected by the high floods, NGH-II was laid on the eroded section of the mound at a distance of about 45 meters south-west of NGH-I. Natural soil was encountered at different depths of 2.25 m in NGH-I and NGH-III and 0.90 m. in NGH-II. While NGH-I and NGH-III yielded six occupational layers (Fig. 2), NGH-II exposed three occupational layers above the natural soil.

STRATIGRAPHY

Since the stratigraphy of NGH-I and NGH-III is almost identical, for convenience the layer-wise sequence of NGH-I is given in Fig. 2. Charcoal samples collected in this trench from Layer 5 at a depth of 1.90-2.00 m give a ^{14}C date of 2580 ± 80 YBP, (Calibrated 2760 – 2510) as determined by Birbal Sahni Institute of Palaeobotany, Lucknow (Appendix-1).

Layer 1 with a deposit of 15 cm of dark grey soil constituted the surface humus. The deposit comes under regular cultivation and yielded potteries of Red ware, Black ware, black slipped ware and Black-and-red ware along with a few iron nails and hop-scotches.

Layer 2 with an average thickness of 55 cm is a deposit of compact and hard black soil that develops vertical cracks on the section when it gets de-hydrated. The ceramic assemblage in this layer includes potteries of Red ware, Red slipped ware, black slipped ware and Black-and-red ware. Antiquities include iron chisel, nail and fragments; fragments of copper and glass bangle, beads, and hop-scotch along with a few graffiti mark potteries.

Layer 3 is a deposit of 35 cm of compact hard dark brown soil. It yielded potteries of black slipped ware, Red slipped ware and Black-and-red ware. Some potsherds bear graffiti marks. The antiquities are iron nails and fragments, beads of carnelian and shell.

Layer 4 with a deposit of 40 cm of compact brown soil yielded potteries of black slipped ware, burnished Black ware, Red slipped ware, burnished Red ware and Black-and-red ware. Some have graffiti marks. One specimen of white painted Black-and-red ware from this layer at the base is an important find. Antiquities include iron nails, knife, terracotta hop-scotch and spindle whorl.

Layer 5 is a deposit of 55 cm of light brown soil that yielded potteries of Red slipped ware, burnished Red ware, black slipped ware, burnished Black ware and Black-and-red ware of both burnished and un-burnished variety. This layer yielded 20 potsherds of white painted Black-and-red ware along with one specimen of white painted Red ware. Hop-scotch and pottery with graffiti marks continued. The antiquities are clay sling ball, fragments of iron, hop-scotch, spindle whorl, beads of shell and carnelian. However, towards the lower portion of this layer there is a marked difference in the antiquities that include bone points, animal bones with grooves and different stages of cutting and polishing, antlers with cut marks, ring stones and hammer stones, three microliths, and a Neolithic celt of basalt. Other miscellaneous finds include both charred and uncharred bones.

Layer 6 atop the natural soil is a deposit of 25 cm of dark brown soil mixed with patches of charcoal and ash. The potteries are red slipped, black slipped and burnished Red and Black ware, and Black-and-red ware along with some specimens of plain Red ware. White painted Black-and-red ware continues here. A few specimens of mat-impressed potteries have also come from the lower levels of this deposit. The antiquities recovered from this layer are two Neolithic celts and four microliths along with lumps of reed-impressed burnt clay and charred and un-charred bones.

Knobbed lids found in various pottery types that continued to exist throughout the occupational deposit except in Layer 6 constitute an important feature in the ceramic assemblage of the site.

POTTERY ASSEMBLAGE

Red ware

Red ware, which constitutes a dominant pottery type in India, continues to prevail all through from the bottom to the top. It constitutes 63.13% of the total excavated potteries. The layer-wise distribution of this pottery is 11.36% in Layer 1, 73.63% in Layer 2, 63.49% in Layer 3, 68.06% in Layer 4, 75.14% in Layer 5, and 74.36% in Layer 6. The characteristic shapes of this ware are bowl, basin, dish, vase, jar, *handi*, etc (Fig. 3). The fabric is from course to medium and fine with both thick and thin section. Few potsherds have paintings in black both in the inner and outer sides of the pots. Sometimes the ware has a thick slip in the outer side. The clay is tempered with fine grain sand, straw and husk that also speak about the use of grain. Potteries were made on fast-turned as well as slow-turned wheels. All are well-fired except a few in course fabric. Jars with splayed-out rims and convex bowls with featureless rim are the important shapes in this pottery type. Incised horizontal and oblique lines and

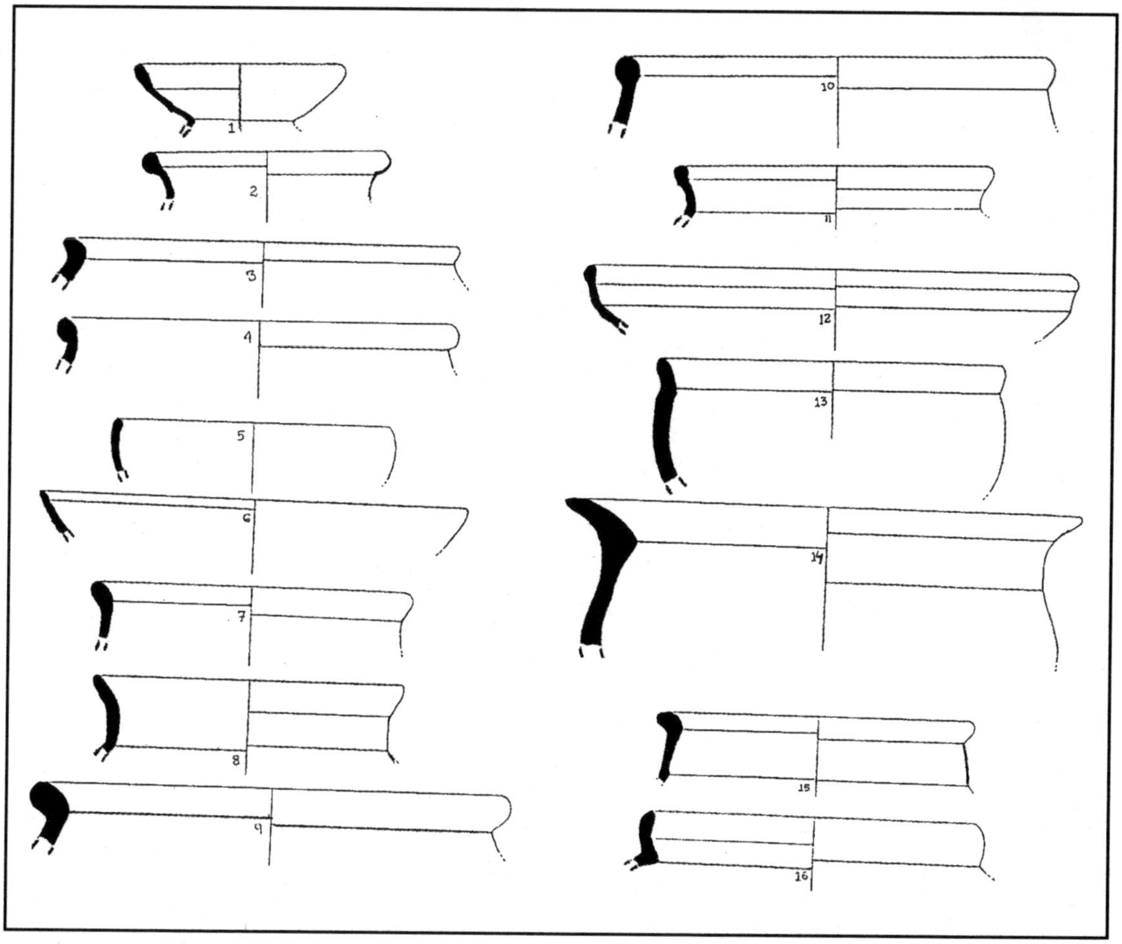

Fig. 3. Red slipped ware: 1- Layer, (1) 2-9 Layer, (2), 10-12 Layers (3), 13-14 Layer (4), 15-16 Layer (5).

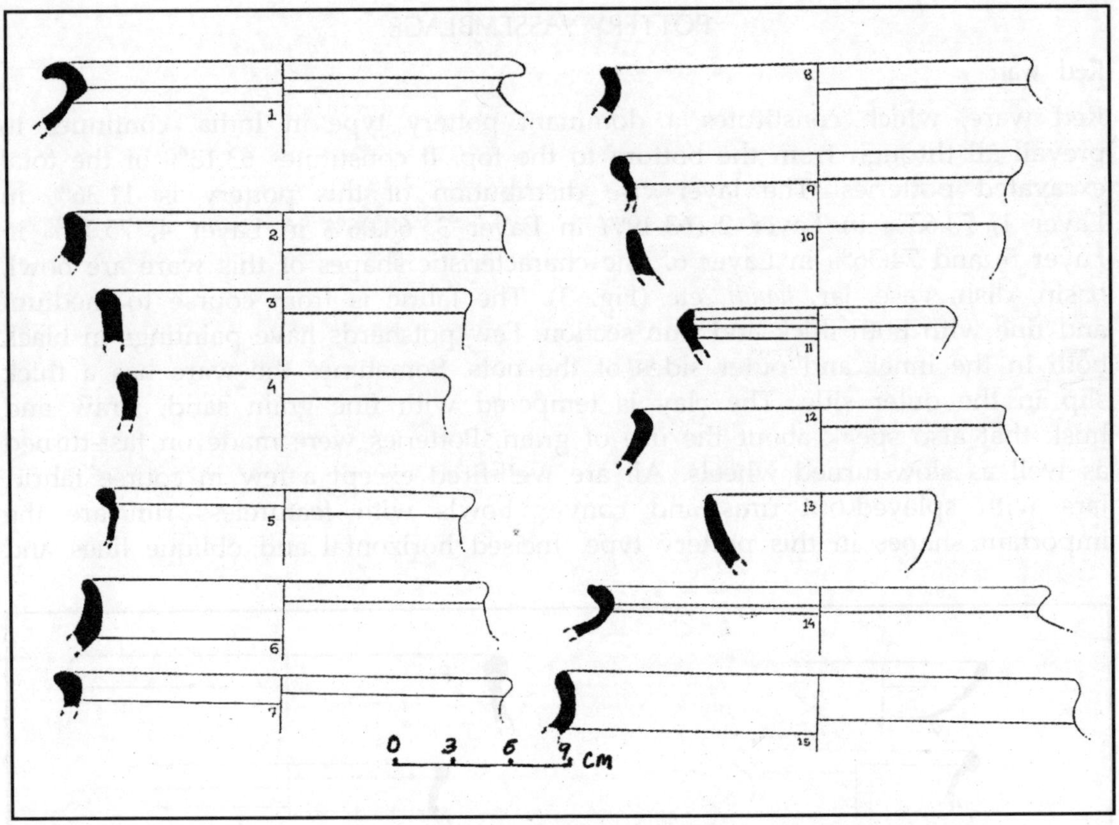

Fig. 4. Red ware : 1-7 Layer (2), 8-11 Layer (3) & 12-15 Layers, (4).

series of thumb impressions in the outer side of the pot are some of the decorations of this ware. Some grooved lines are also found in the lower neck portion.

Red slipped ware

Red slipped ware is the next important pottery type of the site. It constitutes 6.28% of the total excavated potteries. The layer-wise distribution of this pottery is 4.10% in Layer 2, 9.17% in Layer 3, 5.93% in Layer 4, 6.35% in Layer 5, and 7.46% in Layer 6. It is absent in Layer 1. The various shapes of this ware are bowl, basin, dish, vase, jar and *handi* (Fig. 4). The vessals are made of clay treated with a thick red slip on the exterior side, which is subsequently polished and fired at a high temperàture. The wares are sturdy and produce a metallic sound when the fabric is thin. Majority of pots in this ware are quite heavy and thick in section. The clay is levigated and tempered with husk and sand. The pots are decorated with incised and appliqué designs before application of the slip. Slip is clearly visible in the section of the pot. The colour varies from dark red to pink. They are course, medium and fine in fabric. Vase with flaring mouth and in-turned or out-turned rims is the dominant shape. The *handis* have out-turned rims. A Blak painting on the inner surface of some sherds is a noticeable feature. Some potsherds also have post firing graffiti marks.

Black ware

Black ware is another important ware of the site. It constitutes 6.47% of the total pottery recovered from the trench. The layer-wise distribution of this pottery is 9.81% in Layer 1, 7.22% in Layer 2, 6.46% in Layer 3, 3.83% in Layer 4, 5.78% in Layer 5, and 5.3% in Layer 6. The wares are course to medium and fine in fabric. The important shapes of this ware are bowl, dish, vase and jar. Bowl with featureless rim is an important pottery type of this ware. Potteries were made on fast-turned as well as slow-turned wheels. All are well fired except a few in course fabric. Grooved lines are found in many of this ware. Jars bear horizontal incised lines on the exterior surface.

Black slipped ware

Black slipped ware constitutes 0.92% of the total assemblage. It is 1.66% in Layer 2, 0.19% in Layer 3, 0.34% in Layer 4, 4.62% in Layer 5, and 1.86% in Layer 6. Like Red slipped ware this ware is also absent in Layer 1. It is from medium to fine in fabric. Slip is noticed both interior and exterior side of the pot. The important shapes in this ware are bowl, basin, dish, vase and jar (Fig. 5). All pots are wheel made. Pots are made of levigated clay and well fired. Bowl is the dominant shape with both featureless and out-turned rims. Decoration includes horizontal incised lines on the exterior surface of the pots.

Black-and-red ware

Interestingly, Black-and-red ware like Red ware prevails all through from bottom to the top. As the name implies, the ware has a black interior and red exterior. It constitutes 23.20% of the total pottery assemblage next to Red ware. It is 78.81% in Layer 1, 13.3% in Layer 2, 20.66% in Layer 3, 21.81% in Layer 4, 8.09% in Layer 5, and 12.06% in Layer 6. This ware is more in Period-II than in Period-I. Their percentage is more in every layer may be because they are more fragmentary than other potteries. The ware is medium to fine in fabric. All are prepared of well-levigated clay, well potted and well fired. The important shapes are bowl, dish, small vase and cups. A few miniature shapes are also there. Bowl and dish are the dominant shapes of this ware (Fig. 6). Some bowls are with featureless rim. Some wares of fine fabric have grooved incised lines made on fast moving wheel. There is the punch decoration in the exterior side of a big bowl. Some potteries of Period-IB are burnished. Burnished potteries are totally absent in Period-I. This ware is the hallmark in the Chalcolithic assemblage at Golabai.[9] Paintings in white are found in the inner surface of some pots.

Painted pottery

The excavation at Nuagarh produced the largest number of painted potsherds so far discovered in Orissa. With a total of 61 painted potsherds it constitutes 0.376% of the total excavated potteries. While the paintings are found both in Red slipped ware and Black-and-red ware, they are more in Black-and-red ware (Fig. 7). All are found in Period-I. The potteries were painted in creamy white pigment invariably on the inner side or on the rims or on the neck portion of

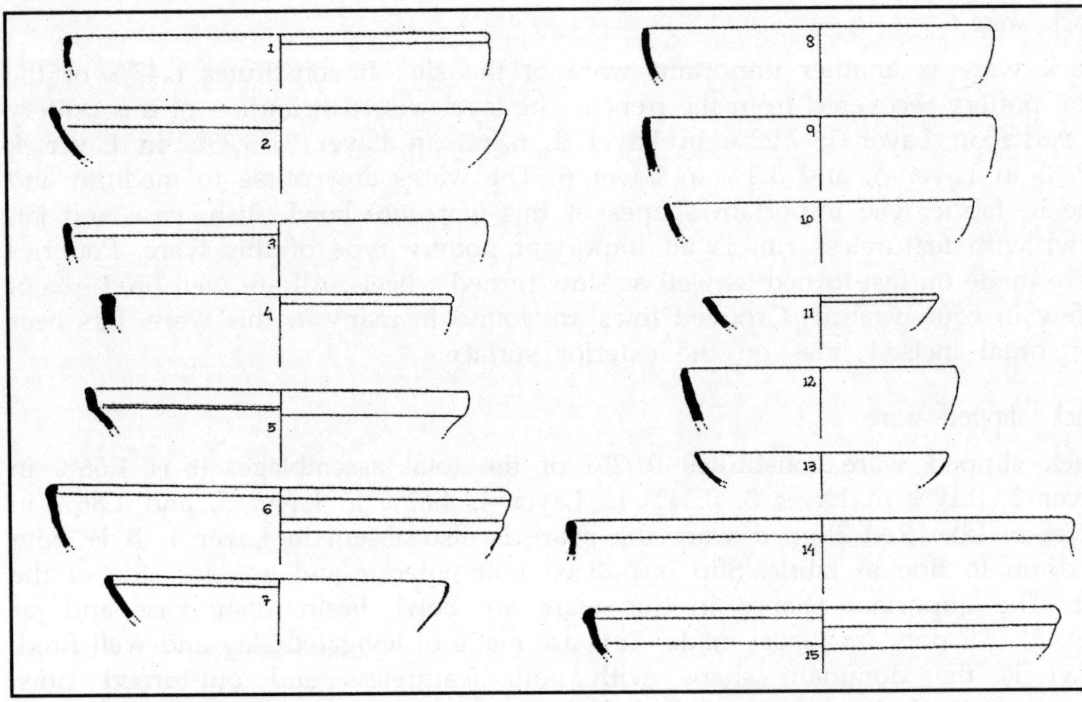

Fig. 5. Black slipped ware: 1-8 Layer (2), 9-13 Layer (3) & 14-15 Layer (4).

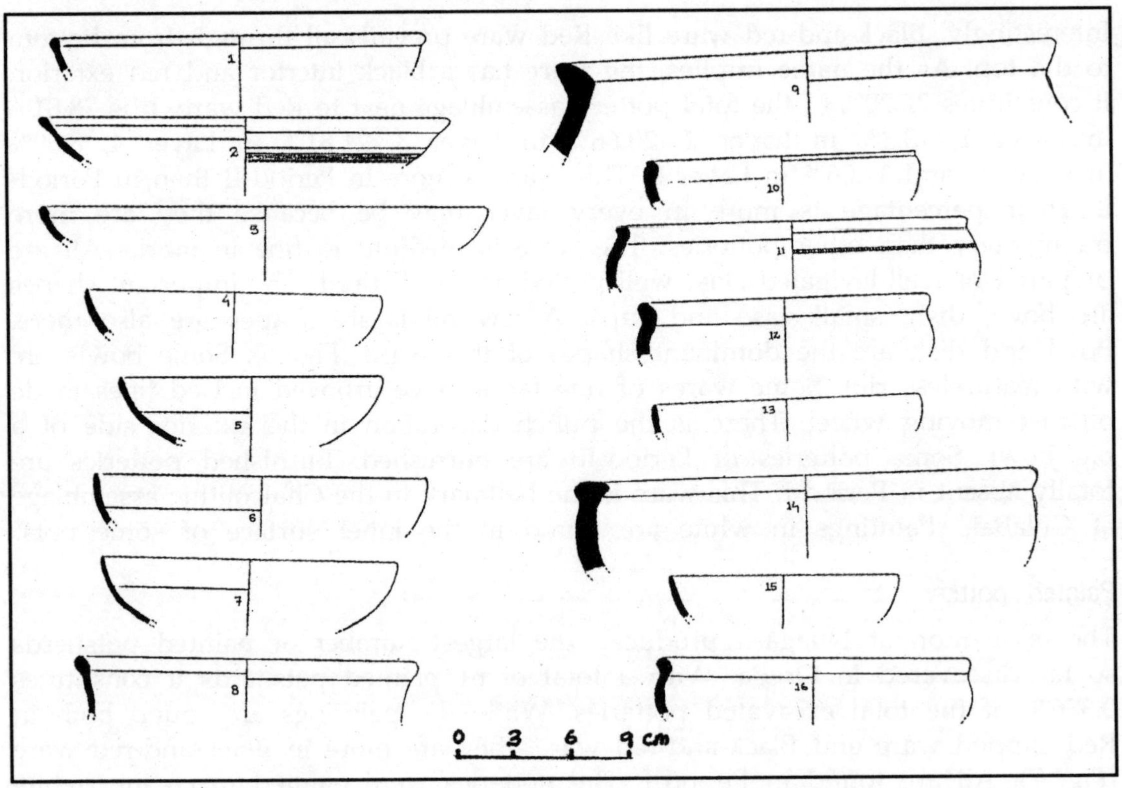

Fig. 6. Black-and-red ware: 1-6 Layer (2), 7-11 Layer (3), 12-14 Layer (4) & 15-16 Layer (5).

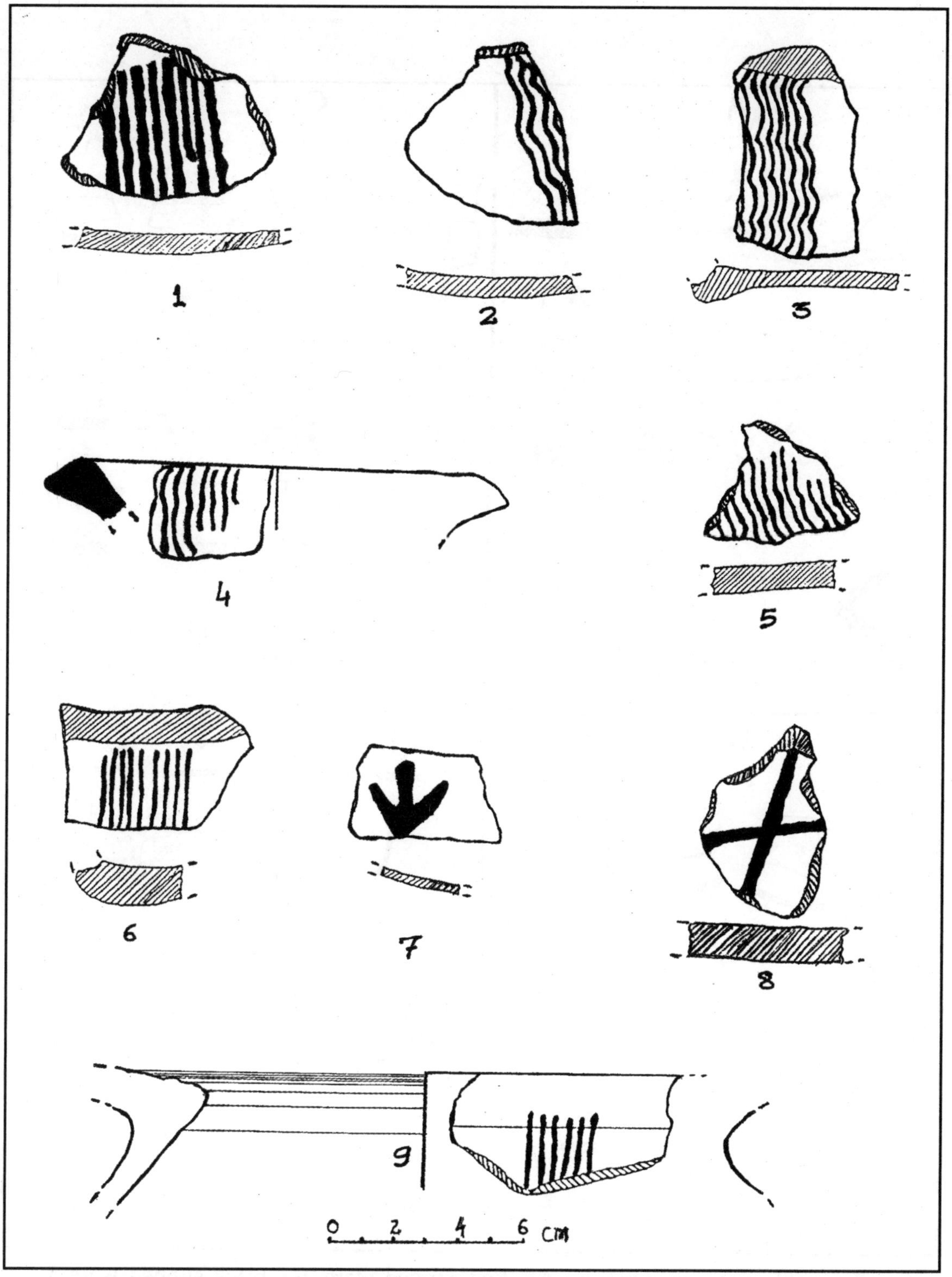

Fig. 7. Painted pottery: 1 & 2 - white painting on Red ware, 3, 4, 5, 9 - white painting on Red slipped ware, 6 white painting on black slipped ware, 7 black painting on Black-and-red ware & 8 - ochre Painting on Red ware.

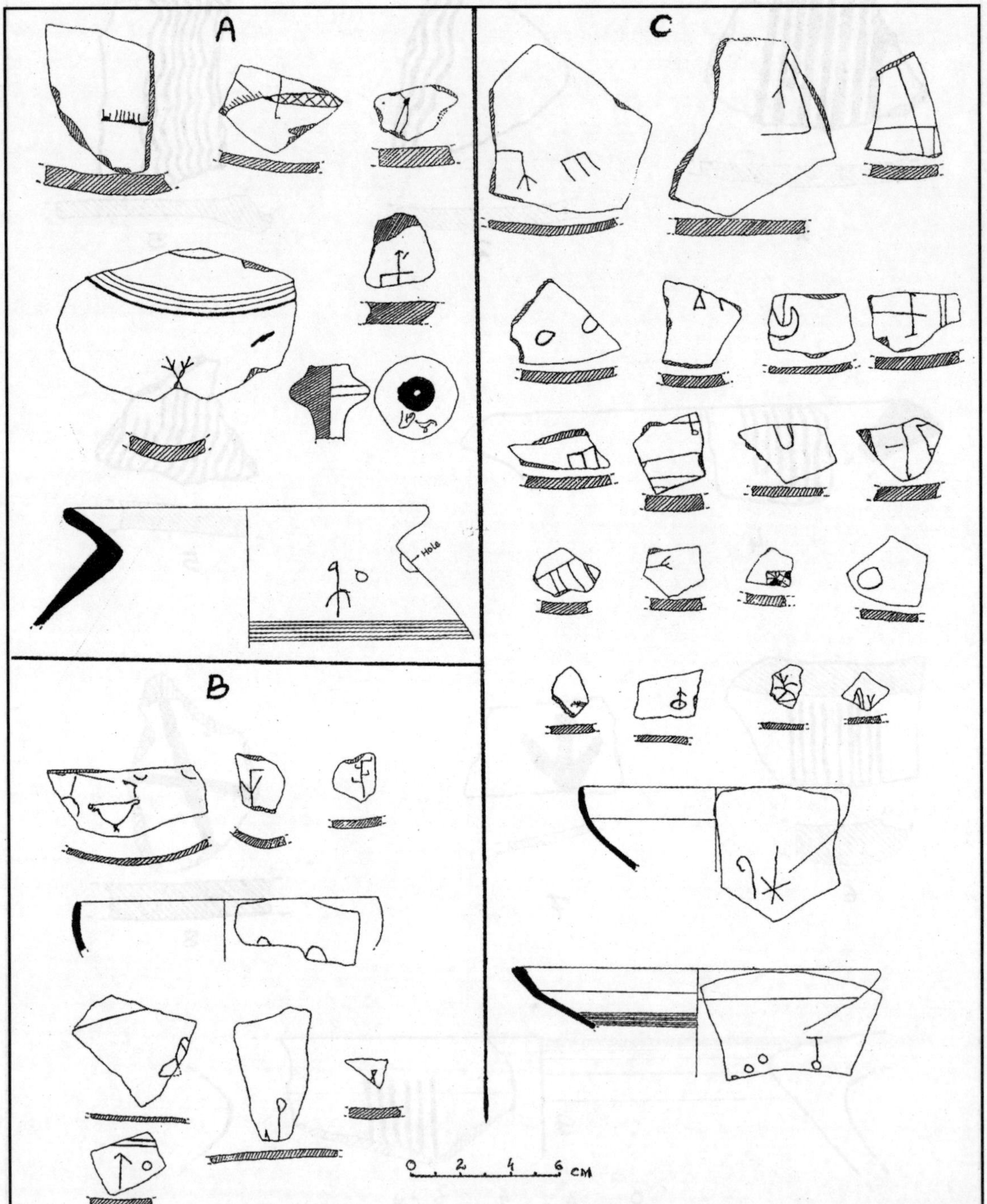

Fig. 8. Graffiti marks in potteries: A - Red slipped ware, B - black slipped ware, C - Black-and-red ware.

the pots. The painted designs are dots, rows of wavy as well as straight lines and zig-zag lines and the shapes in which such paintings are found are bowl, vase and jar. The motif of an arrowhead in black on the outer red surface of a Black-and-red ware is interesting. Another Red slipped ware has a painting in ochre. The paintings were executed after application of slip and firing of the pots. Similar painted potteries have also come from Khambeswaripalli,[10] a Chalcolithic site situated at a distance of about five kilometers from Nuagarh in the upstream of the Mahanadi. Bhejidihi,[11] another Chalcolithic site in the Mahanadi valley has reported painted potteries. But in Bhejidihi the paintings are in black on Red slipped ware and Black-and-red ware like the painted potteries of Period-II at Pandu-Rajar Dhibi.[12]

GRAFFITI MARK POTTERY

The excavation produced a fairly good number of sherds with graffiti marks. These are the post-firing scratches on the outer surface of the pots. With a total of 73 pieces graffiti marked potteries constitute 0.45% of the total pottery assemblage. The marks are found in Red slipped ware, black slipped ware and Black-and-red ware (Fig. 8). Graffiti marks are found more in Black-and-red ware than in other wares. They are found in the potteries of both the periods. The marks are both geometric and non-geometric. Some marks are naturalistic like fish and bird and some are anthropomorphic. A few identifiable marks are ladder, arrowhead and circles. Similar graffiti mark potteries are also reported from Manamunda-Asurgarh[13] and Narla-Asurgarh, where it is found only on Red slipped ware and Black-and-red ware and not on black slipped ware as in Nuagarh.

CULTURE SEQUENCE AND CHRONOLOGY

Taking into account the aforesaid cultural materials and the ^{14}C determination from Layer 5, two-fold culture sequence of the site may be proposed with two sub-phases in Period-I. Period-I represented by layers 4, 5 and 6 have two sub-phases; Period-IA represented by the deposits of Layer 6 and Period-IB with the deposits of Layer 4 and Layer 5. Cultural materials in both the sub-phases remain almost the same except for iron in Layer 6, whose occurrence may not be entirely ruled out. However, with the existing material evidence the deposits in Layer 6 may be ascribed to a Late Chalcolithic Phase. In the next sub-phase Period-IB, whose beginning is precisely dated to the 6th century BC as per the ^{14}C determination, we see the introduction of iron in a limited scale along with all the material assemblage of the earlier period. Iron, painted pottery, burnished pottery, and pottery with a variety of post-fired graffiti marks is the hallmark of this phase. Potteries are fast wheel-turned and medium to thick in fabric. Fine fabric potteries are found in Black-and-red ware and in a few specimen of red slipped and black slipped ware. Unlike other sites painted potteries are found in red slipped, black slipped and Black-and-red wares. Paintings are found in the pigments of white, ochre and black. Since this sub-phase presents cultural traits of both Late Chalcolithic and Early Iron Age phases it may be termed

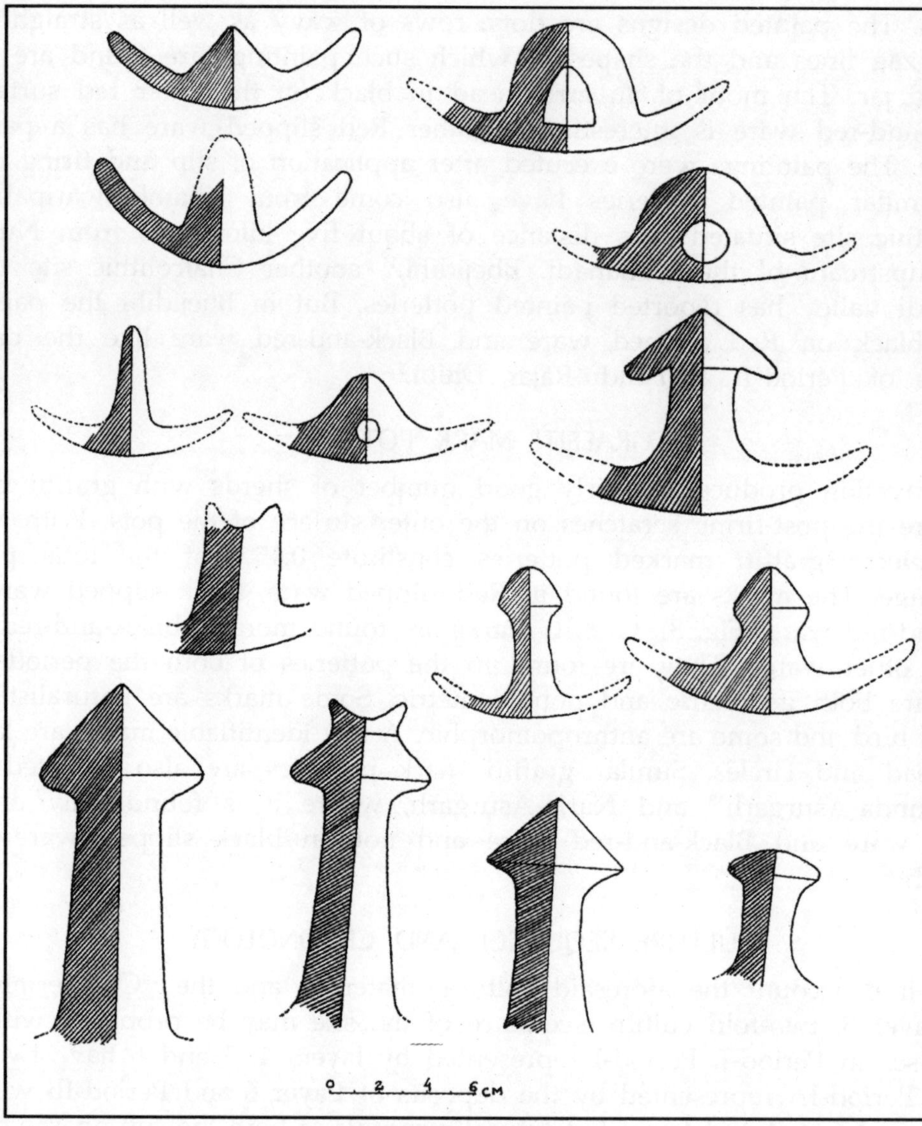

Fig. 9. Knobbed lids.

Ferro-Chalcolithic. Such a terminology proposed taking into account the present material evidence from a limited excavation is entirely provisional and subject to correction in a future large-scale excavation of the site.

Period-II represented by the habitational materials of layers 1, 2 and 3 witnessed a significant change in the ceramic assemblage of the preceding period. The pottery assemblage is mainly represented by plain Red ware and Red slipped ware followed by a lesser percentage of Black-and-red ware and black slipped ware. Finer quality of red slipped and black slipped ware predominate in layers 2 and 3. Painted potteries of the preceding period are totally absent. Post-firing graffiti mark potteries, however, continue to exist more particularly in Black-and-red ware. The use of iron is more common that includes nails, chisel, knife, and several fragments of unidentifiable shapes along with a few slags. Since

Black-and-red ware continue to exist even in Layer 1 when the site was abandoned we are restricted to ascribe a time period of 1st century AD to the upper levels of Period-II

Hence the chronology of the site may be ascribed from the Chalcolithic period to the 1st century AD Iron was introduced in the 6th century BC as ascertained by the ^{14}C determination.

DISCUSSION

In Indian archaeology a host of 'Asura' sites are found in the Ranchi district of Jharkhand state (erstwhile Bihar).[3] Barring a few sites in the Chakradharpur area (8 sites) of Singhbhum, 110 sites are reported from Ranchi district only and their concentration is more in the Khunti area. Owing to their diverse archaeological materials such as ancient burnt bricks, iron implements and slags, potsherds, stone implements, cinerary urns, silted-up tanks, etc the local Mundas regard these antiquities to have belonged to the 'Asuras' who preceded them in the region and as such antiquities do not belong to them. It is also interesting to note that an iron smelting tribe called the Asuras is found in the Ranchi district but their connection with the Asuras of the Munda tradition is not clear. According to Sarat Chandra Roy[4] (Roy, 1915: 229), who first reported these Asura sites, the Asura sites are i) invariably located on elevated tracts of land conveniently situated on the banks of water course and eminently suited for defence; ii) with foundations of brick buildings, large tanks, cinerary urns, copper ornaments and stone beads, copper celts and traces of iron smelting; iii) with a wide chronological horizon ranging from the Stone Age, Copper Age to the Early Iron Age[5] (Roy, 1915 : 253). In 1944 Amalananda Ghosh revisited many of these sites reported by Roy and undertook an excavation at a site called Kunjal. Ghosh[6] exposed a mud-brick structure with four rooms and showed that the cultural affiliation of the site was with iron-using culture and not with the three stages of culture which Roy had proposed[7] (Chakrabarti, 1993: 55). In 1964-65 Sunil Chandra Ray excavated another Asura site at Saradkel[8] (*IAR*, 1964-65). Ray also came out with only one cultural level of an iron-using community with two occupational periods. As regards the age, Ray ascribed to the early centuries of the Christian Era, and to be very precise to the Kushana Period of occupation in the upper Gangetic Valley. It was subsequently confirmed by radiocarbon dates.

Thus, the Asura sites in Ranchi belonged to an advanced group of iron-using people who came to the region in the early centuries of the Christian Era to exploit local iron ores[9] (Ghosh, 1989: 293).

Coming to the Asura sites in Orissa, three sites including the present one have been excavated so far for diverse archaeological interests. In view of the above discussion on Asura sites in Ranchi the results of excavation of other Asura sites in Orissa need to be discussed for a better understanding of the archaeology of Asura sites in India.

Narla-Asurgarh (20° 03′N and 83° 22′E), in Kalahandi district, with a massive earthen fortification extending over an area of more than half-a-square kilometer was excavated by Dr. N.K. Sahu of the Post-Graduate Department of History, Sambalpur University in March 1973.[10] The fortification is almost square in plan with four wide gates in four cardinal directions. On the eastern side of the fort there is an extensive lake, water from which was brought through two sluice gates to fill up the moat on three sides of the fort – northern, eastern and southern. River Sandul, a tributary of the Tel, flowing on the western side of the fort serves as a natural moat. The excavation yielded evidence of structural activities in brick, punch-marked coins (50 in number) of both silver and bronze of Pre-Mauryan, Mauryan and Post-Mauryan Period; beads of chalcedony, agate, carnelian, and coral; iron objects like hooks, door hinges, arrowheads and axes; potteries of Red ware, Red slipped ware, black slipped and black polished ware (NBP-?), grooved ware; terracotta figurines, glass bangles, and Neolithic celts (what the excavator called two pieces of chopping implements made of polished stone were found ... supposed to be the tools of the Neolithic man). Taking into account the material evidence of the site the excavator assigns a time period from the 3rd century BC to 5th century AD.[11] He is of the view that Asugarh was an important centre of the Atavika territory during the time of Asoka for recruitment of the mighty Kalingan army and in the 4th century AD the fort was under the sway of Vyghraraja of Mahakantara whom Samudragupta claimed to have defeated in the course of his South Indian campaign.

Archaeological site of Manamunda-Asurgarh (20° 49′N and 83° 56′E) is situated by the side of the confluence of river Tel and Mahanadi on the right bank in Boudh (erstwhile Phulbani) district. The mound measures 1.5 km long and 0.5 km wide. Excavation conducted by the Post-Graduate Department of History, Sambalpur University in 1981[12] and 1990[13] unravelled material culture of the site extending from the 4th century BC to 5th century AD. The excavation of 1981 under the joint auspices of the Post-Graduate Department of History, Sambalpur University and the Department of Archaeology, Deccan College, Pune in February 1981 was a part of the "Search for Lanka" project of Dr. H.D. Sankalia. Dr. Sankalia envinced interest in the excavation on account of two copper plate charters of the 11th century AD, namely, Sonepur charter[14] of Somesvaradeva and Mahada charter[15] of Somesvaradevavarman that refer to this locality as Lanka and the Chief as *Paschimalankadhipati*. The excavation of 1981 reported material culture over a period from the 1st century AD to the Post-Gupta Period without reaching up to the natural soil.[16] But the excavation of 1990 dug up to the natural soil by the present author yielded material culture from the 4th century BC to the 3rd century AD. The important finds from the excavation include a Mauryan imperial silver punch-marked coin of the 3rd century BC; iron objects of knife, dagger, spear-head, arrowhead, axe, nail, door clamps, hinges and sickle; beads of carnelian, quartz and coral; potteries of Red ware, Red slipped ware, Black ware, black slipped ware, Black-and-red ware and black slipped grooved ware with or without a central knob. Some red slipped potteries bore post-firing graffiti marks. Structural activities in brick were an important activity of the site. The bricks were well fired and were made of clay mixed with straw and husk. Their size varied from 32 cm to 26 cm in length and from 23 cm to 20 cm in breadth with a uniform thickness of 5 cm. On account of a habitational deposit of one meter below the punch-marked coin the excavators assign the beginning of the settlement in the site to the 4th century BC.

In this context another Asurgarh site not excavated so far may be referred to. Not very far from Narla-Asurgarh is another fortified ancient settlement at Kharligarh (20° 27'N and 83° 33'E) in Tusra tehsil of Bolangir district. This site is also locally known as Asurgarh and Gumagarh. Here, the river Raul takes Roman 'U' turn one kilometer before discharging into the Tel. Thus, the river serves as a natural moat on three sides, south, east and north, of the site and the western side being protected by a massive earthen rampart measuring 400 meters long (north-south) and about 12 meters high with a gateway at the centre made of large-sized bricks. On exploration the site yielded evidence of structural activities in large-sized bricks and cultural materials like copper punch-marked coins, iron objects and implements, saddle querns, hop-scotches along with potteries of Red ware, Red slipped ware, Black ware and Black-and-red ware. The site, thus, conforms to a similar settlement pattern and material culture.

The Asurgarh sites in Orissa discussed above indicate to a material culture of Early Iron Age except Period-IA of Nuagarh. People occupied the sites at a stage of material advancement and sophistication assignable to a period of 400 to 600 years during the Pre-Christian and the early centuries of the Christian Era. Use of iron, punch-marked coins, and potteries of black slipped and Black-and-red ware remains the hallmark of the material assemblage of these sites. Except Nuagarh all other Asurgarh sites were fortified metropolises, where large-sized bricks had been extensively used for construction of fortifications and the settlement inside the fortification. The sites were strategically located in the Middle Mahanadi Valley (along with its major tributary, the Tel) which also served as the lifeline of communication and trade from the hinterland to the coastal plains and vice-versa. All these sites were abandoned and deserted after the 5th-6th centuries AD as evident from the account of Hiuen Tsang, who did not make any reference to these metropolises when he visited this area in the first half of the 7th century AD.

REFERENCES

1. G. Ramdas, "Kumersingha Plate......", *Journal of Kalinga Historical Research Society (JKHRS)*, Vol. I, no. 3, 1946, pp. 229-36.
2. P.C. Rath, "Notes on important archaeological sites, Asurgarh in Sonepur state", *JKHRS*, Vol. 1, no. 4, 1947, pp. 387-89.
3. S.C. Roy, "A note on some remains of the ancient Asuras in the Ranchi district", *JBORS*, 1, 1915, pp. 229-53.
4. S.C. Roy, "Distribution and nature of Asur sites in Chottanagpur", *JBORS*, 6, 1920, pp. 393-423.
5. S.C. Roy, *op. cit.*, p. 253.
6. A. Ghosh, *An Encyclopaedia of Indian Archaeology*, Vol. 1, 1989, Munshiram Manoharlal Publisher Pvt. Ltd., p. 293.

7. D. K. Chakrabarti, *Archaeology of Eastern India, Chhotanagpur Plateau and West Bengal*, Munshiram Manoharlal Publisher Pvt. Ltd., pp. 54-56.
8. *IAR*, 1964-65.
9. A. Ghosh, *op. cit.*
10. N. K. Sahu, "Asurgarh", in S.C. Behera (ed.), *Interim Excavation Reports*, Post-Graduate Department of History, Sambalpur University, 1982, pp. 1-8.
11. *Ibid.*, p. 6.
12. S.C. Behera, "Manamunda", in S.C. Behera (ed.), *op. cit.*, pp. 16-22.
13. *Indian Archaeology 1989-90: A Review*, pp. 80-86.
14. *E.I.*, Vol. XII, pp. 237-42; *E.I.*, Vol. XXVIII, pp. 321-26; S.N. Rajguru (ed.), *Inscriptions of Orissa*, Vol. IV, 1966, pp. 268-75.
15. *E.I.*, Vol. XXVIII, pp. 283 f.
16. S.C. Behera (ed.), *op. cit.*, p. 21.

TEMPLES OF WESTERN ORISSA

Prafulla Kumar Nayak

INTRODUCTION

Western Orissa comprises the modern districts of Jharsuguda, Deogarh, Sundargarh, Sambalpur, Bargarh, Nuapada, Kalahandi, Bolangir, Sonepur and Baud Kandhamal. These territories were included in the kingdom of South Kosala from early times. This tract of land has experienced the rule of various dynasties in different spans of time. These dynasties left their indelible imprint in this land in the field of administration, society, religion, art and architecture, etc. The rulers not only constructed monuments but also patronised the building activities like forts, palaces and temples. The peaceful co-existence of several diverse sects, the royal patronage and the eclectic attitude of the generous kings caused the construction of temples in large number distributed throughout Western Orissa. The capitals had been temple towns in Western Orissa. Hiuen Tsang describes the existence of a large number of Deva temples along with a number of Buddhist *viharas* and Mahayanist monks. The Nalas, Parvatadvarakas, Sarabhapuriyas, Bhanjas, Somavamsis, Telugu Chodas, Gangas and Kalchuris continued the building activities vigorously. Even in Late Medieval Period, the Chauhans of Patna, Sambalpur and Sonepur, the Nagas of Kalahandi, the Paramaras of Gangpur, the Kadambas of Bonai and the later Bhanjas of Baud carried out the tradition of constructing temples. The epigraphic references speak of the existence of a number of temples, which are not traceable now. For instance, Sonepur copper plate charter of Janamejaya mentions particularly about the temples of Kesava and Aditya, which have no trace at present. Many temples are found in ruins, some are razed to ground while few are in dilapidated conditions. While supporting care is not being taken by the different agencies to preserve whatever that is existing, natural and man-made decaying forces are gradually destroying the monuments.

Therefore, the survey of the temple is needed intermittently for documentation. Many art historians have dealt with the temples of Western Orissa, namely, J.D. Beglar, K.P. Jayswal, R.D. Banerjee, K.C. Panigrahi,

N.K. Sahu, D.R. Das, Vidya Dehejia, Donaldson, Stadner, etc. All have concentrated on the main temple centres and due attention has not been given for the peripheral temple art. The Late Medieval Temples have not also been taken up. Hence, whatever that has been said regarding the temples of Western Orissa needs to be studied intensively. The author is fortunate of availing of such an opportunity of a survey of the temples being funded by the UGC under the SAP. The author is thankful to the Post-Graduate Department of History as well as to Prof. S.C. Panda, Co-ordinator, DRS, for taking up the publication work of this report.

The author has done the survey work within the limitations of funds and time. The report is divided into two parts – Part-I: Temples of Early Period (early period to 13th century AD) and Part-II: Temples of the Medieval Period (14th century AD to 18th century AD). Some of the temples like Saintala, Belkhandi etc. have been left out and some new ones like Surda *Panchayatana* temple, Pantnagarh temples and Sauntpur temples have been included. The report is based mainly on field study supported by the published works of the Art Historians. The study is limited to the Architectural style and Sculptural programme.

PHASE – I: EARLY TEMPLES

GANDHARADI TEMPLES

Gandharadi is situated on the right bank of Mahanadi. It is 14 km away from Baud. A metal road approaches it from Sonepur to Baud. At a distance of about 35 km from Sonepur towards Baud there is a village named Junhapank on road. The temple site can be reached by covering 5 km towards Mahanadi from this place. Gandharadi was a place of importance during the rule of Bhanjas. Its name occurs in the inscriptions as "Gandhatapatti" and "Gandharavadi". This place has the prized possession of two identical temples of high artistic merit and architectural technique. The two temples are so much similar that these are termed as twins. One is a perfect duplicate of the other except the *Ayudha*. Among the twins one is dedicated to Nilamadhava and the other to Siddhesvara.

The temples are erected on a simple platform, which measures 91 feet in length and 58 feet in width. The historians are of the view that originally the temples were the central shrines of a *Panchayatana* plan. They base their opinion on the remains of four subsidiary shrines in the four corners of the temple. The remains of shrines are not there excepting the holes where probably the *lingam* was once installed. At present three holes or so-called *Sakti-pithas* are visible at three corners. The fourth one is not discernible. Further, *Panchayatana* temple complexes are of various types, namely, Siva *Panchayatana*, Vishnu *Panchayatana*, Ganesa *Panchayatana*, Ravi *Panchayatana* and Sakti or Devi *Panchayatana*. Siva, Vishnu, Devi, Ganesa, and Surya enshrine the five temples. The temple complex is named after the deity enshrined in the central temple. At places it is observed that in Siva *Panchayatana* all five are dedicated to Siva and *lingam* is found in all five temples. But here only three remains of Siva shrines are noticed. If there was another one it comes to four and if the Siddhesvara is added the total comes to five. But the presence of Vishnu temple adjacent to the Siddhesvara temple deviates the *Panchayatana* plan. Further, besides the presiding deity Nilamadhava, there are other Nilamadhava images found in the frontal hall. One is a prototype, though smaller in height as compared to the main image. The author was informed from the priest that there is a legend of transporting of such an image from this place to Kantilo by boat and that was installed in that temple. The present image of Nilamadhava at the Nilamadhava temple of Kantilo exhibits close iconic similarities with the second image of Gandharadi temple. There might be other images, which were taken away or buried under ground. So the proposition that it was a *Panchayatana* complex, though not impossible, requires discovery of further evidence. Peculiarly it is famous as *Charisambhu,* which indicates the presence of four Saiva shrines. The remains of three shrines and the extant Siddhesvara temple make it four. So it is better to be satisfied with the idea of *Charisambhu* till the discovery of other shrines and plan programme.

The *pista* is a lofty one, the wall that displays the three sections – *pabhaga, jangha* and *baranda.* The *jangha* is adorned with *mundis* and pilasters. The temples consist of a *Vimana* and a *Jagamohana* each. The *Vimana* rises upward from the pista. It consists of three essential elements, namely, *bada, gandi* and *mastaka.* The *bada* comprises the *pabhaga, jangha* and *baranda.* The *pabhaga* is composed of four mouldings, which are *khura, kumbha, patta* and *basanta.* The *khura* is decorated with *chaitya* motif while the *kumbha* is adorned with *champaka* leaf motif. The *jangha* is vertically divided into five segments. The *jangha* is *pancharatha.* The *kanika* of the *jangha* has engaged pilaster designed with *vajra mundi* at the lower part and garlands on the top. The *anaratha* is decorated with slender miniature shrine having the *sikhara* comprising successive horizontal mouldings crowned by the *vajra mastaka.* The *raha* of the *jangha* is ornamented with large *vajra mastaka.* On each side of this *vajra mundi* is found offset pilasters. Above the *vajra masataka* and just below the upper part of the *baranda* is carved a *kalasa.* The *baranda* is constituted of a large moulding with a recess at the top.

The *gandi* moves tapering upward till it meets the *bisama.* The *gandi* also exhibits a *pancharatha* plan quite in conformity with the plan of the *bada.* The *kanika* pagas are divided into seven *bhumis* by *bhumi amalas.* The *bhumis* are composed of four *bhumi* baranadikas and adorned with *chaitya* motifs. The *amaratha pagas* likewise divided into horizontal *barandikas.* They are decorated with triple *chaitya* motifs connected with a fillet or narrow rectangular bar. The *raha paga* rises with a *vajra mastaka* just above the *baranda.* The *raha* also has *bhumi barandakas* and five successive *chaitya* motifs in an alignment on each *bhumi barandika.* In the front *raha* above the *jagamohan* roof was a triangular window, which is missing now. The *pagas* meet on *bisama* or *vedika.* On it is found *beki,* which contains female figures in place of *bhara bahaka.* The female figures or *mandira* charinis are placed above the *raha paga* of each side. The *beki* is surmounted by the *amalaka,* which holds the *khapuri* above it. As *kalasa* is absent, the *ayudha* is placed on it. The Siddhesvara contains an *akasa linga* built on stone and the Nilamadhava temple possesses a *chakra* made of stone on respective *ayudha.*

In front of the sanctum is the *Mukhasala* or the *Jagamohana*. The *Jagamohana* is rectangular and having a two-tiered sloping roof like that of Parsuramesvara temple. It has a *trianga bada* and a *pancharatha jangha*. The side-walls of the temples accommodate two latticed windows, one on each side. The blank space above the windows or *gavaksa* is carved three-*rekha vimanika* each separated by a pilaster. This *gavaksa mandana* is not found in other temples of Western Orissa. *Naga/Nagi* uprights flank the *gavaksa* on *raha*. The lower portion of the Naga/ Nagi *stambhas* is depicted with *gajakranta* or *gajasimha* motif.

The twin temple having similarities stone by stone is a marvel in ancient Indian architectural history. It proclaims the super and superb architectonic skill of the celebrated architects of Orissa.

SURDA TEMPLE

The village Surda is located to the south-east of the town Bolangir. The temples are found on a rocky out crop at the end of the village Surda. There are five old temples, one small modern *mandapa* and recently built *Mukhasala* before the main temple. Modern structures have been added. Many colours have been applied for the beautification of the temple.

Most important are the five old temples which are arranged in *Panchayatana* plan – main temple in the centre, and four small temples at four corners. The main temple is called Kosalesvara temple. All the temples of the place were of *rekha* style. The main temple stands on a platform about two feet high. Originally there was no *Mukhasala* but in recent years a *Mukhasala* has been added. The temple faces east and in front, there is a small porch. The height of the temple is about 35 feet. The platform measures 17 feet x 13 feet. All the temples have been constructed with sizely dressed stones. It has all the principal elements, viz, *pista, bada, gandi* and *mastaka*. It possesses a *trianga bada* and *triratha gandi*. On the three sides on the *raha* of the *jangha*, there are niches topped by *kumbha* motif. The niches are meant for installing deities. The *Vimana* is a square cell of six feet in length and width. The temple raises upward straight to a great height and then takes prominent curve near the top terminated by a *vedi* or *bisama*. The *pagas* of the *bada* are aligned with that of the *gandi*. The style of elevation of the temple suggests a date of 9th/10th century AD. On the entrance to the *Jagamohana* is the image of Gagalaxmi. The entrance doorway has three ornamental bands. On the lintel is carved the images of Gagalaxmi in the centre. The ornate doorjamb possesses *nagasakha, puspa sakha* and *mithuna sakha*. The *dvarapalas* are placed on both the sides of the entrances. On the left of the inner side of the entrance is found the image of Ganesa. On the right the figure of Kartikeya. The porch of the entrance looks like a projected eave. There is a small kanti in between *bada* and *gandi*. The placement of Ganesa and Kartikeya on sidewalls of the entrance has been a *characteristic* feature of many temples of this locality. For example, the entrance of Kosalesvara temple of Baidyanath and the entrance of Kapilesvara temple of Charada possess the images of Ganesa and Kartikeya.

The *bada* ends with the *baranada*, which has three mouldings. The *gandi* is plain. The *gandi* meets the *bisama* or *vedi* at the top wherefrom the *mastaka*

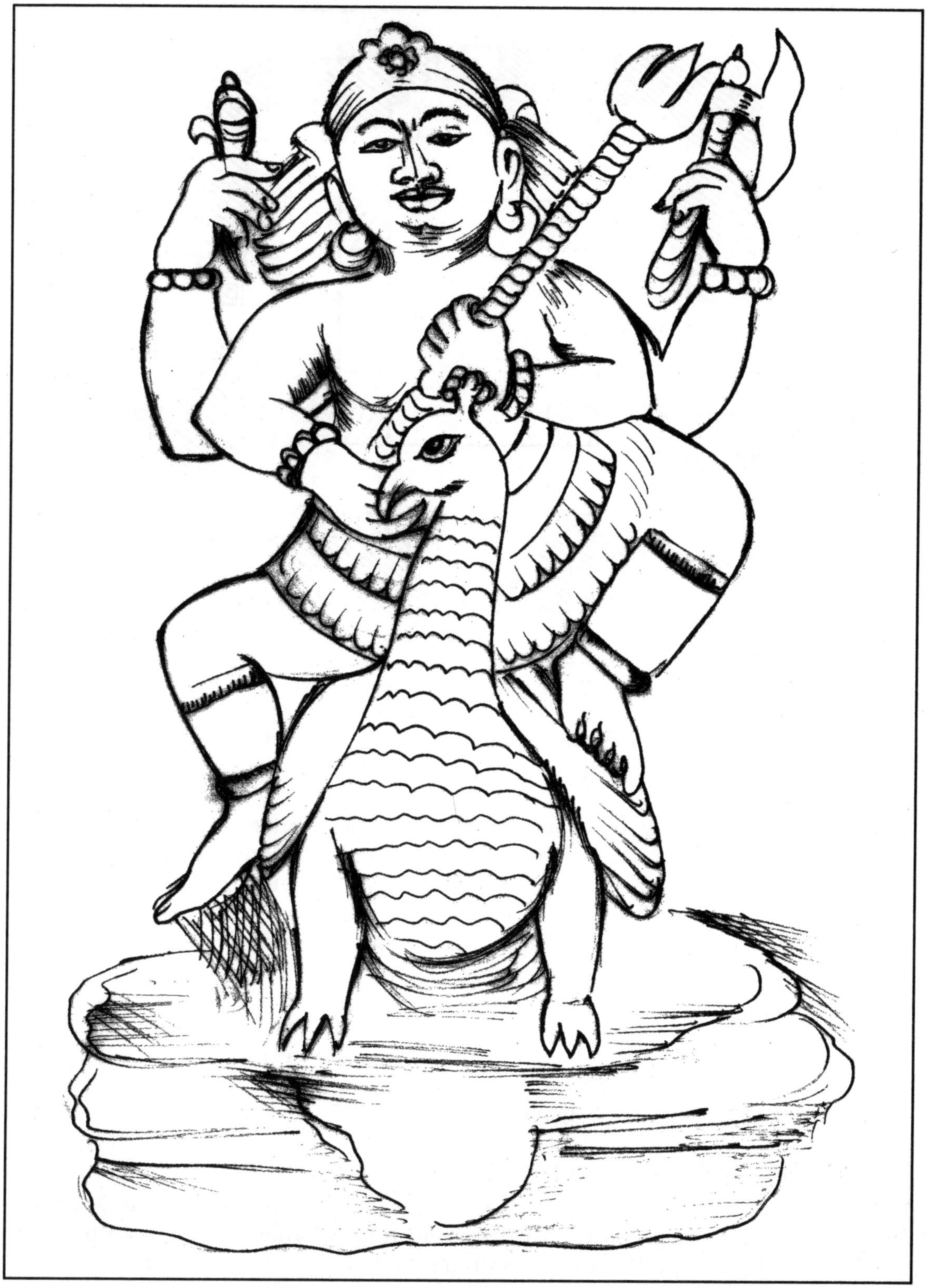

Fig. 1. Kartikeya, Charada Temple.

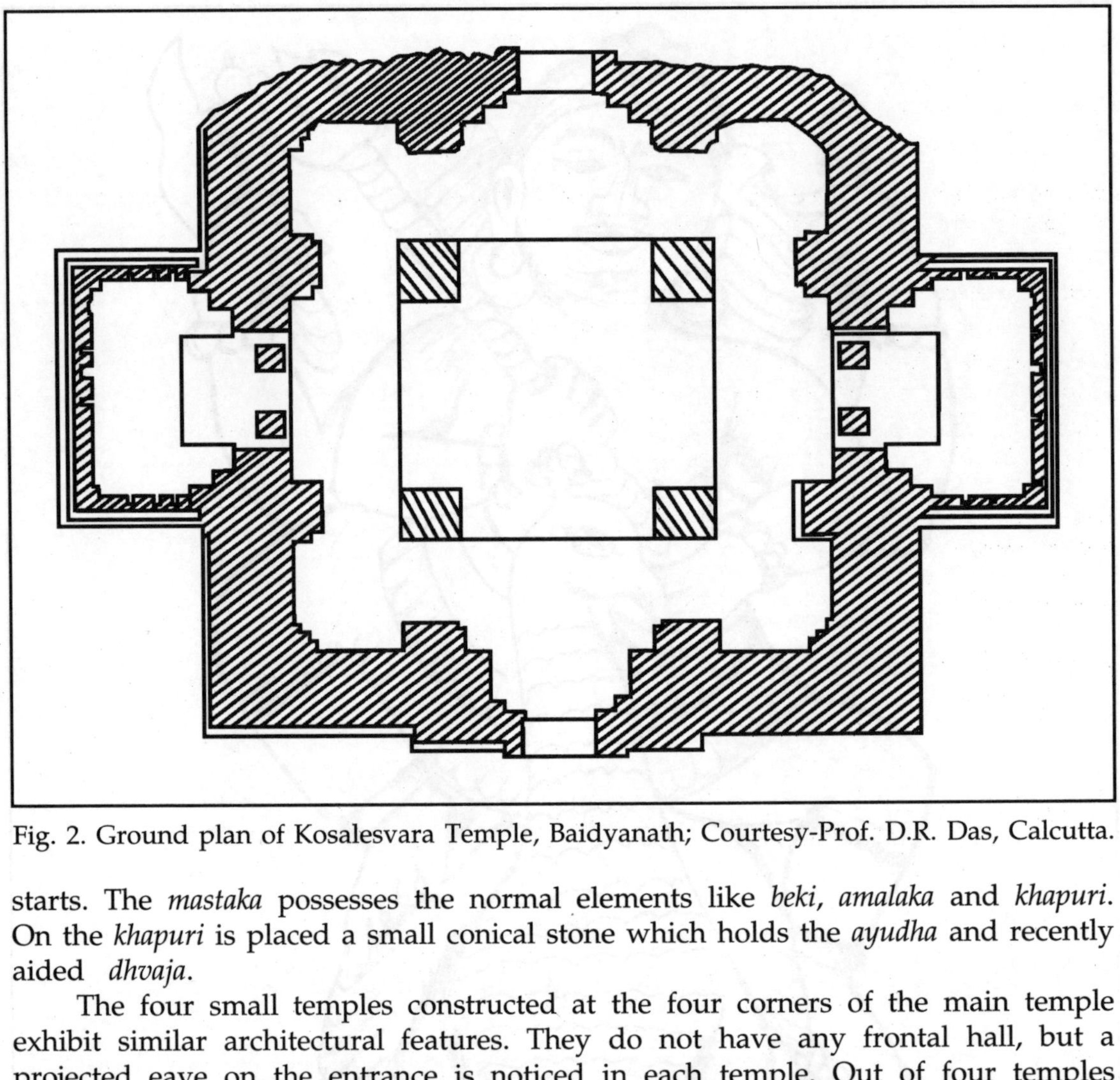

Fig. 2. Ground plan of Kosalesvara Temple, Baidyanath; Courtesy-Prof. D.R. Das, Calcutta.

starts. The *mastaka* possesses the normal elements like *beki*, *amalaka* and *khapuri*. On the *khapuri* is placed a small conical stone which holds the *ayudha* and recently aided *dhvaja*.

The four small temples constructed at the four corners of the main temple exhibit similar architectural features. They do not have any frontal hall, but a projected eave on the entrance is noticed in each temple. Out of four temples two are in the front side and other two are behind the main one. The temple at present enshrines different deities like Bhairava, Chandi, Subhesvara and Kharsuanbudhi. The Sabhanesvara temple on its outer wall has a three-lettered inscription which reads as 'Sayana'. The *triratha gandi* and *trianga bada* are early features. But its elevation and height suggests a date of early 10th century AD. The temple complex belongs to Siva *panchayatana* variety. The temples of Bhairava, Chandi, Subhesvara and Kharsuanbudhi are of 16 feet, 15 feet, 15 feet and 13 feet high, respectively.

PATALESVARA TEMPLE OF BUDHIKOMNA

The temple of Patalesvara exists in the village Budhikomna in the Nuapada district. It can be located on the road leading from Khariar to Raipur in between Khariar and Nuapada. The temple is built in bricks and faces east. Donaldson opines that originally there was a pillared *mandapa* and an *antarala* within the temple proper. But now only the temple and *antarala* are present.

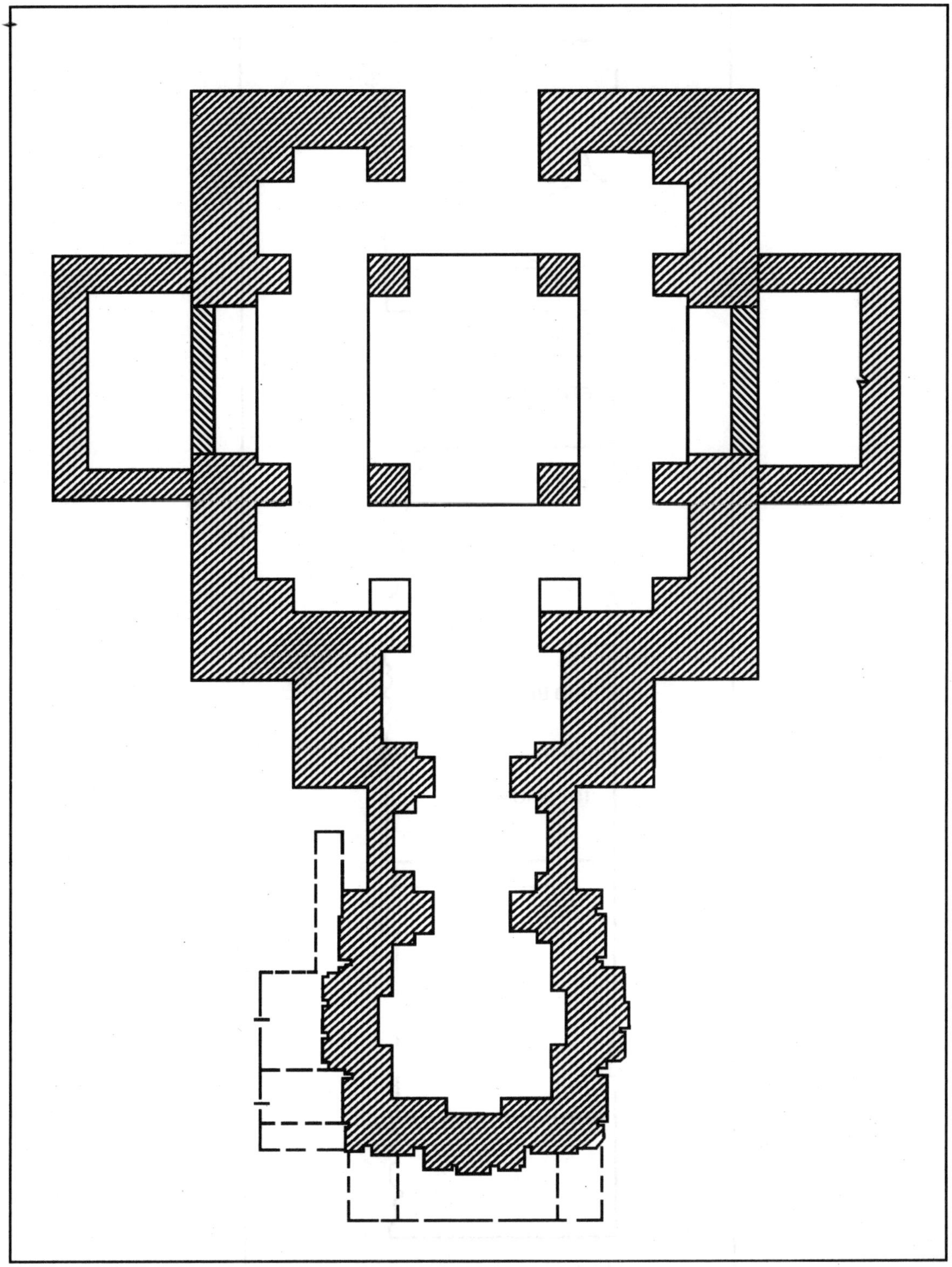

Fig. 3. Ground plan of Kosalesvara Temple, Charada; Courtesy-Prof. D.R. Das, Calcutta.

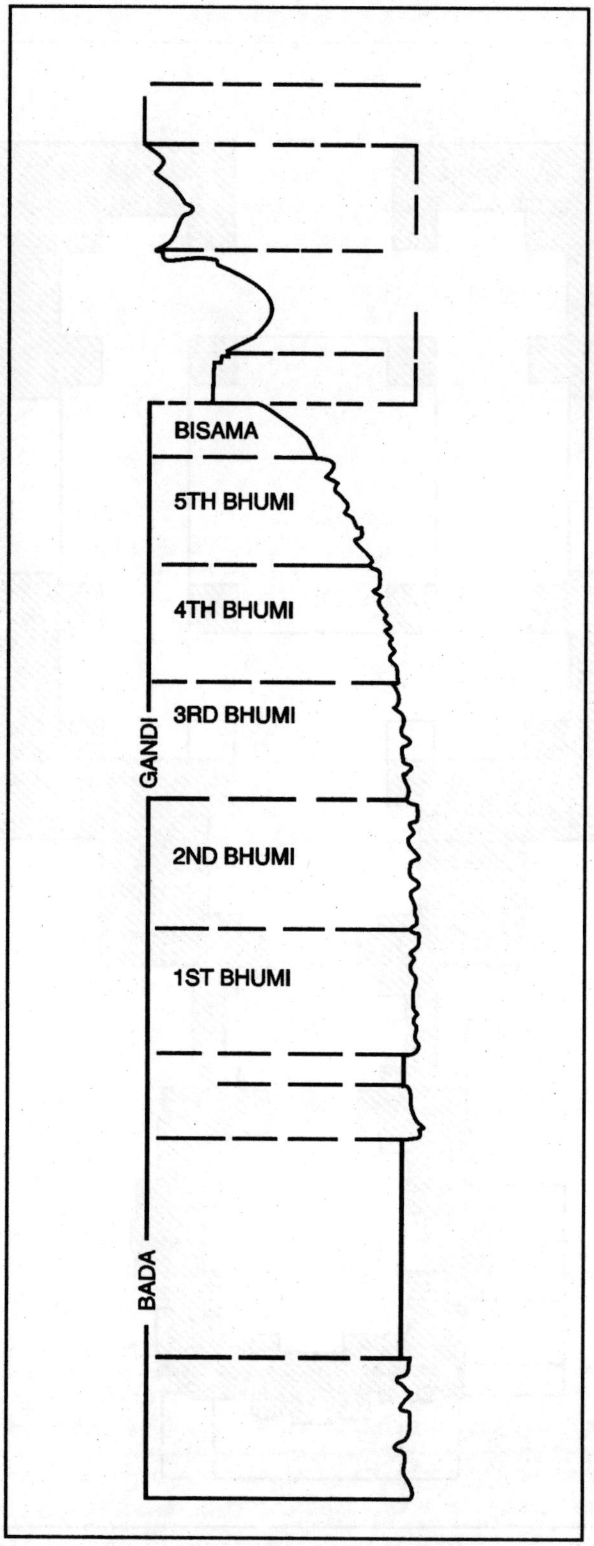

Fig. 4. Profile of Kosalesvara Temple, Charada;
Courtesy-Prof. D.R. Das, Calcutta.

The temple stands on the ground without *pista*, and tapers upwards up to an altitude of 45 feet. The ground plan of the temple is star-shaped, which is formed by two intersecting squares. The squares measure 13 feet on each side. The temple has three principal divisions – *bada, gandi* and *mastaka*. The *bada* is divided into five parts – *pabhaga, tala jangha, bandhana, upara jangha* and *baranda*. Both the *janghas* are of equal height, i.e., 3 feet 7 inches. Due to stellate design the *kanika* and *anuratha* are more prominent than *raha*. The *pabhaga* has three mouldings. In the *kanika pagas* are found *vajramundis*, and within the *chaitya* design, the figures of *nagas, yaksass*, etc are seen. The *anuratha* is designed as a plain pillaster on the *jangha* portion. The *bandhana* has a single moulding. A *khura*-shaped moulding succeeded by a depression forms the *baranda* from where the *gandi* moves upwards. The *kanika* of the *gandi* possesses six *bhumis*. The *bhumi amalas* end abruptly without covering the width of the *kanika*. The *gandi* exhibiting a *pancharatha* plan terminates at the *bisama* wherefrom the *mastaka* rises. The *mastaka* is a later renovation by the Department of Archaeology, Government of Orissa. The *mastaka* contains the normal features like *beki, amalaka, khapuri, kalasa, ayudha*, etc. The door-jambs to the sanctum are intact. The *lalatabimba* has a representation of *abhiseka* Laxmi flanked by elephants pouring water. *Abhiseka* Laxmi occupies the central position in the *Navagraha* panel. On the right side of her are carved the figures of Ravi, Soma, Mangala, Buddha, Brihaspati and on the other Sukra, Sani, Rahu and Ketu. The door frame contain two courses of decoration. The river Goddess Ganga and Yamuna are sculptured in high relief. The inner course of the frame is decorated with creeper and lotus medallions. The temple is a beautiful specimen of the stellate group of temples.

KANSIL TEMPLE

The village Kansil is in the close vicinity of Ranipur Jharial. It had a mound, which was excavated in 1973 by the Department of Archaeology, Government of Orissa, and from where remains of the temple were unearthed. This temple was known in the locality as Chhelia temple.

From the excavation it was known that the temple had a *Vimana*, an *antarala* and a *Mukhasala*. It was erected on a high platform. The temple has a stellate device. The temple externally shows *pancharatha* plan. Internally the sanctum is square in shape. The entrance doorway is plain. The *pabhaga* has three mouldings. It is built of bricks and is a Siva temple. Donaldson fixes the date of this temple to the 9th century AD and D.R. Das assigns this temple a date of 11th century AD.

BAUD TEMPLES

The present town Baud, now the district headquarters, is situated on the right bank of river Mahanadi. As it occupies a place in the Middle Mahanadi Valley, it has a definite link with the Upper and Lower Mahanadi Valley and this played liasoning role in transmitting and assimilating the cultural trends from one end to the other end. Baud and its vicinity are replete with monuments and sculptures of Brahmanical, Buddhist and Jaina sects. Thus, it forms an antiquarian belt.

The town itself preserves monuments of ancient period. At the outskirt of the town is found a temple complex. Beglar who visited the temple in 1874-75 AD first reported the temple complex.[1] The Ramesvara temple, which was probably the main temple, has already been heavily damaged and was completely renovated by the time of Beglar's visit. It had then a sanctum, a *mandapa* and a portico though in ruins. At present these structures are not there. The present temple faces east. What is more interesting is Beglar's report of another nine shrines which were in decay and contemporaneous with the main one. These shrines are described to have surrounded the main temple of Ramesvara.

Besides this group of temple, there is another group of three temples erected at a distance in the same premise. These temples stand independently. These three temples, all identical in look, are dedicated to Siva and known as Bhuvanesvara, Kapilesvara or Sapnesvara and Siddhesvara or Paschima Somanath. Bhuvaneswar and Kapilesvara face the east but the Siddhesvara has a reverse orientation (i.e., west facing). A keen observation of the layout of the temple indicates that each of the three temples was originally constructed at the corners of rectangle. The fourth one was perhaps completely destroyed. The temples were built of purplish red durable sandstone. Each of these stands on a high platform having a *Vimana* and a projected porch in front. The temples are approached by a flight of steps. The temples have no vestibule or frontal hall unlike the other stellate temples. They have four fundamental elements, viz, *pista, bada, gandi* and *mastaka*.

The *pista* or platform of the temple is high. The *pista* is stellular conforming to the shape of the sanctum. It is a most uncommon feature as the platform of the temples is mostly rectangular or square. The *pista* measures 4 feet 1 inches in heights. It consists of four stylized base mouldings, viz, *khura, kumbha, kani* and *basanta*.

From the *pista* grows the *bada*, which moves upward having the usual sections of *pabhaga, jangha* and *baranda*. The *pabhaga* has five mouldings, namely, *khura, kumbha, patta, kani* and *basanta*. The *khura* is adorned with *chaitya* arch motifs and vase and foliage motif is found in the *kumbha* moullding. *Patta* is a thin flat moulding. A *champaka* leaf placed vertically in the *kumbha* connects the *chaitya* motif found in *khura*. The upper three mouldings are connected with a perpendicular bar, which accommodates small figures in it. *Kani*, which is decorated with scroll work, has not taken the pointed shape.

The *jangha* section is 4 feet 3 inches high. Each facet is 2 feet 8 inches wide. Every facet of the *jangha* possesses two miniature *khakhara* shrine and a pilaster in outer flank. Each replica of the *khakhara* contains *pabhaga, jangha, gandi* and *mastaka*. This elongated *khakhara* shrine forms the *paga* of the *jangha*, which is noticed for the first time in this temple. The trunk (*gandi*) of the miniature *khakhara mundi* is composed of five courses of moulding. It is crowned by a *kalasa* flanked by rampant lion being mounted by a rider. The pillaster above the outer flank of the each facet contains a base, shaft and a capital. The base, which has been described as *tala bandhana* by Donaldson, consists of multiple string-courses topped by a pitcher. On this pot is found an engraving of an elongated 'S'-like design in a slanting way. Above the pot is found the standing figure of a maiden carved in high relief. It occupies the lower portion of the shaft, the upper part of which preserves a *kirttimukha* and a scroll-work. The *kirttimukha* is shown dripping the chains of pearls. The capital is decorated with the dwarfish atlantis. The *bada* is terminated by the *baranda,* which consists of two mouldings and a wide recess on it. The niches on the *jangha* are empty. There are some detached figures of Brahma, four-armed Nataraja in the *bhujanga trasita* pose dancing on *Apsmara purusa,* Ganesa, Chamunda, etc lying in the premises.

Though the *gandi* exhibits stellate device, its elevation reflects the use of *rekha gandi.* Like *rekha* spire, it also rises perpendicularly upward up to certain height and takes a sharp bend at the top near the *bisama.* The veritical three segments on each side of the *bada* are closely aligned with the three *pagas* of each facet of the *gandi* and thus in total it makes an eight-pointed stellar form. The *kanika pagas* of the *gandi* were divided horizontally into five *bhumis* marked by five *bhumi amalakas.* Each *bhumi* consists of four *bhumi barandikas.* The inner *pagas* are also divided horizontally into a number of *barandas* but here, in place of *bhumi amala, pheni* demarcates one series of mouldings from the other. In other words, the *bhumi-amalaka* is replaced by *pheni* with petals device. The *bisama* or the *vedi,* the meeting place of the *gandi,* also assumes an eight-pointed stellar form corresponding to the star shape of the *gandi* for which at places depressions are found in the circular edge of the *bisama.* The vertical *pagas* are sub-divided into narrow vertical chases. The successive *bhumi baranadika* or horizonal superimposed mouldings are decorated with *chaitya* arch or floral designs. The triple *chaityas* one above the other being interlaced by the fillets or ribbons are the standard decorative motifs here on the *gandi.* The body of the *gandi* is highly ornate. It is replete with the delicately executed filigree works on the *pagas* ascending towards the *bisama* at the top. The *bisama* holds the *mastaka* which includes a *beki,* an *amlaka,* a *khapuri,* a *kalasa* and a *dhvaja.* The Paschima Somanath temple possesses a *chakra,* unusual to a Saiva shrine.

The *vajra mastaka* or *bho* motif is carved above the entrance porch. This is also called *sukanasa,* which is projected from the eastern *raha* on frontal *paga* and placed on the entrance portal. The base portion of the motif has a tricellar motif. The middle cell is a larger one. Probably these three empty niches were being used for housing divine figures. The central cell or niche is crowned by an elongated *khakara mundi,* which encroaches into the *chaitya* medallion. At the top of the *bho* was *kirttimukha* issuing the strings of pearls from its mouth and a chain with a ball at the bottom.

A shallow projected portico in front of it negotiates the *garbhagriha.* Two pillars in front and one pilaster on each sidewall support the roof of the porch. The pilasters have figures carved in alto-relievo and decorated with scroll patterns. The pillars have a *ghata pallava* base. The shaft is octagonal, each facets of which are designed with scroll works. The upper part of the shaft is depicted with the *kirttimukha* emitting strings of pearls and bell on a chain. The capital of the pillar has an octagonal platform succeeded by a cushion and abacus. The door-jamb contains a *trishakha* frame, which includes the *manusya kautuki shakha.* On the bottom of the outer jamb are installed the four-armed *dvarapalas* endowed with *kapala,* trident rosary, etc. On the *dvaralalatabimba* of the architrave is noticed the depiction of the image of Gajalaxmi seated in *lalitasana* flanked by elephants. Her right hand is in *abhaya mudra* and the left carries a lotus. The architrave contains a *Navagraha* panel wherein the figures of Rahu and Ketu have been peculiarly represented. Rahu is represented by a head only in place of a half-bust figure. The Ketu also is shown seated cross-legged, trunkless figure rather than a serpent tail observed in later temples.

The exterior of the temple is replaced with small decorative motifs. The most prominent feature of the ornamentation programme is the depiction of the beautiful female figure standing in *tribhanga* posture embellished with the choicest ornaments. The belles with their well-proportioned physical contour and inviting looks, still now, serve as the arrestress of the attention of the devotees. The caryatids are found on the capitals of the pilasters, also in the recesses of the temple. In some examples, their erotic nature has been emphasized as they are represented showing their enlarged *lingam*. Donaldson records some erotic rituals like *purascharana, maithuna, sringarana,* etc on the temple body.[2] Among the vegetative motifs, *ghatapallava*, floral design, *vina* creeper with climbing human figures and other scroll works have been employed. The *kalasa* flanked by pouncing lions with riders is a novel motif found here.

The cult icons are not rare in the temple. Ganesa, Gajalaxmi, Nataraja, etc are depicted in the temples. The small figures of Lakulisa are represented in different *mudras*. A sitting goddess holding a lotus is represented in many places of the temple. It may be a variant of Tara.

The Baud temples exhibit high standard of architectural skill and remarkably exquisite carvings. It has close similarities with Muktesvara. K.C. Panigrahi[3] and other scholars unequivocally proclaim its contemporaneity with Muktesvara. The stellate plan is exhibited in fullest form in Boudh temples. In Muktesvara temple, only the ground plan of the *Mukhasala* is star-like.[4] Muktesvara has a frontal hall, which is inchoative of *Pidhadeula* or *Jagamohana*. It is absent in Baud. It seems that in coastal areas, the architecture started adopting the inclusion of *Pidha deula* and left the stellate form as evidenced from the ground plan of the *Mukhasala* of Muktesvara temple. So Muktesvara may be placed after Baud temples though the temples may be assigned a date of 10th century AD.

The temples have entry through the portico. It is strange to observe that the interior of the *garbha griha* is also built in stellar design, quite in conformity with the external plan. More astonishing is the *arghya patta* or *yonipitha*, where the *linga* is enshrined, is also made in stellate in keeping with the format of the temple. It is fantastic to notice that the base of the shaft of the *linga*, which is under-ground, also is octagonal and star-shaped. However, the upper visible part of the *linga* is as usual round in shape. The *yoni pitha* and the *linga* are made of black chlorite stone.

The concept of the temple planning, particularly of Baud temples, is thought provoking. The *pista* is octagonal, the temple both externally and internally octagonal, *bisama* is octagonal, *Sakti pitha* octagonal, the basement of shape of the *linga* (the visible representation of Lord Siva) is also octagonal. All these are neither accidental nor experimental. It has a deeper meaning. All are made eight-pointed. The number 'eight' is adopted here in every important sphere. It has a close connection with the cults of Saivism Lakulisa and Mattamayura.

The *Kausitaki Brahmana*[5] refers to the eight names of Siva, namely, Rudra, Sarva, Ugra, Asani, Mahadeva, Isana, Bhava and Pasupati. The Saiva pantheon of Pasupata sect worship the *Asta murtis* of Lord Siva. The Tewar inscription[6] of Gayakarns opens with an invocation to the eight forms of Siva. The Pasupati temple inscription of Jayadeva[7] (Nepal) describes the gift of an eight-petalled silver lotus to the God so that the eight forms may be accommodated on its petals. The "Sdok Kak Thom Inscription" of Udayaditya Varman[8] refers to the offering of an *asta puspika* daily to the *Astatanu,* i.e., eight forms of Siva by the royal priest. Banahbhatta[9] also informs about the worships of eight forms of Siva by *asta puspikas.* The *asta puspika* obviously means *asta dala* or eight-patalled lotus flower. *Asta dala* and *sodasa dala* are popular *Yantras* (mystic diagram) on which the deities are installed and worshipped. The eight-pointed plan of the temples may be taken as the symbolical representation of *asta dala* or *asta puspika,* which was favoured very much by the *Pasupatas* for the worship of *asta tanu* or *murtis.* These eight forms are described on eight *Siddhis* in Horsha stone inscription. It is known that Pasupata Saivism was flourishing in this area. The representation of Lukulisa in various *mudras* in the temples of Baud, Patnagarh and Ranipur-Jharial is clear evidence of the popularity of the Pasupata sect. The eight-pointed plan of the temple is very likely the innovation of Pasupata priests who probably wanted to install their God on *asta dala asthanas.* In consultation with the *Sthapatis* (architects) the eight-pointed plan was devised which was later on experimented and materialised. The temple became a *yantra.* The *Astatanu,* giver of *Asta Siddhi,* presided over it. A number of temples having eight-pointed plans were constructed in South Kosala (Madhya Pradesh and Orissa). Even the *Mukhasala* of Muktesvara exhibits a star-like ground plan. The ceiling of the *Mukhasala* of Muktesvara is decorated with the carving of an eight-petalled lotus medallion, each petal of which is occupied by a *matrika* and the last petal accommodates *virabhadra.* This suggests *Tantrik* affiliation. Though the point of view of R.D. Banerjee[10] about the triangular plan of the placement of the temple is not suitable in case of Baud temples, the eight-pointed plan of temples is a definite pointer to a mystic diagram (*Yantra*). Here is the *Lingam,* which is installed on a *Yantra.* So the affiliation of the Baud temple with *tantricism* may not be impossible though it looks improbable at present.

Beglar[11] reports that there were other nine shrines existing in dilapidated condition during his visit. So, in total there were twelve temples excluding the main temple, i.e., Ramesvara temple. It is inspiring to think that at that place there was a group of *Astaparivara* temple, the main temple of which was Ramesvara. The other group of temples, which are under our discussion, might have been a *panchayatana group* or a *charisambhu* group of temples.

CHAUSATHI YOGINI TEMPLE AT RANIPUR-JHARIAL

In Orissa there are two Chausathi Yogini temples. One is at Hirapur in Khurdha district and the other is Yogini temple at Ranipur-Jharial, which is being discussed here. These temples are the products of *Tantrik* school. These are usually circular in size and devoid of any roof.

The temple at Ranipur-Jharial is also circular having a diameter of 53 feet 8 inches externally. The thickness of the wall is 4 feet 10 inches, which houses in its inner-side the *Yoginis* in the niches. The height of the wall is 8 feet 3 inches. The *pabhaga* consists of three courses of stone. The wall composed of five courses of stone dressing and the niches of the temple cover three courses of the stones. The interior wall contains 5 feet 4 inches niches. There is a *mandapa* in the centre, which is occupied by a Nataraja image. The *mandapa* is 6 feet 10 inches square and 1 feet 8 inches high. Probably the Nataraja was the presiding deity of the *Yoginis*. The Nataraja image is eight-armed and three-headed. He is shown dancing on the back of his mount bull that is couchant. The snake is held above his head by his two upper hands. The main right hand is shown in *gajahasta mudra*. The corresponding left is broken. The other right hands hold trident and kettle drum. The left hands carry a skull and a rosary. The God is in a pose where the knees are apart and feet nearer. The lord is heavily be-decked with jewels, an unfrequented feature on Siva icons. He wears cylindrical crowns on his three heads, neck-lets, and necklaces garland his armlets and anklets. A beaded girdle is also traced around the waist just above the bottom of the garland. The eyes are half closed. He is shown in *urddhvalinga*. The face reveals contentment. The God is engaged in *ananda-tandava* bestowing blissfulness upon the world. To the right below the foot is carved a small figure of Ganesa.

The image is carved out of slab in high relief and measures 4 feet 7 inches in height and 2 feet 4 inches cm in width. Donaldson observes a small seven-headed human figure, which was near the *Yogini* No. 32 when Beglar visited the site. Beglar has noticed 53 *Yoginis*. At present 48 *Yoginis* are in existence. Out of these, 20 *Yoginis* are four-handed and 28 are two-armed. They are carved out from rough sand stones. All are exhibited in similar dance posture where knees are kept apart and the feet together. But the hands display various poses. The lord Siva in the centre also is depicted more or less in a similar position. The placement of legs forms a posture of classical dance "in stance assumed at the start of each set of movement, thus the *Yoginis* are poised as if ready to perform dance." The representation and placement of the Siva in the centre of the circle of *Yoginis* is in conformity with the textual prescription. The depiction of Siva and the *Yoginis* in dancing posture is a peculiar iconological feature almost unfrequented elsewhere. The general measurement of the height of the *Yoginis* is 3 feet. They have a conical headdress. A sizeable number of *Yoginis* are endowed with animal heads. Now there are 12 zoocephallic *Yogini* images. Beglar has reported 14 such representations.

The *Yogini* in No. 14 who is bigger than the other images had either six or eight arms as reported by Beglar[12]. (Now all heads are broken. The figure is placed in niche no. 13.) By the help of her two hands she was pulling open her mouth. She stands on a prostrate human figure. Donaldson identifies it with Chamunda. Another six-armed image has been noticed by Beglar, which bears the number "21". One hand is placed at her navel and other holds sword, rosary, mace and *vajra*. The rest-on is broken. Beglar reports only one three-headed *Yogini*

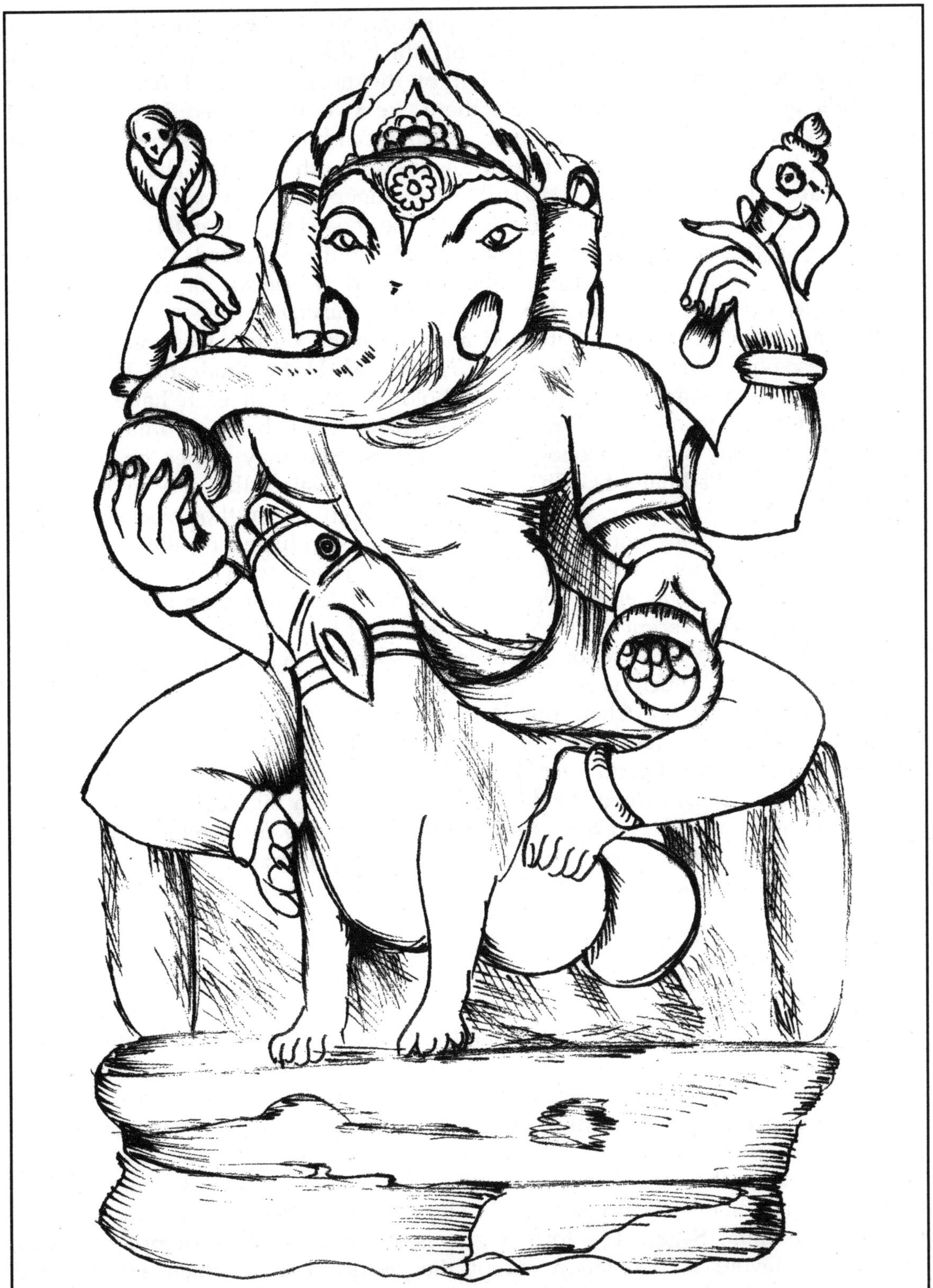

Fig. 5. Ganesa, Charada Temple.

with two arms. Clarles Fabri gives the photograph in plate No. LXXXI of the three-headed *Yogini* with four arms out of which the upper right holds a trident and upper left carries a rosary. The left of the normal pair of hands holds a *kamandalu* and the rest is broken. So there are two three-faced *Yoginis* (nos. 1 and 12). The first one may be termed as *Sarvatomukhi* and the second one may be termed *Brahmani*. As many as fifteen *Yoginis* are with tridents. The zoocephallic *Yoginis* are: the cat-faced (*Marjari*), the tiger-faced (*Vyaghri*), lion-faced (*Simhanana*), the elephant-faced (*Gajanaris*), the boar-faced (*Varahi*), the snake-faced (*Sarpasya*), the bear-faced (*Riksanana*), the buffalo-headed (*Vrisanana*), the cow-faced with horns (*Gomukhi*), the horse-headed (*Hayanana* or *Hayagriva*), the antelope-faced (*Mrigasira*) and the goat-faced (*Ajanana*).

Beglar refers to another goat-faced and lion-faced figure. The animal-headed *Yoginis* resemble very much Lokhari *Yoginis* of Uttar Pradesh. The Yogini no. 2, which is missing, was two-armed holding lotuses in each hand. She has been depicted riding a chariot drawn by seven horses. It has a definite link with Sun God who has similar iconographic features. She may either be identified with Chhaya or Padmahasta. Charles Fabri who visited the site in early 60s did not mention this figure. It was not there when the author visited the site in 1972 as a student in connection with study tour conducted by the Department of History, Sambalpur University. Charles Fabri refers to a four-armed image one of whose hands was either placed on her vital organ or pointing to it (Vide, plate LXXXIII). The recent survey conducted by J.K. Patnaik does not refer to such an image. Beglar's report also lacks such a description; after all, his description is very much sketchy.

The entrance of the Chausathi Yogini temple is to the east. It is 6 feet 5 inches in height and 5 feet 2 inches in width. Beglar[13] observed that there might be an entrance to south and pointed to a portion where the uniformity of the courses of stone is disturbed. Donaldson[14] also gives a similar view. Dehejia is of the same opinion. The portion is still there and clearly discernible. The present entrance was a later device. The temple may be ascribed to the early 10th century AD on the basis of stylistic consideration and historical observations.

LIYAHARI TEMPLE OF RANIPUR-JHARIAL

Ranipur-Jharial is in the sub-division of Titlagarh and situated at a distance of 32 km from Titlagarh town. John Campbell visited the place in 1853 when there were "about 120 temples". Beglar visited the site in 1874-75 when there were about 94 temples in existence out of 120 temples. In 1990, the total number of temples were 52. However, there were 50 temples in existence in 1998. The temples are plain and majorities are of *rekha* order. Recently renovation and restoration work is going on. Among the lot there are two *Khakhara* temples. One is found on the top of the large out-crop of rock near the *Chausathi Yogini* temple and another is on the south-east slope near the Somesvara temple edged on the tank Raital Sagar. The former one is a small one. The temple is plain, simple and devoid of decoration except the *chaitya* motifs, which are depicted on the body. The latter one is the larger one and is known as Liyakhai *deul* or Liyahari *mandir*. The body of Liyakhai *mandir* also is devoid of ornamentation.

The temple is 20 feet 8 inches in length and 17 feet 5 inches in width and 22 feet in height. The temple has all four elements. It stands on a platform and has a simple *pabhaga* about 1 feet 10 inches high. The *jangha* measures 4 feet 7 inches. It is succeeded by a *baranda* consisting of three mouldings. The *gandi* is plain except the depiction of *chaitya* motif, which starts from the *baranda* and extends upwards to the *gandi*. The *bada* exhibits a *triratha* and *trianga* plan. The *gandi* has no *ratha* plan. The *chaitya* above the entrance is more prominent than other such motifs. The *khakhara mastaka* is demarcated by a *khandi* or recess. The front portion is rectangular which has three entrances separated by pillars and pilasters. The temple might have been dedicated to the Sakta goddesses, as the temples of *Khakhara* order are known to have been enshrined by goddesses.

INDRALATH TEMPLE OF RANIPUR-JHARIAL

It is the tallest temple among the temples of Ranipur-Jharial. The temple is built of bricks and stands on a high platform. The height of the *pista* is 4 feet 4 inches. It is rectangular having a size measuring 90 feet in length and 37 feet in width. The temple comprises of a sanctum and an *antarala*. The *Mukhasala* has been razed to the ground. The sanctum is square, each side of which measures 10 feet. The temple faces east. The *Vimana* has the usual four vertical sections, viz, *pista, bada, gandi* and *mastaka*.

The *bada* of the temple consists of five divisions, namely, *pabhaga, tala jangha, bandhana, upara jangha* and *baranda*. The *pabhaga*, the lower-most part of the temple, has four mouldings namely *khura, kumbha, patta* and *basanta*. In length it is 5 feet 9 inches. The *tala jangha* is higher than the upper one. The *bada* is not only *panchanga* but *pancharatha* also as it has five vertical divisions. On the *raha* is found the *vajramundi* and a large *chaitya* above the niche. The niche on the *raha paga* is empty. Two pilasters are found on the sides of the niche. The pilasters serve as the frame of the niche. *Kanika pagas* look similar to that of *raha*. The *anurathas* are multi-faceted shafts. The *raha* is framed at the corners by pillars coiled around by the tail of the *naga*. Below the *baranda* moulding and above the *naga stambhas* are found small *kirttimukhas*. The *gandi* rises from the *baranda*, which is marked by thin mouldings. The *gandi* or *sikhara* displays *pancharatha* plans having five vertical segments. The *rathas* or *pagas* of the *bada* correspond to that of the *gandi*. The *kanika* of the *sikhara* is divided into nine *bhumis*. The first *bhumi* contains two *barandikas* but successive *bhumis* above it have one *barandika* each in between the two *bhumi amalas*. The *bhumis* are flat fillets with a small *chaitya* motif. The *anuratha* is adorned with small *vajramundis* arranged one above the other. The *raha* has the *chaitya* medallion on its body. The *Parsvadevatas* are not found now. The *chaitya* medallions above the niche of the southern wall have a figure of *Varaha* and that of northern wall contains an image of Nrisimha. The *chaitya* medallion of the western side is occupied by an image of Hanuman holding the mountain in place of Trivekrama. This suggests that the temple was a Vaishnava one. The *sikhara* of the temple has a mutilated *mastaka*. It raises up to a height of 75 feet. The temple may be dated to 10th century AD tentatively. The Sandhisthala of the temple contains replicas of *rekhavimana* in the lower portion and a figure of a female deity in the upper portion on the north side.

The body of the temple contains a number of small scenes related to the activities of child Krisha. For instance *Putana badha, Kaliya dalana, Pralambasura badha* by Balarama, four-armed Vaishnavi deity, Nrisimha, Varaha, etc are noticed. Along with these, figures connected with Siva like Lakulisa, Nataraj, etc are also depicted. But the preponderence of the Vaishnava divinities points it to be a Vaishnava shrine. K.N. Mohapatra opines that the temple was presided by the lord Gopal. In the interior of the *antarala* are gathered some scattered images of Buddha, Kartikeya, Hara-Parvati, etc. A small *Jagamohana/Mukhasala* is found in front of the sanctum. It is square and small in size and 43 feet high.

The name of the temple Indralatha spontaneously reminds the name of the Somavamsi king Indraratha who might have been the builder of the temple.

MOHANGIRI TEMPLE

Mohangiri is a small village situated to the north-east of Bhawanipatna at a distance of 56 miles. A small rivulet named Kaliaganga flows nearby the village. On the bank of this stream there is a dilapidated temple dedicated to Siva on an earthen mound. This present temple has been built in place of the old one. It is said that a forest guard was told in a dream to excavate the mound. The dream was narrated to the ruler of the area. Accordingly, the mound was excavated and the remnants of an old temple were discovered with the *linga*. The present temple was built with the materials of the old temple. The foundation of the old temple is still visible around the present small one. The presiding deity is *lingam*, which is believed to be a *Swayambhu* (self-created) one. The *Sakti pitha* is circular. As the old temple is completely demolished it is difficult to determine the elevation of the *sikhara*. From the rest of the foundation it appears to have been a sanctum of square size. Kedarnath Mohapatra, who visited this place, informs that the architectural scheme resembles that of the Parasurameswara of Bhubaneswar. If he is to be believed then we have to attribute an early *rekha* elevation to the sanctum.

In front of the sanctum is found the *Mukhasala*, which is rectangular in plan. It is a pillared hall of eight pillars and four pilasters. The pillars are plain and square bearing *ghata pallava* design on their top. The long horizontal beams of stones are also noticed in the *Jagamohana*. Whether it had a flat roof or multi-tiered roof cannot be ascertained now. Presently it is covered with straw and tiles. The interesting features of the *Jagamohana* are the pillars and the inscription on the floor besides some geometric diagrams very akin to different *Yantras* of Sakta cult. S.N. Rajguru has reported about two inscriptions. P.C. Rath deciphered the name as Sphita Chanda. However, S.N. Rajguru has read the name Sphita Chanda as Chitra Chanda. The first inscription read by S.N. Rajguru is;

L. I. *Sri mudgala kulasya (sya)*
II. *Chitra Chandra.*

And the second is "*Vyuha Bhairava*". But at present only one is noticed there which is written in a single line. The local people reported that a few years back a Saheb took it away to Calcutta. The *Yantras* are still visible. The *Yantras* and the name "Vyuha Bhairava" point unmistakably to *Tantrik* worship prevalent in that place. The remains of *amalaka silas* noticed in the stone heaps near the temple and the pond suggest the existence of a number of shrines there. It is evident from the sculptures available there. The hole on the sizely cut stones indicates that the temple was erected in the system of interlocking stones. Iron clamps might have also been used for the purpose. It is also evident from the arrangement of monolithic pillars and lintels of the *Jagamohana*.

The entrance of the sanctum is flanked by the Saiva *dvarapalas* – Nandikesvara and Bhringi. The interior walls are adorned with sculptured panels consisting of the figures of deer, swan, *gandharva* couple, Ganesa and a bull. Some panels also depict the churning of ocean by the gods, the exile of Rama Laxman and Sita and other images related to Rama theme. The outer walls of the sanctum contain the niches to house the *Parsvadevatas*. A two-armed Ganesa is found on the southern wall. Kartikeya is housed in the western niche. He is two-armed and mounted on peacock. The northern niche accommodates a unique image if she is considered as a *Parsvadevata*. It is a standing image of a female of peaceful appearance. She is two armed and is adorned with a *karanda mukuta*. *Kundala* and *hara* are placed in the ear and around the neck of the image. The right hand is in *Abhaya mudra*. The lady is shown feeding his breast to a baby who is standing near her. This image cannot be that of a *Parsvadevata*. To us it appears to be a *Matrika* image. Such an image is noticed in Mathura museum, which was collected form Kagarola in the Agra district. The image is of Vaisnavi, who is holding a mace in her upper right hand and a *chakra* in her upper left hand. The normal right hand is in *varada* pose. In her normal left hand she is supporting a standing baby who is shown touching the breast of the mother. Garuda is shown seated to the right. The image of the Divine Mother of Mathura museum is four-handed, whereas the image of Mohangiri are two-armed. But the basic motherly feature is strikingly similar in both the icons. The Mathura icon belongs to the Medieval Period. From the above discussion it is clear that the image is a *Matrika* image, and it may not be far removed in date from that of Mathura museum. The image was wrongly placed as a *Parsvadevata* during the building of the present temple. The image of northern *Parsvadevata* might be laid littered in the mounds. As the local architect could not find the image of the northern wall, they picked up this image and housed it in the northern niche of the *Parsvadevata* of the modern structure.

Besides these, there are some sculptures – both secular and sectarian – found scattered near the temple area among which mention may be made of a Lakulisa image, one four-armed Durga and one eight-handed Durga. The local people keeping them in separate rooms are worshiping the latter two images. The former one is noticed in debris near the pond. This image also exhibits medieval features.

The use of large monolithic pillars and lintels, the adoption of interlocking system of stones, the inscriptions of Mudgala Dynasty, the *Matrika* image and

Lakulisa image indicate a date of the 8th century AD. In other words, the old temple of Mohangiri was a contemporary to the temple Parasurameswara.

Though the temple and *Mukhasala* have been completely removed, the existing eight pillars and four pilasters connected above by lintels and beams appear to be original. The pillars are highly stylized. The lower portion of the pillar is square. In the middle it becomes a *Purnaghata* with over-flowing leafy scrolls at four corners. Then it is succeeded by the other decorative mouldings. At the top again it is square surmounted by a square capital. Vidya Dehejia places the temple in formative Phase-B, i.e., 8th century AD.

SANKUSHGARH SITE

The site is situated on the confluence of Rahul and Budha at a distance of 10 miles from Madanpur-Rampur in Kalahandi district. In the site are found a number of sculptures scattered here and there. The images of Umamaheswara, the *Alasakanyas* like *Dalamalikas* and *Salabhanjikas* are found in Sankushgarh. Presently, these pieces are taken away from Sankushgarh and are kept in the college premises of Madanpur-Rampur. A beautiful image of Parvati is preserved along with the above-said images. It has also been brought from Sankushgarh. The image is shown seated in *lalitasana* on a pedestal.

There is another remarkable Saiva image found installed in a house. The house is recently built and the image found in the site was placed by the local people as the presiding deity of the so-called shrine. The image is four-armed out of which one is broken. The other three hold a *khatwanga*, an *aksamala* and *dambaru*. The facial expression is grave but not furious. The eyes have bulging eyeballs. The god wears a conical crown, a necklace and earrings. An elliptical halo made out of lotus petals covers the back of the head. He is represented in ithyphallic form. The god is surrounded by garland-bearers, fly whisk bearers, and is attended by Siva *ganas* with other devotees. The image contains a rosary, an attribute of Saumya aspect, and exhibits *Urdhvalinga* – a characteristic of Ghora aspect. This image may be taken as that of Siva, the great *yogin*. The discovery of Saivite sculptures in plenty points to the existence of a Saiva shrine in Sankushgarh, which may also belong to the 8th/9th century AD.

SOMESVARA TEMPLE OF RANIPUR-JHARIAL

Ranipur-Jharial in ancient time was known as Ranipadra and was an important pilgrimage centre where a large number of temple remains were traced. Some are in situ, some are restored recently and many are in ruins. Among all the temples, noteworthy are Somesvara temple, Indralath temple, and sixty-four Yogini temples.

The Somesvara temple stands on the sloping part of a rocky hillock. The temple rises from a low plinth. It faces east. It has two components, *garbhagriha* and *Mukhasala*. In between is found a small plain *antarala* (vestibule), which connects both the structures to each other. The *garbhagriha* or *Vimana* is 12.6 feet square and has a *triratha gandi* and *trianga bada*. The *bada, gandi* and *mastaka* are intact. The *bada* has the three elements – *pabhaga, jangha* and *baranda*. The

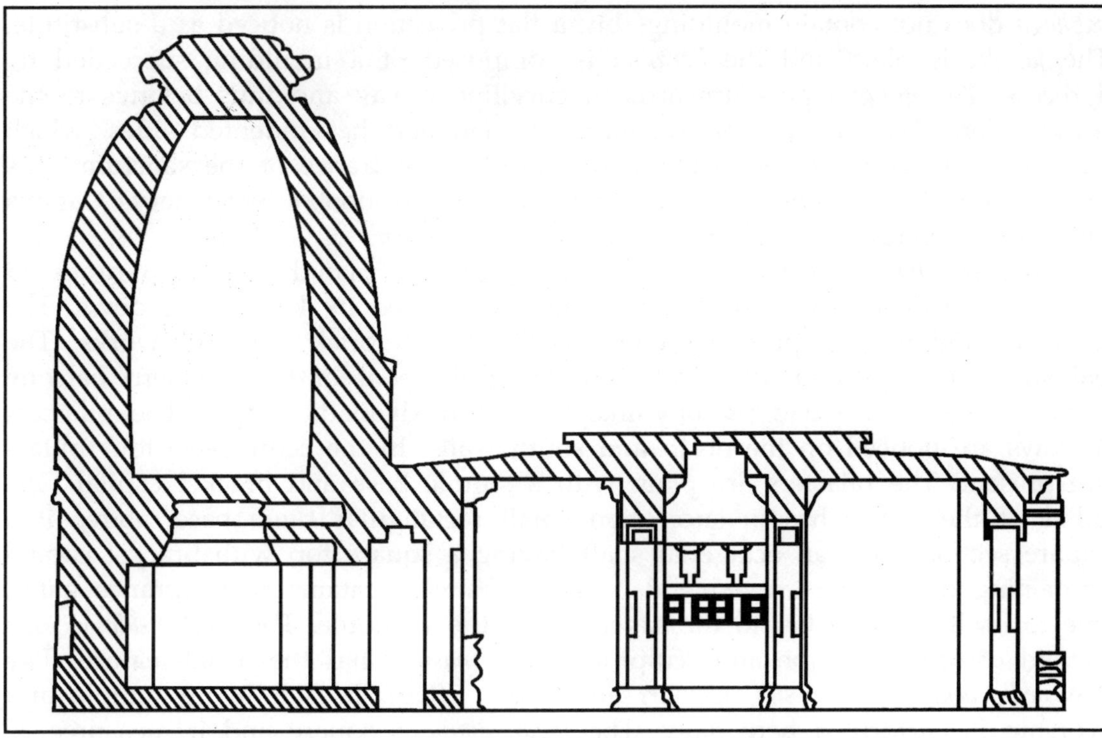

Fig. 6. Sectional Elevation of Somesvara Temple, Ranipur-Jarial; Courtesy-Prof. D.R. Das, Calcutta.

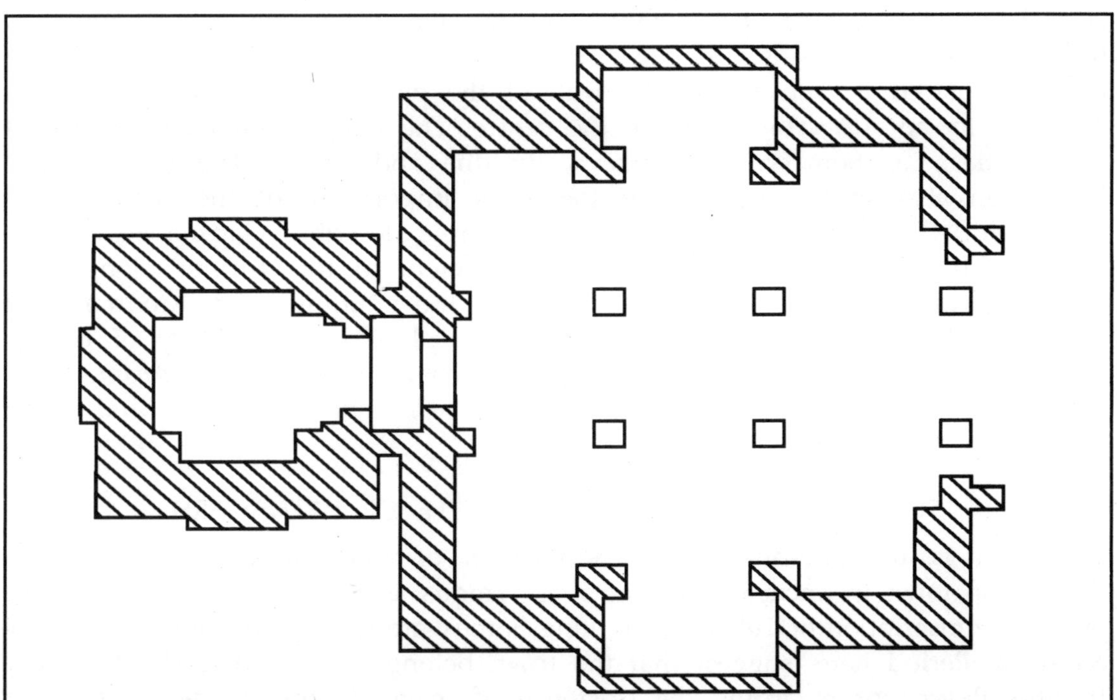

Fig. 7. Ground plan, Somesvara Temple, Ranipur-Jarial; Courtesy-Prof. D.R. Das, Calcutta.

pabhaga does not contain mouldings but a flat projection is noticed as a substitute. The *jangha* is plain and the *baranda* is composed of a moulding succeeded by a recess. The *gandi* tapers upwards in curvilinear way and thus belongs to the *rekha* order. The *garbha griha* is square in plan and has indented sides, which extend to the vestibule. The circular frame of the entrance of the sanctum rests on the stone lintel. Under the lintel there is an inscription of Saivacharya Gagana Siva. The sanctum is enshrined with a Siva *lingam*.

The *Mukhasala* or *Jagamohana* is also square in plan having two projected balconies on north and south sides, which are closed by latticed windows. The latticed windows are probably later creations with brick masonry works. The balustrade railings and small pillars holding the roof of the northern balcony indicate that it also had balcony like that of Baidyanath temple. The pilasters in rows are noticed on the north and south walls. In the centre also four pillars are present. The pilasters are plain with a simple base and bracket capital. The pillar of the centre has in succession small rectangular *khura* base, above it a square section, then an octagonal shaft having a square top with bracket capital containing downward curved ends. The *Mukhasala* contains two entrance gates, one to itself and another to the sanctum via the vestibule. The *Mukhasala* is also devoid of ornamentation and sculptures. The *mastaka* has the usual features like the *vedi*, *beki*, *amalaka sila*, *khapuri* and *dhvaja* (flag). It is a living temple and worship is performed here daily. The *Jagamohana* is square and it measures 27 feet in length and breadth while the central space created by the four pillars in it is 9 feet square. The introduction of the *antarala* seems to be a novel item in Orissan temple architecture. To the inner side of the entrance doorway there is a detached image of Durga, which is now worshipped by the devotees. A figure of a small *Nagini* is also found near the sanctum door and a small Buddha image is placed in a niche on the wall of the passage. The sanctum lintel is occupied by an *Abhishaka* Laxmi in the centre. The temple contained images of four deities, i.e., Somesvara, Kartikeya, Buddha and Laxmi. The Bilhari stone inscription also speaks high about the great importance of the sacred place (Ranipadra). The inscription found in this temple describes Gagana Siva as its builder. The *Tirtha Kanda* of *Krityakalpataru* refers to this further along with Viraja, Purushottam and Mahendra. It shows the antiquity and importance of the place. In art history it occupies a unique place in the history of temple architecture because of varieties of temples such as hypaethral, *khakhara*, *rekha*, *Jagamohana* with plain sloping roof without *pidha*, brick temples and other temples.

SOMESVARA / KOSALESVARA TEMPLE OF PATNAGARH

Patnagarh is the sub-divisional headquarters of Bolangir district. It was a flourishing town in ancient days and was famous as Kuanripatna. The presence of a stone inscription of Teluguchoda king Somesvaradeva, an old temple of early Medieval Period here, suggest that the town belongs to a very early date. The traditional account regarding the existence of seven *Tantrik* maidens and their esoteric practices further attests to the ancientness of the place. Later on it became the capital of Chauhan Dynasty of Orissa. The fort area of the town contains many temples, among which the Somesvara temple, Patnesvari temple and Samaleswari temple are noteworthy.

The Somesvara temple, also known as Kosalesvara temple, is the oldest one. It has undergone many alterations, repair and reconstruction. The temple is heavily plastered. Axially it is divided into two parts. The *Vimana* or sanctum and the *Jagamohana* or the frontal hall. There is an additional structure in front of the *Jagamohana*, which is known as *Nandimandapa*. The *Vimana* is 14 feet 8 inches square. The exterior of the temple is rigorously plain. The *Jagamohana* is rectangular. But Donaldson describes that the *Jagamohana* is 27 feet 6 inches square. It has a lateral transept on both the north and south wall. The projection of the transept measures 4 feet 6 inches. Donaldson observes this portion as an improvement upon the portion of Ranipur-Jharial. The *Nandimandapa* is composed of four designed pillars carrying the roof. It is 8 feet in length, 8 feet in width and 8 feet in height. Each pillar has a square base, which is divided into three mouldings. The centre of each side of the square platform is carved with a *chaitya* motif. Inside the *chaitya* motif are found the depictions of *kirttimukha*, human heads, Ganesa, etc. Above the platform stands the shaft, which exhibits *kirttimukha* emitting pearl string courses, which move the mouth of another. In between the *kirttimukha*s, the whole facet is filled with the fretwork of criss-cross patern. The octagonal part is surmounted by a *ghata pallava* motif, which is crowned by an abacus. The abacus is connected with a portion of the plain square pillar. The abacus has two projections wherein is found the carving of eight-petalled flower design. This eight-petalled lotus rosette is found in Sauntpur, Budhikomna, Adbhar and Kharod.

The pillars of *Jagamohana* can be divided into three categories: (1) plain pillars, (2) pillars with base relief, and (3) pillars without base relief. The plain pillar has a low pedestal. The pillar is composed of three divisions, square shaft topped in the *ratha* design. It is crowned by a plain band surmounted by a *triratha* design. The capital is plain and square. The other group includes the pillar having a plain square portion. On it are four rampant lions at four corners. It is succeeded by a band containing *chaitya* motif. On this band are found *kirttimukha*s with *alamba* design. The lower portion where the four lions are depicted contains small niches which house small figures. The third category of pillars is well finished. These pillars have square shaft richly carved with floral pattern, scroll work, *chaitya* motif, etc. Above it are found standing lions at four corners. In between two corner lions, is a small niche on the lower portion. These niches house figures of Ganesa, Kartikeya, Mithuna couple, Lakulisa and the scenes of Krishna *lila*, *Naga*s and Siva Parvati, Gauri, etc. This position is succeeded by a flat band containing the heads of lions engraved in low relief. Above this is found an *alamba* device. On the top the pillars are the square capitals, which have *alamba* motifs.

Though the architectural framework of Patnagarh *Jagamohana* tallies with that Baidyanath and Charada, the pillar designs display close affinity with the pillars of Sauntpur and Pujaripali. The projected *chhatris* (*chhayay*) at the top of the corner of the *Mukhasala* are found with the images of flying *Gandharvas*.

A bull was placed on the centre of the *Jagamohana*. In 1974, when the author visited the place the roof of the *Jagamohana* was not there. The *Jagamohana* was open.

The temple of Patnagarh, like the temple of Baidyanath, Charada and Sauntpur, contains life-size images, which are found attached to the walls of *Jagamohana*. At the entrance of the southern balcony there is a beautiful female figure found busy in removing her clothes. To the side is chiselled a parrot on a stand. Though oval halo is noticed behind the figure, which is an insignia of divinity, it may be taken as a *suka sarika* maiden than as a deity. An image of *Ardhanarisvara* is kept on the north wall. The hands are broken. The lower portion has disappeared. The face and the body show a clear demarcation of male half to the right and the female half to the left. Flying *Gandharvas* are carved at the top of the slab. A life-size female figure about 6 feet high is kept against the south wall of the *Jagamohana*. The figure is headless. Out of four hands two are broken and the rest are placed in front of her body. She is standing on one foot. The raised left leg being bent rests on the right knee portion. A female attendant is found on the lower portion of both the sides of the deity. It is strange that not a single ornament or jewellery is found on her body except the *Yajnopavita*. Probably she is performing penance. Donaldson identifies the deity as *Tapasvini* Parvati. Behind the missing head, an elliptical halo radiating rays is carved. To the right side of the halo is found a *linga* and to the left is noticed a four-armed Ganesa. Most peculiar is the presence of nine heads at the top of the back slab. The nine heads are taken to be the representation of nine planets by Donaldson and others. But it may well be identified with Nava Durga also. The *Mukhasala* of Baidyanath temple also has a standing two-armed female figure. It is also headless, and above the missing head are carved nine heads in a row. Another four-armed figure is kept within the *mandapa* of which the right leg and back arms are broken. Donaldson describes, "He originally had his missing leg raised and resting on his weapon while crossing his arms in front of his body, a rare iconographic form Orissa." He places the temple in the time period of 9th/10th century AD. There is a large platform near the temple on the step of which an inscription is engraved. It has recorded that the village Ghasarani was donated for regular supply of flower to the lord Somesvara by the king Somesvara, identified with the homonymous king of Teluguchoda Dynasty who was ruling in 11th/12th century AD. This time may be assigned to the construction of this temple also.

In the niche of northern wall is installed an image of four-armed Bhairava which holds in its upper right a *trisula* and a rosary in the matching hand. The right hand of the normal pair displays the *varada* posture while on the left below is seen a dog sitting. In the western niche is found an image of four-handed Siva with his mount bull. A male figure is engraved below which can be taken as a devotee. Four-armed Ganesa is found in the southern niche. Recently, while digging near the Patnesvari temple, two small images were unearthed.

These two images resemble so much in style and representation with that of the tribal hunters shown in the railing of the balcony of the Baidyanath temple that it can be taken as replicas of the latter. The hairs are arranged in cork-screw curls. They wear loin cloth and are equipped with bow and arrow being accompanied by a dog. The sculptures can be taken as a definite pointer of its contemporaries with that of the Baidyanath temple.

S.S. Panda[15] refers to a panel, fitted to the left side of the *Jagamohana* entrance, depicting "procession of seven females carrying a chhatri". To the east of the outskirt of the fort area, an interesting image is worshipped under a tree. It is a male figure having eight arms and a ferocious face. The left hands hold Agni, *vajra*, *sarpa* and *khetaka* while the right hand possess *khadga*, *musala*, *trisula* and *danda*. The deity stands on a prostrate human being. Often Virabhada is found associated with *Sapta Matrika*s. The number of *Matrika*s varies from 8 to 16. Here the deity surrounded by female figures may be taken as *Matrika*s and the male figure may be identified with Virabhadra.

KOSALESHWAR TEMPLE OF BAIDYANATH

Baidyanath, a small village, is picturesquely situated on the bank of the Tel river and is only 5 km south-west of Hardushol Chhak, the nearest bus stoppage on the Sonepur Bolangir Road. This is a place of pilgrimage and is famous for the temple of antiquarian value. The temple is named after its presiding deity Kosaleswara and is situated at the end of the village. It consists of a *Vimana* (sanctum) and a *Jagamohana*, which are square in plan. The original sanctum where the *lingam* had been previously installed is now no more. The present temple, which contains the *lingam*, is of a *Bhadra* type[16] and appears to be a modern one. The foundation of the original sanctum is still visible around the present cella. The *Jagamohana*, a rare gallery of medieval Orissan art, was once in a dilapidated condition but now is renovated by the Cultural Affairs Department of State Government of Orissa. What type of *gandi* it had originally is difficult to ascertain as it is completely destroyed. Even the earliest photograph[17] supplied by B.C. Majumdar fail to convey any idea of its *gandi*. Generalizing the architectural style of the temples of the variety in Western Orissa, we may presume that the present *Mukhasala* might have contained a like that of Somesvara temple at Ranipur-Jharial and the sanctum might have been a *rekha* type temple[18] as found in Charada.

The *mandapa* has a stone doorway at the entrance and an elaborately ornamented doorframe to the west, i.e., to the sanctum. It has twelve engaged pillars, which form the square interior and a raised *vedika* in the centre of the *mandapa* having four pillars at four corners. The *vedika* is 14 feet square in plan. The doorframe on the eastern entrance possesses three bands of scroll works. The lintel of the architrave contains a figure of Gajalaxmi. Here Laxmi is shown seated in *lalitasana* with the right leg hanging down the pedastal and the left by rests on the pedastal. The inner course of the frame has lotus rossette and filigree works. The architrave has one male figure after one female. The entrance gate to the west also is lavishly carved. At the base of the doorframe are found the *dvarapalas* in both side accompanied by river goddesses Ganga and Yamuna. The *dvarapalas* are 40 inches in height and the river goddesses measure 42 inches. It is a rare feature of Orissan temples where large-sized *dravapalas* are attended by river goddess of about equal size. They are also placed on the projecting jambs and not on the inside jamb. On the lintel of the inner frame is found a *navagraha* slab. The broad beam above the inner frame is depicted with a fine image of *Anantasayi* Visnu.

The twelve engaged pillars are plain. But the four pillars in the central are ornate. The pillars at the base are undecorated and square in shape. They rise from a *Ghata pallva* pedestal. The upper portion of the pillars is octagonal and carved with standing lions alternating with *Kirttimukhas* dripping pearls from their mouth. Above the design, two more courses of floral work are found. They are *dhanu ganthi* and *mali phula phadika* scroll work. It is surmounted by *alamba* motif with *Kirttimukha* on the eight facets above which is the bracket capital having a larger *alamba* device at the base.

Inside the sanctum is the *linga*. Behind the *linga*, the back wall contains rows of detached sculptures, which were fixed on it when this new structure was built. The row includes the figures of Uma-Maheswar, Ganesa, and Kartikeya, etc. This type of arrangement is found in the sanctums of Mohangiri and Patnagarh also.

The small space between the two structures indicates the presence of a vestibule before the entrance to the cella. The temple also faces towards the east as in the case of all Deva temples. The style of the building is very massive. Heavy stones have been used in the construction of the structure. The stones are dressed one after another without mortar. Small iron beams and hinges have been employed here. In some places of the *Jagamohana*, bricks also have been used. The bricks, being very large and hard, suggest an early date. The upper part of the inside walls of the *Jagamohana* contain sculptures carved out of bricks. The ceiling was supported by four sculptured pillars inside. The peculiar feature of this *Jagamohana* is the porch-like projections on both sides of the walls. It is an oblong verandah raised like a pedestal covered with a flat roof supported by two small pillars. The outside of the verandah is attached by a railing of small stone-uprights wich also contain sculptures. The coping of this railing is very heavy. The lower portion of this raised verandah has a railing-like structure. In totality it looks like a balcony. These two balconies on both the sides make the hall lighted by permeating light and air from outside. The *mandapa* has two entrances. The one on the front and the other is on the back leading into the sanctum. The *Jagamohana*, unlike the temple of Gandharadi does not stand on a raised platform, but the structure rises from the ground. It is now bereft of roof and only the *bada* portion or the vertical cube is now in a surveyable condition. The *Jagamohana* consists of *Panchanga bada*[19], i.e., the cube has been divided horizontally into five parts namely *pabhaga*, lower *jangha*, the *bandhana*, the upper *jangha*, and the *baranda*. The *pabhaga* contains four mouldings – *khura*, *patta*, *kani*, *basanta*. Like Gandharadi temple and Baud temple, *Kumhba*-designed moulding has been adopted here. The basement of the *pabhaga* is decorated with small and plain *chaitya* motifs. Both the lower and upper *janghas* are plain. Only two pilasters of brick are seen raised upwards starting from the beginning of the *tala-jangha* to the ending of the upper *jangha*, being encircled by a curling snake of which the hood is not prominent. It may be taken as a variation of

Naga pillar. In the *pabhaga* portion, between second and third mouldings, there are small *chaitya* motifs. *Bandhana* consists of a plain moulding which divides the *jangha* into upper and lower parts. The *baranda*, which demarcates the *Gandi* from the *bada* contains three plain mouldings. Then onwards is the roof of the *Gandi* no shape of which can now be traced. Another peculiarity of this temple is that unlike other temples, the outer surface of the *Jagamohana* is less sculptured whereas the inner side of the wall is sculptured with beautiful life-size figures. In front of the *Jagamohana* there is a small recently made porch where a *Nandi* of black chlorite stone has been kept. Previously it was kept outside the *Jagamohana* in open as informed by local people.

While entering the premises of the temple one can see the Gajalaxmi image on the lintel of the eastern gateway. The stone pillars, which support the lintel, now look plain. This Gajalaxmi representation is found in many temples of Siva and Vishnu in western as well as in Eastern Orissa. From a study of the symbols of the royal seals of Somavamsis, B.C. Majumdar[20] was led to believe that Matangi Mahalaxmi was the household goddess of the Kosala Guptas (Somavamsis). This goddess was introduced by Sarabhapuriya kings for the first time in South Kosala. Later on the representation of the Goddess Gajalaxmi was continued by the Somavamsi monarchs in their seals and structures. The depiction of Gajalaxmi in the lintel of the entrance became popular and was adopted by other royal dynasties.

In the lintel the goddess is sitting on a lotus pedestal with her right leg hanging down and left being placed on the pedestal touching the right thigh. In the left hand she is holding a full-blown lotus and is attended by two attendants from both sides. Two out-flanking elephants (one on each side) are shown above her head raising their proboscis upward and pouring water on her head. In the premises of the temple there are some images lying uncared for. Among them there is a broken image of a lady, the lower portion of whose body is completely destroyed and the upper portion up to the waist is intact. She is standing in a *bhanga* pose. Only one hand of it is intact which rests on the waist. Beaded garland is visible around her neck. She may be identified as Kumari or Mohini. An *Ardhanarisvara murti*, which was previously inside the temple and now lying in the premises, has been very much damaged. There is no doubt that it was once a fine piece of sculpture. But due to the ravages of nature and the carelessness of the visitors, the glaze and the charm of the figure is gone now. The image is four-handed out of which three hands are broken. The only remaining hand is holding a *Khatvanga*. In the female part, jewelled ornaments, lady garments, elaborate ear ornaments, female lead dress, decorated girdle and a prominent breast have been shown. While the male part contains a *sarpa kundala* in the ear, *Jata mukuta* on the head, *Sarpa valaya* (armlet), a sacred thread passing through the chest and rest is plain. A Nataraja figure, which is now broken into two pieces, is kept in a slanting position on the side of the boundary wall. It has ten arms out of which four arms are lost. Two pairs are intact. The uppermost pair holds a snake over his head. The next pair of hands (from the top) holds *dambaru* and a *japamala*, respectively. The third left hand carries fire and the lower left hand a *naga* with raised hood. The lower

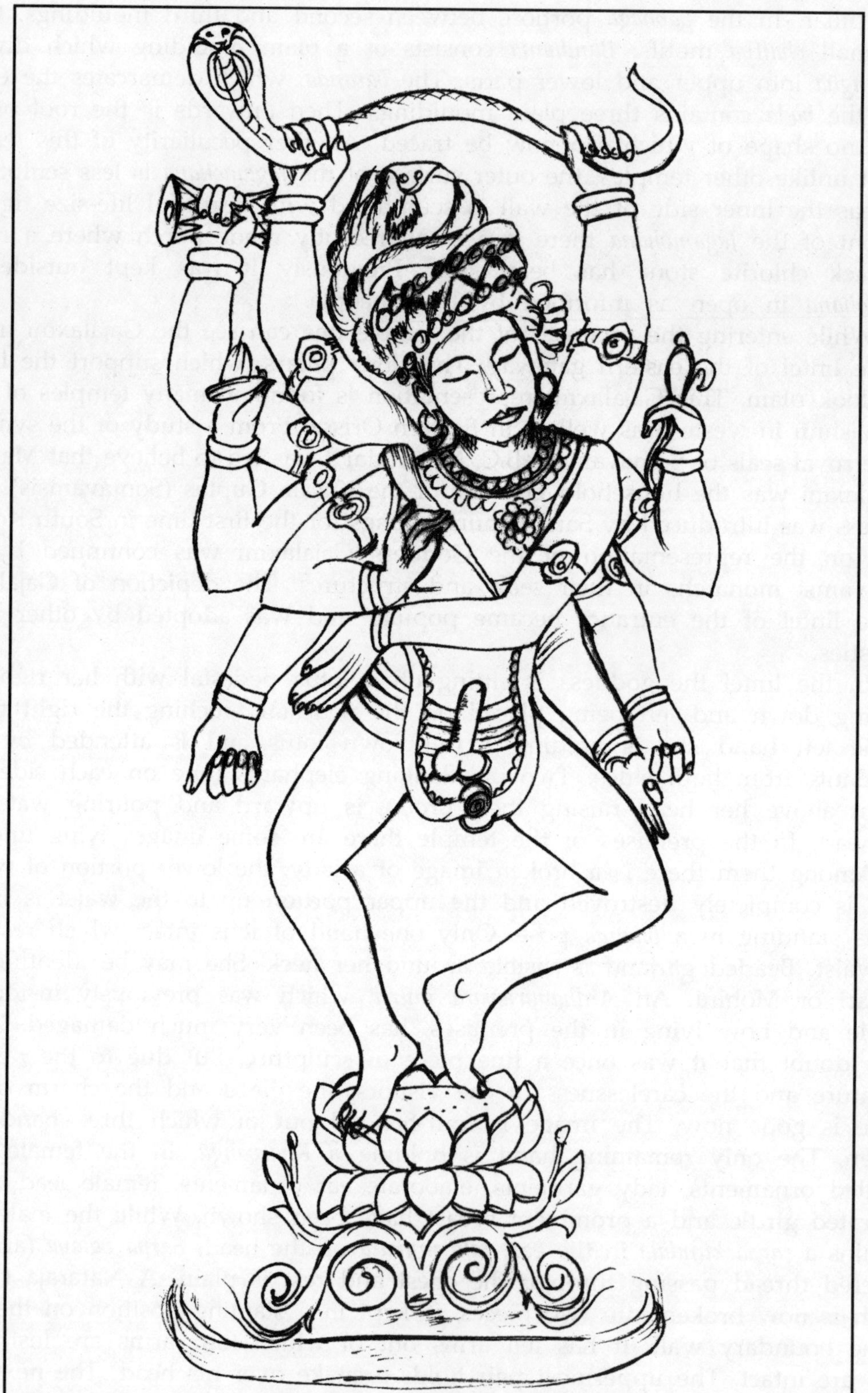

Fig. 8. Nataraja, Charada Temple.

portion contains a standing bull behind the image. On both sides are seen attendants – one female sitting on the right and the other male standing on the left. Another small figure is shown attached near the knee of the image.

Some other stray images are also found there. Among them a large-sized recumbent bull carved out of rough stone, a *linga* containing a small sitting figure in it (*Mukhalingam*) within a square *Saktipitha*, and a two-armed standing images holding a *parasu* and an indistinct object are found.

The outer side of the *Jagamohana* is devoid of sculpture except on the uprights of the railing of the balconies. Some beautiful sculptures, which exhibit various aspects of social life of the tribal people, are found here. There are also found the cult images of Ganesa, Garuda, etc. Besides these, in the southern balcony a fighting scene of a divine figure with an animal is carved on an upright. The animal is standing on its hind legs and jumping towards the man. The front legs of the animal are on the thigh of the man. Another divine figure is seen fighting with a bull in a separate upright. Many indistinct figures can be traced in the body of the upright of the balcony. These figures have been identified with Krishna killing the demon Kesi and Vrsa.

In the northern balcony there are some important scenes carved in the uprights of the railing. Here is depicted the domestic life of the tribal people. A man wearing a loincloth on his waist portion is seen standing, holding a bow and an arrow in the left and right hand, respectively. A dog is seen accompanying the man. This is definitely a hunting scene of a tribal man. A female figure with a waistcloth is shown here holding in the left hand a typical tribal winnowing fan. A child stands on the right side of the female. Among others a male figure is sitting with his legs out-stretched to form a lap to make his child sit comfortably. Two female figures are seen on the sides of the male figure. It also undoubtedly represents a scene of the day-to-day life of a rural family. These three sculptures depict the domestic life of a rural folk life of Western Orissa in realistic manner. This type of representation is not found in any temple of coastal Orissa. Fabri, Panigrahi, Dehejia, Donaldson and N.K. Sahu have overlooked this group of sculptures. The author for the first time brought this sculpture to the notice of the scholars[21]. To the left of the outer side of the balcony there is figure of an erotic couple. Both are sitting naked locked in the act of love. This looks crude now. That it was once a fine piece of art goes without saying.

Inside the *Mukhasala* there are some rare specimens of medieval Orissan art, which remind us of our glorious heritage of classical art. Just to the left of the entrance of the *Jagamohana* a two-armed image of Kartikesvara is found attached to the wall. The figure is shown seated on a peacock with a spear in his hand. Charles Fabri[22] speaks of its unusual representation of the hairstyle, i.e., "wig" style of hairdressing. Generally Kartikeya as a *Parsvadevata* is found attached in every Siva temple in the outer surface of a sidewall. But he is shown here on the left side of the entrance gate. Among the ornaments, he is found wearing a necklace around his neck and a decorated bracelet on his wrist. Charles Fabri, however, has given much emphasis on the hairstyle of the figure and opines that the hair has been dressed in the "wig" style, which is a typical fashion of 6th century AD.[23] But the temple cannot be dated back to 6th century AD as it is not corroborated by other evidences. In the front of this Kartikeya image, a large Ganesa image is seen attached to the wall. This figure is in a dancing pose having six arms. We find two other cult images, one on the northern wall and the other on the southern. The important image is that of the northern wall which is a composite figure of Hari and Hara. The image is four-armed. The normal pair of hands is seen in *barada* and *abhaya mudra*. But the upper pair contains the *Ayudha* of both the gods. The right hand is seen holding a trident – the prominent feature of Siva, while the left hand is shown with a *chakra*, the characteristic attribute of Vishnu (Hari). This image suggests the unity of the two divergent cult, i.e., Saiva and Vaisnava. The other figure is of a lady, which is yet to be identified. It is a two-armed figure but both the arms have been broken. Above the head of this figure a row of nine heads is found carved. On both the sides she is attended by two females. Very likely it is Sakta Goddess representing nine Durgas. Nearer to this a headless image is found who is seen standing wearing girdle, armlets, bangles and *sari*. The feet are ornamented by anklets. The right hand is in *barada mudra* and the left hand rests on the waist. This may be a divine figure probably of Parvati. This image is inside the north balcony. In this balcony is found the depiction of an erotic couple[24] carved beautifully on a polished stone. The male and female both are standing naked facing each other. The male figure holds in his right hand the left foot of the female. They are engaged in amorous play of love and are kissing the lips of each other. Charles Fabri describes it as follows:

> In the case of lovers I could like to draw attention not only to the beauty of the shape of the standing lovers but the gentleness and tenderness with which the man holds in his hand the lovely foot of the girl – most unusual composition to which I know no parallel. Indeed it would be false to call this an erotic image, this is not eroticism. This is loving tenderness, love in its full sense.[25]

As the hind part of the male figure is attached to the wall and the female clings to the body of the male having raised her left foot and placed on the right palm of the male, the sculpture may be called as a variation of *vriksadhirudhaka.* While the male looks normal, the female appears to be very passionate. In front of this sculpture a figure is seen gracefully carved. Here one can notice the deliberate tendency of the artist to twist the body into sinuous attitudes. The figure is in a *bhanga* pose having prominent breasts. The right hand rose upwards holding a portion of *sari* and the left rests on the waist within which also a portion of her *sari* is visible, probably engaged in removing her clothes. On the left side is carved a wooden stand (*rukha*) on which a parrot is sitting. The head of the parrot is lost. A similar figure is also found in the temple of Kosaleswara temple of Patnagarh.[26] This can be identified with *suka sarika* or *suka vilasa*, one of the arts of female pastime. Not far from this, a female figure is very delicately carved on a pillar of the balcony. This is a lovely lady re-adjusting her head ornament with her hand by looking into the mirror.[27] The mirror is damaged.

These types of *Alasakanyas* are seen depicted on the southern balcony also. A female under the foot of the tree, is carved standing at ease, the left leg of

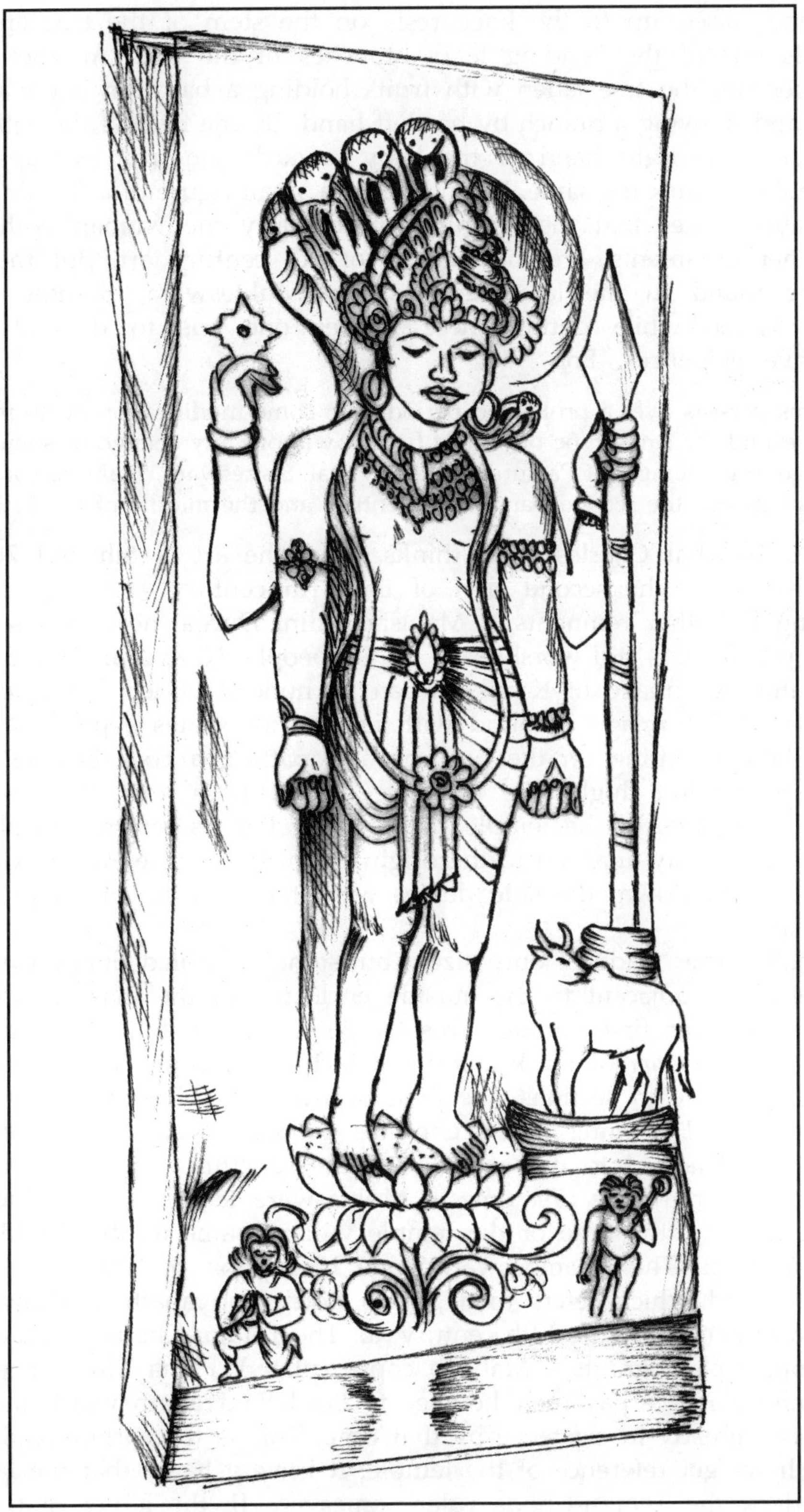

Fig. 9. Harihara, Charada Temple.

whom being raised up to the knee rests on the stem of the tree and the left hand holds one of the bending leafy branches of the tree. Another female is standing beneath the tree laden with fruits holding a baby on her waist by the right arm and drawing a branch by her left hand. By the help of the right forearm she is raising the right hand of the baby towards the fruit perhaps to make the baby able to pluck the same. Behind her is a small figure of a female attendant. Charles Fabri opines that these figures, particularly the woman with a mirror adjusting her ornaments, are masterpiece of 6th century art. But these female figures are found in the later temples like Mukteswara, Brahmeswara, and Lingaraj, etc. So while dating these figures one has to depend on other corroborative evidences. For,

> certain forms persists over a prolonged period with some modification or no modification at all. So we find the same type of female figures without any change or sometimes with slight change in the temple of Parsuramesvara, Vaital, Sisireswara, Brahmeswara, the dates of which is between the second part of 7th century and the middle of the 11th century.[28]

Therefore, what Charles Fabri thinks to be the art of 6th and 7th century may be the art of the second part of the 11th century AD.

Among the other remnants, a Mahisamardini Durga, now in a small porch inside the premises, is still worshipped by the people. Near it an image of Ganesa is also found. An image of Kartikeya can be noticed under a tree just outside the boundary. This image is found with its two associates – peacock and cock. Kartikeya here is sitting on the peacock and patting a cock by the left hand, which is on his left thigh. The presence of Kartikeya with two mounts also suggests a later date of the temple. These three figures referred to above were very likely previously attached to the original sanctum as the *Parsvadevatas*. When the temple broke down, the side deities were taken away and kept separately for worship.

A small shrine made of only sizely out-stones is called Subheswara temple, which is situated adjacent to the outside enclosure of the main temple. People say that the builder first founded this temple and then built the main temple. Within this is a *lingam* of black chlorite, which lends some antiquarian interest. The *lingam* is made in sections, the joint of which has been done by a socket-cylinder system. The lintel of its entrance contains a *navagraha* panel, which originally was attached to the entrance of the sanctum. The representations of nine planets occur for the first time in Mukteswara temple.[29] If we judge taking this panel in view, the time of the temple will be same as that of Mukteswara or posterior to it. The Khambeswari Stone Inscription of Bhanudeva I[30] is the first lithic record which refers to a gift to Lord Baidyanath. It shows that the lord was well known by the 13th century AD. The Telugu-Choda rulers of Sonepur in their copper-plate grants – Mahada copper-plate,[31] Patna Museum plate[32] and Kumarisimha plate[33] – pay their homage to Lord Baidyanath which indicate that the God was already in existence by that time. This is the earliest known source from which we get reference of the temple. It is very likely that the temple was constructed by the Telugu-Choda ruler Somesvara II, the issuer of the Mahada grant. The Telugu Choda rulers call themselves "Baidyanatha-Pada-Pankaja-

Bhramara" or the bee on the lotus feet of Lord Baidyanath. Hence, the temple may be ascribed to the last quarter of the 11th century AD, i.e., the ruling period of Somesvara II.[34]

KAPILESWARA TEMPLE OF *CHARADA*

Charada is situated 5 km west of Binka, a Tahsil headquarters of Suvarnapur district of Orissa. The temple complex is on a rocky outcrop. Like many other temples, the temple of Charada also has a beautiful legend about the self revelation of the *Lingam*/Lord Siva in Charada. It is said that the Ganga king Anangabhimadeva was suffering from an incurable disease. He was advised to go on a pilgrimage. The king, after consulting his *Rajaguru* and astrologers, thought to start his religious tour towards Western Orissa. In course of his tour he reached Charoda area and encamped with his retinues at a place called Rahela. People say that the place earned the name Rahela because of the stay of the king at that place. In the night the king saw a dream. In the dream Lord Siva appeared before him and instructed him to take a dip in the nearby *ghat* of Mahanadi, which was a pious place capable of exhausting all sins, after which all sins would be wiped out and his disease would be cured. Then he would proceed backwards from the bank. On the way there would be a rivulet. After crossing the rivulet he would discover a long thread of a cobweb extending westward being wreathed by jasmine (Jui) flowers. The king would then meet a cowherd who would lead him to the origin of the long wreath of flowers. There the king would find the lord. The lord had been established in the form of *lingam* by the famous sage Kapila. So He is there as Lord Kapilesvara.

It was a strange dream. The king got up in the morning and acted upon the divine order of the Lord. He went to the Mahanadi and had taken his bath in the nearby *ghat*. To his utter consternation, he felt relieved of the disease after the bath. The disease was cured. The bathing ghat today is known as *Papaksaya ghat*. People now also believe that bathing at this place during eclipse days is auspicious and sin removing. Being obliged by the blessings of the god he followed further instruction of the dream. He marched backward, found the rivulet which he crossed. He saw a wreath of flowers in a bushy *jungal* which was extended towards the west. There he met the cowherd. The king followed the flowered thread. The cowherd showed the way. At last he reached a rocky hillock where he could see a heap of jui flowers covering a raised small stone. The king went there and took out the flowers. He saw the lord in the form of *lingam*. He was awestruck, his hairs became erect and he prostrated on the ground before the *lingam* with tears of joy. Then and there the king ordered his officers for the construction of a temple of the ever compassionate god. He stayed there till the temple was constructed. After the completion of the temple, learned Brahmins were brought for its consecration. Divakara Sadangi, who was proficient in *Vedas* and *Vedangas,* was made the *Hotri* of the consecration ceremony. The king left for his capital from a place Udle after making proper arrangements for the daily worship of Lord Kapilesvara Siva.[35] The place Udle (which means "flied or went") now is known as Urlle situated close to the *Papaksaya Ghat*.

The temple consists of a *Vimana* and a *Jagamohana*. The *Vimana* is square and measures about 5¢10^{2}[36] on each inner side. The outer side measurement is about 10¢3^{2} x 10¢3^{2}. But unlike Patnagarh, Sauntpur and Vaidyanath, the *Vimana* here is original and more or less intact. It faces east. In between the *Vimana* and *Mukhasala* is the vestibule. The sanctum has the three principal parts which are prominent, viz, *bada*, *gandi* and *mastaka*. The platform is very low. The *Vimana* possesses a *trianga bada* namely *pabhaga*, *jangha* and *baranda*. The sanctum displays a *pancharatha* plan. The vertical segments of the *gandi* correspond with wall to that of the *bada*. The *pabhaga* has four mouldings. The *jangha* measures 5 feet in altitude. The *baranda* comprises a large *khura*-type moulding above which is noticed a *kanti* (recess). Out of the five *pagas*, the two *kanika pagas* look like pilasters having moulded base and the top contains hanging festoons from the *Kirttimukha*. The *anuratha* possesses a *Khakhara mundi*. The niche of the *anuratha* surmounted by a number of small tiers (*pirhas*), in succession with gradual receding in size. The niche in the *raha* is a simple superstructure crowned by a sloping roof. The *raha*-niches contain Ganesa, Kartikeya and Parvati in southern, western and northern sides, respectively. The *Parsvadevatas* appear to be later in date. The proportionate ratio of the *kanika, anuratha* and *raha* is 1:2:4.[37] The demarcation between the *pagas* is made by the *dhara* recesses. In *kanika pagas* is noticed a number of spans created by the ribbed right angled structures (*bhumi amalakas*). The span (*bhumi*) is composed of three-and-a-half *bhumi barandikas*.

The *gandi* above the *baranda* rises as a curvilinear spire. The *Vimana* measures about 28 feet in hight. The *gandi* is heavily plastered and its body contains some erotic figures in stucco, naturally of later date. The *gandi* ends with the *bisama* which also exhibits a *pancharatha* plan. The *mastaka* rises from the *bisama*. It comprises the *beki*, *amalaka*, a *khapuri* with a top designed with petals of full-blown (*Vikasita Padma*) lotus. It is surmounted by a small *amalaka* above which are a metal *kalasa*, *ayudha* (trident) and *dhvaja*. The elements of the *mastaka* above the large *amalaka* are found in the Chauhan temples of Late Medieval Period. It suggests that this temple has been repaired whenever necessary during the Chauhan rule. The doorframe like that of the temples of Baidyanath, does not contain the river goddesses but possesses the Siva *dvarapalas* at the appropriate places. The sanctum is negotiated by the vestibule which has direct access to the *Jagamohan* or *Mukhasala*.

The *Mukhasala* is a pillared *mandapa* with twelve engaged pillars and four pillars in the centre. It is square in shape and it measures 24¢10^{2} x 24¢10^{2} externally and 19¢3^{2} x 19¢3^{2} internally.[38] It makes a lithic frame very much akin to that of Baidyanath. The *mukhamandapa* has the main entrance in the east between two engaged pillars. On the northern wall of the broad entrance is fixed the image of Kartikeya and on the south is found the figure of Ganesa. Ganesa is represented riding on the back of his mount rat. The rat is an over-size one. Kartikeya also is shown riding his mount peacock. The *Mukhasala* possesses two *gavaksa* projection, one in the north and the other in the south. This has been walled up and plastered. That these two were originally the two balconied porches as at Baidyanath is clearly evident from its remains existent in the plinth of the southern wing. The extended two sides when closed by the brick screen have created an alcove where the *Nayikas* have been placed.

The pillars are highly ornate. Recently the pillars were burnished with various colours which conceals the minute details of the scroll work. The pillars have three distinct parts, viz, base, shaft and capital. The pillar emerges from a *ghatapallava* placed on a square pedestal. The shaft of the pillar is octagonal. The two courses having square cut, diamond-shaped design surround the shaft in the middle which divides it into two halves. The lower portion has in its each facet a *kirttimukha* and stooped lion figure alternately. The string of pearls are hanging issued from the mouth of the *kirttimukha*. The facets of upper half preserves the *kirttimukha* heads and the multi-stringed garland of pearl beads swings from mouth to mouth of these *kirttimukhas*. A bell suspended from each garland is noticed in the *alambas*. The capital is an octagonal slab divided into two having octagonal cross-section. The capital is crowned by a bracket having upward curved ends. It contains *bhara raksakas, chauri bearers* and *vidyadhara*.

The doorframe towards the west which leads to the sanctum is composed of four courses of scroll work. The Gajalaxmi is depicted on the lintel. The flanked pilasters possess entwined *naga* figures. The second lintel has a beautiful representation of *Sesa Sayi* Visnu.

In the *Mukhasala* there are graceful sculptures very artistically carved. An image of *Hari Hara* is attached to the wall of the *mandapa*. The image is four-armed and carved in high relief on a stone slab. The god is represented in *Sthanaka Samabhanga* pose. Below the slab is depicted the figure of bull to the right and an attendant is sketched to the left. The uper right hand holds a trident and the upper left a conch. A *gana* attendant is noticed on the right side. Garuda, the vehicle of Visnu, is delineated in the left side. The image is 4 feet 10 inches high and 1 feet 10 inches wide. Another standing image of *Ardhanarisvara* is also found in the *Jagamohana*. It stands in *Samabhanga* posture. The bull and attendants are found in both sides. The right upper hand carries a *parasu* and the lower is in *varada* pose. The left upper hand catches either a mirror or a *pasa* and the lower one holds a part of the garment. A *gana* is depicted on the right and the lion on the left. The size of the image is 16 inches by 20 inches. A large size image of Siva in *sthanaka* pose is also found here. It is two-armed of which the right hand is broken and the left is akimbo. He wears *jatamukuta*. The *Prabhavali* is sketched behind. The bull and an attendant on the sides of the god are carved. The image has an height of 4 feet 10 inches and width of 1 feet 6 inches. Another figure of importance is of Nataraja. The deity is ten armed and dancing blissfully. The uppermost pair of hands hold the snake in an arched form. The next pair to it catches a kettle-drum in the right and a spear in the left. Then the normal pair (3rd) of which the left is in *gajahasta* while the right is on the chest. The right hand of the fourth pair is raised upward perhaps showing *abhaya* pose and the left extends downwards displaying *varada* postures. The left hand of the lowest pair moves downward and the right hand also has a similar movement wherein the thumb touches the ring finger. To the right side is carved a skeletal figure and to the left a female. A bull is depicted behind the legs. The figures of *Alasakanyas, Dalmalikas,* etc were also noticed in

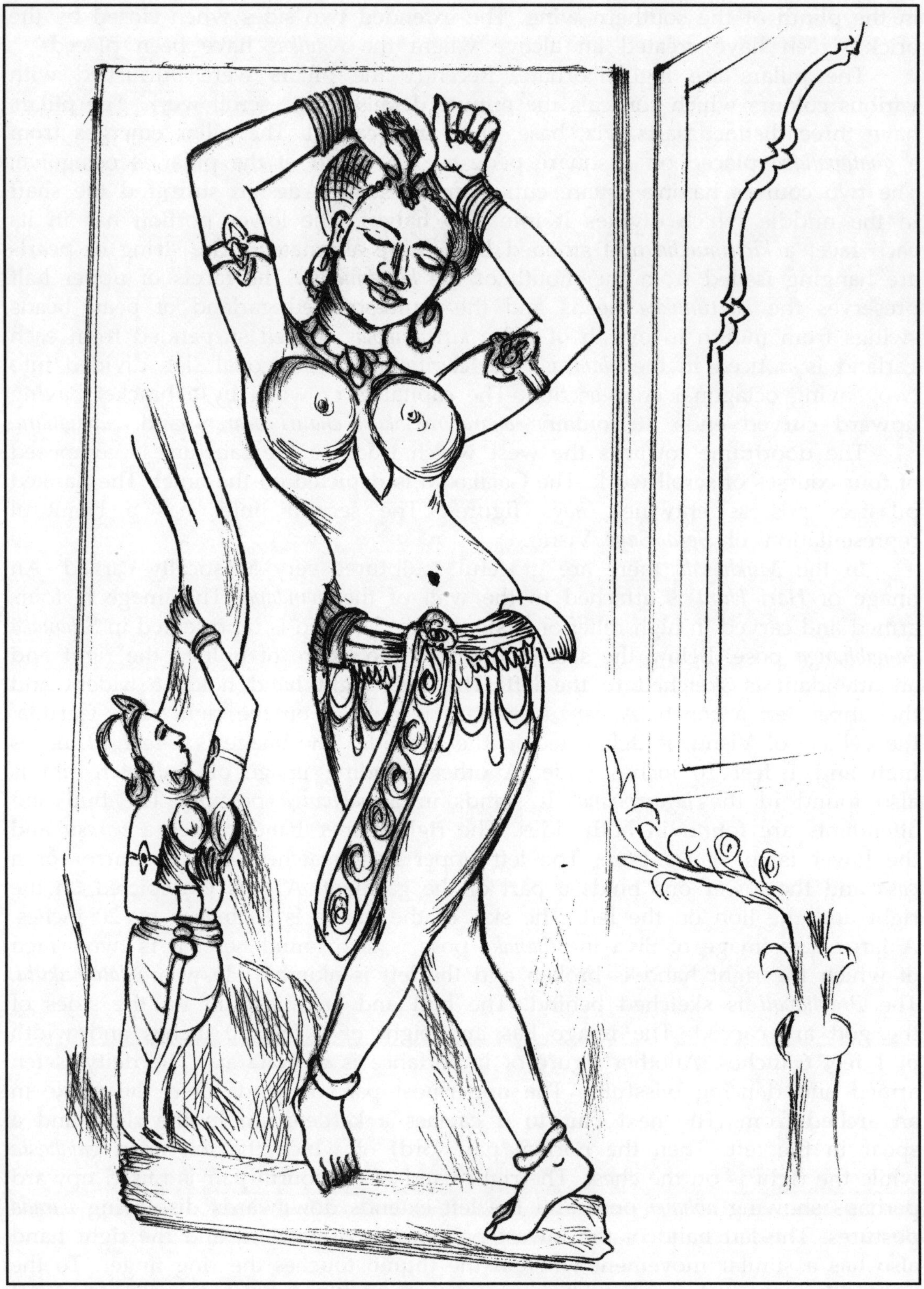

Fig. 10. Alasakanya, Charada Temple.

the *mukhamandapa* of Charada as at Vaidyanath. A standing four-armed image of Ganesa eating *modakas* from the pot is very realistically sculptured. Donaldson[39] refers to an image of Agni in the temple premises. It is a four armed image standing in *tribhanga* posture. Flames radiate from his head. The head is missing and the right hand is broken now. There was another four-armed image when the author visited the place in 1974. The upper pair of hand holds a *khadga* in the right and a *kharpara* in the left. The lower right carries a knife and left possesses some-thing unidentifiable. The head radiates flame behind it. The figure was known there among the local people as that of Jvalamukhi.

At present the temple complex is filled with additional structures of modern times. More than of 25% of the population of the villagers are *Pujakas/Thanapatis*. It is gathered from the *Pujakas* that there were twenty-two villages which are donated for performance of differnet kinds of services to the lord, viz, Phulmuthi was donated for supply of flowers perpetually, Sankara was granted *maufi* for blowing conches before the lord, Gurdula was given for washing and cleaning of the premises, kitchen etc. This reminds us of 36 kinds of services (*Chhatisaniyoga*) arranged by Anangabhima III for Jagannath temple at Puri. However the close similarity observed in the architectural style and sculptural programme of Charada temple with that of Baidyanath temple, also of Patnagarh suggest strongly the contemporaneity of the former with the latters. On epigraphical consideration the date of Baidyanath may be fixed in the later half of 11th century AD.[40] As the temple of Charada has close similarities in architectural style and sculptural programme with that of the emples of Vaidyanath, the time of the former may be placed in the 11th century AD D.R. Das[41] fixes the date of Kapilesvara temple of Charada in between last half of 9th century AD and first half of 10th century AD T.E. Donalson[42] favours a date of 10th century AD for the temple of Charada. Vidya Dehejia[43] assigns a date of 9th century AD to the temple. In the temple complex of Patnagarh there is an inscription belonging to Telugu Choda king Somesvaradeva who was ruling in 12th century AD. The pillared *mandapa* with lateral transept forms a style of its own. In this type of architecture, the earliest occurrence of the balconied window or lateral transepts is noticed in Gyraspur temples as reported by Krishnadeva.[44] Even the *mandapas* with twelve pilasters and four pillars are also found in Gyraspur. Ruins known as *Ath khambha* (8 pillars) and *char khambha* (4 pillars) are of also there in Gyraspur.[45] Maladeva temple at Gyraspur possesses a pair of non-functional balconied windows. These temples belong to 9th century AD (Pratihara Period).[46] The Kalikamata temple at Chittorgarh also has a closed hall with lateral transepts. In Ambikamata temple[47] at Jaget in the district of Udayapur are noticed latticed windows in the lateral transepts. The Sun temple at Varman in Sirohi district also has this architectural device. The temples of Rajasthan and Solanki temples also have adopted the style. Percy Brown refers to *nal mandapa* and says that "it is so called because it has created subsequently over the *nal* or staircase leading into the interior of the building."[48] It suggests that originally the simple entrance from all sides of the *mandapa* were projected, then staircase was added after which it was transformed into a porch and gradually it developed into balustraded balconies. Its evolution first started in

8th/9th century in the Pratihara age, then in Rajasthan and subsequently became developed in 11th century AD. It entered into Orissa through Central India. *Pārsva Kaksa* in the developed temple may be taken as another evolute of this which is adopted in the temple of Khajuraho. So an 11th century date ascribed to the temple having this type of architectural pattern in Orissa/Western Orissa may be quite reasonable.

The Telugu Chodas ruled Western Orissa in the second-half of 11th century AD. They style themselves as *Vaidyanatha Pada Pankaja Bhramara* (the bee on the lotus feet of Vaidyanath) in their copper-plate charters, which suggest their deep devotion towards Lord Baidyanatha. Very likely the Kosalesvara temple of Baidyanath has been built by them. As the temple of Kapilesvara of Charada is very akin to the temple of Baidyanatha, it seems that the former was also built by the Telugu Choda rulers. Mahada plates[49] of Somesvara II record that Somesvara II was not only *Vaidyanata Pada Pankaja Bhramora* but also has made grant for Vaidyanatha *Pritikamartha*. Somesvaradeva III issued Kumarisimha charter[50] which was granted for the longeivity of his parents. The Patna museum charter[51] records the donation of Phulmuthi and Daholi for pleasing Lord Narayana Bhattaraka. Both the villages were under Charada *visay*. The people of the village Baniabandha were addressed while making this grant. It is known from the Gopalpur charter (set II) of Somavansi king Janamejaya I issued in 10th regnal year that Jalasayana Narayana was popular during his time. Perhaps the Lord Narayana Bhattaraka of the Patna musuem grant and the Jalasayana Narayana of Gopalpur charter are same. The king granted villages situated in Charada *visaya* to Lord Narayana to gain loyalty and popular support of the section of people who were devoted to Narayana. It appears that the Lord Kapilesvara and His temple were not that popular and important at that time. It might have been that there was no temple in existence at the time of the grant. Probably afterwards Somesvara III, as he was also Saiva by faith, might have thought of building a Siva temple at Charada.[52] Due to Kalachuri invasion he had kept himself engaged in protecting the kingdom for which he could not devote full time for the construction of the temple at Charada. It is also not improbable that the temple might not have been completed in entirety. After him the Kalachuris might have showed their indifferent attitude towards its completion for the Kalachuris were also often at war with the imperial Gangas. Anangabhima Deva III conquered this territory and according to the legend might have given the finishing touch to the temple. He re-consecrated the Lord Kapilesvara and made arrangement for the daily worship. Curiously the village Phulmathi, which was granted for pleasing Narayana, was later on granted for supplying flowers to the Lord Kapilesvara. At present also the local tradition is alive though not followed in actual practice.

In view of the above discussion it appears that the temple was constructed during the time of Telugu Choda rule after the architectural pattern and sculptural style of the Baidyanath temple in about the closing part of 11th century AD. Later on Anangbhima Deva III fulfilled all formalities left beforehand and arranged necessary requirements for the management of the temple for which he is portrayed as the builder of the temple in the legend.

KOSALESVARA OF SAUNTPUR

Sauntpur is situated at a distance of about 15 km from Bolangir town. It has an ancient temple complex. A number of sculptures belonging to Saiva and Vaisnava sects have been discovered there. Sri Ram Chandra Mallick refers to two ancient temples of Samantapur. At the outskirt of the village are found the ruins of ancient temples like *navagraha* slab, temple pillars and door jambs. All are broken. Loose sculptures like Bhairava, Ardhanarisvara and Ganesa are also noticed. It seems that if not more at least two temples were there as per the observation of S.C. Mallick. Present Sauntpur is the corrupt form of ancient Samantapura. It appears that the temple had a *Vimana* and *Mukhasala*. The temple once contained a pillared *Mukhasala*, which is evident from the existence of pillars. The pillars are very much similar in carving and shape with that of the *Mukhasala* of Somesvara temple of Patnagarh. Two pillar are intact. The pillars are rectangular having small niches at four sides. The first pillars contains the figures of a female standing at the door peeping through a half-closed door, a seated male worshipping a Siva *linga*, a *yaksa/gana* in meditative pose and a male seated cross-legged with folding hands. The second pillar has the representations of a therio-anthropomorphic *naga* figure with folded hands, a *nagini* in a similar pose, another *naga* figure and Ganesa in all four sides. The images of Trivikrama and Narasimha suggests the existence of an ancient Visnu temple and the images of Nataraja and Bhairab described by P.C. Rath indicates the presence of a Saiva shrine in the past. An image of Ardhanarisvara is also seen in the temple. The Saiva temple was known as Kosaleswar temple. The present temple, which is a modern structure, is also named after that of the old one. The iconic trait of the sculptures of Sauntpur remind us about the massive life-size images of the temple of Baidyanath situated near Sonepur. The temple of Baidyanath is also known as Kosaleswar temple. Another temple of the same name is found at Patnagarh. This temple also abounds in big sculptures. The treatment of mass in Nataraja, Bhairaba and Sun God of Sauntpur is conspicuous in the images of Nataraja, Ardhanarisvara, Kartikeya and Ganesa of Baidyanath. Further, the treatment of Tribikrama Narasimha and a few other images have close affinities with the sculptures of Patnagarh and Charada.

It appears that these temples – Kosaleswara of Vaidyanath, Kosaleswara of Sauntpur, Kosaleswara alias Someswara of Patnagarh and Kapileswar temple of Charada are contemporary. Even they can be taken as the products of one school. The Surya image of Sauntpur shown standing in a peculiar way and holding a lotus bud exhibits the characteristics of southern solar iconography. The absence of high boots is also a southern trait. Probably it is a product of Telugu Chodas who carried the southern trend with them. The Kosaleswara group of temples may be ascribed to Telugu Chodas who were ruling over Sonepur and Patnagarh area in the 11th/12th century. So the old Siva temple of Sauntpur may be assigned to 11th century AD and the Vishnu temple may be attributed to the *Ganga* kings who occupied the area in 13th century AD.

Besides this there is another temple of 20th century dedicated to Goddess Sauntei, the protectress of Sauntpur. She is considered to be the eldest sister

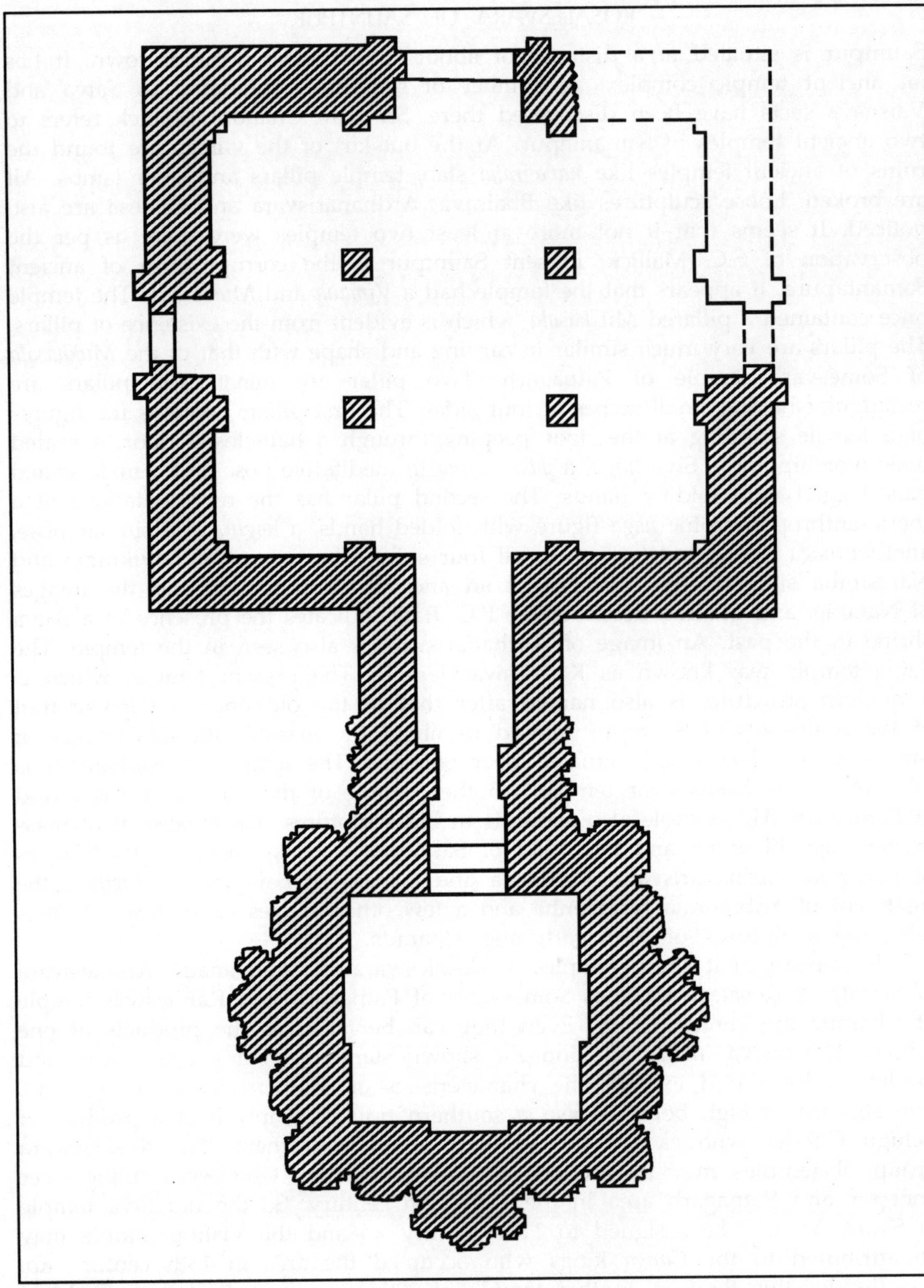

Fig. 11. Ground plan of Narasimhanath Temple, Narasimhanath; Courtesy-Prof. D.R. Das, Calcutta.

of a legendary cult of seven sisters. The other sisters are Samalai, Patnesvari, Suresvari of Sonepur and Kusnei of Kusang, Chandi of Saintala and Mahesvari of Arigaon.

NARLA SIVA TEMPLE

Narla is a suburb, which lies on the Kalahandi-Bhubaneswar road. It is also a Railway station of South-Eastern Railway running from Sambalpur to Rayagada. There is a small temple here of considerable antiquity. The temple stands on the ground. In front was previously an earthen frontal hall, which is a makeshift *Mukhasala*. Now the frontal hall is constructed. It is an earthen walled house having three opening to three sides and another into the sanctum. At present is found a developed structure before the temple. The temple is plastered with lime. It rises from the ground. The temple has a *triratha gandi* and *trianga bada*. The *pabhaga* is plain. The *ratha*s of the *gandi* are perfectly aligned with that of the *bada*. The *raha* of the *janga* has the niches, which houses the *Parsvadevatas*. The *baranda* has three mouldings. Below is the plain flat moulding and on the above is *noli* type moulding. In between is found plane type beads. These *baranda* do not cover the *raha*. On *raha* some type of mouldings are found just below the *baranda* mouldings and above the niche. The *gandi* rises straight to some height and starts bending from all sides from the middle of the *gandi*. All sides of *gandi* meet the *bisama* or *vedi*. On the *vedi* the *mastaka* of the temple is placed. The *mastaka* includes a *beki*, an *amalaka*, a thin *khapuri* in the centre of which is seen small round pedestal. Above this is the *kalasa*, which holds the *ayudha* (trident) and a small *dhvaja*. The interior and exterior of the temple are absolutely plain. In the temple there is an inscription, which reveals that one Madana Mahadeva was ruling this area in the 13th century AD. The temple was built by him and the temple belonged to 13th century AD. Some scholars interpret the date as 12th century AD. On the lintel of the entrance to the temple is carved an image of Ganesa. This is an uncommon device. There is a *Saktipitha* now in the frontal hall having a depiction of eight-petalled lotus on it. This may be taken as a stellate plan. The eight-petalled lotus symbolizes the worship of *Astamurti* of Siva. There are some sculptures of warrior in the temple. The Narla temple contains a *Nritta* Ganapati having six hands in the southern niche, an image of four-armed Kartikeya in the west and a figure of Sarasvati in the north as *Parsvadevatas*. Sarasvati as *Parsvadevata* is unusual.

NARASINGHNATH TEMPLE

Narsinghnath is a place of pilgrimage. Large number of devotees visits the place and pays homage to Lord Bidala Nrisimha, the presiding deity of this place. There is an inscription attached to the wall of the *Mukhasala*, which reveals that Baijaladeva, son of Vatsarajadeva, built the temple.[53] The astronomical combination available in this inscription, when calculated, suggested the date of 1413 AD. Beglar visited this temple in 1974-76 and Bhandarkar in 1904-05.

The temple stands at the foot of the mountain Gandhagiri on the bank of the stream falling down from the mountain. The temple has two structures –

Vimana and *Jagamohana*. These two are inter-connected with an oblong passage. The *Vimana* (sanctum) rises straight from the ground. Thus, the importance is not given to the pista. Other three usual sections, viz, *bada*, *gandi* and *mastaka* are clearly visible. The sanctum is square in size. It rises straight up to some height and takes a prominent bend at the top. The *bada* is five-folded (*Panchanga*) having *pabhaga*, *tala jangha*, *bandhana*, *upara jangha* and *baranda*. The *pabhaga* consists of five mouldings, which are *khura*, *kumbha*, *pata*, *kani*, and *basanta*. The *bandhana*, which divides the *tala jangha* from *upara jangha*, comprises three mouldings of *khura*, *noli*, and *pata*. The *baranda*, which terminates the *bada*, is composed of seven mouldings, which are, from top to bottom, *pata*, *kani*, *pata*, *noli*, *pata*, *pheni*, and *khura*. The sanctum is vertically divided into five segments, viz, *kanika*, *anuratha*, *raha*, *anurath* and *kanika*. *Pidhamundis* are found in the *kanika* and *anuratha pagas* of *tala jangha*. The *raha paga* of *tala jangha* section contains niches wherein the *Parsvadevatas* are housed. In the south, *Varaha* is installed. North contains Trivikrama and Narasimha occupies west niche. There is an image of Laxmi Narayana placed into a makeshift niche within the compound. Narayana seated in *lalitasana* embraces his consort in his left arm. The hand of Laxmi is shown around the shoulders of the god. Other sculptures in low relief are found carved on the rock. The important one is that which is now being worshipped as Durga near the north entrance. The *paga* recesses are filled with the *viralas* and *alasakanyas* or indolent maidens in the lower and upper story. In the upper *jangha* the *pidhamundis* are seen. In the *gandi* section of *anuratha*, are noticed the *angasikhara*s. The *raha pagas* are also decorated with the miniature spires but the east *raha* is adorned with a large *sikhara*. The *kanika paga* is divided horizontally into a number *bhumi*s marked by *bhumi amalaka*s. The *vajramastaka* of bho-type motifs surmounted by Gajasimha are placed on the lower *raha* of other sides. The *mastaka* comprises *vedika* (*bisama*), *beki*, *amalaka sila*, *khapuri*, *kalasa*, *ayudha* and *dhvaja*.

The *Mukhasala* or *Jagamohana* in front of the *Vimana* appears to have undergone heavy modification excepting its fundamental features like four pillars in the centre and the number of pilasters on the inner sidewalls. Originally it was a square structure having four entrances, three on three sides, i.e., east, north and south. The fourth one is on the west connecting the sanctum. Now the doorways on the east, north and towards the sanctum are present. The southern doorways were probably closed and an alcove was created by masonry work wherein the wooden images of Jagannath, Subhadra and Balabhadra are installed. The most striking elements in the *Mukhasala* are its pillars and the doorways decoration. The pillars are square in cross-section and identical in appearance. The shaft of the pillar is square and decorated with semi-lotus medallions intervened with vertical bands of scroll work. At the top, the pillar takes an octagonal shape. The dwarf garland-bearers occupy the four corners leaving the four square space. The pillars are crowned with *ghata pallava* capital. The doorframes of the northern and eastern entrance are carved with great care and artistry.

The doorjambs of the entrance contain three courses of scroll works, viz, *kutila*, *gelaba* and *barajhanjhi*. The *gelaba* band possesses dancing scenes, *linga puja* in the leafy space and frolicking diminutive human figures. In the *barajhanji* scroll the small citrus amidst the plants are noticed. It is surrounded by the *kutila* bands in which are carved the diminutive elephants along with the *vanalata*. At the lower part of the jambs are depicted the *dvarapalas*. Gajalaxmi occupies the central place of the lintel where she is shown seated in *lalitasana* being flanked by elephants above and attendants beneath. The *dvarapalas* wear *jatamukuta* and *sarpa kundala*. Both the *dvarapalas* – Mahakala and Nandi – are four-armed. The *ganas* are found attending both. The usual right hand of Mahakala is in *varada* pose and left hand holds a trident. The upper right catches a rosary and the upper left has a lotus. The main right hand of Nandi displays *varada* and the corresponding left carries a trident. The upper right hand holds a rosary and the matching left carries a *kapala*. The face of Nandi has a short beard. In the adjacent niches are sculpted the images of Ganga and Yamuna. Both are standing two-armed and are flanked by parasol bearers. One of the hands is in *Katyavalamvita* posture and the other holds a water pitcher. They are mounted on their respective vehicles, i.e., crocodile and tortoise.

The eastern doorframe also contains the figure of *Abhiseka* Laxmi seated in *lalitasana* as on the north door. A *navagraha* slab is placed on the Gajalaxmi panel. The *dvarapalas* are two-handed. They stand in *svalpabhanga* pose being accompanied by the female *chauri* bearers. Besides these, an independent standing figure with moustache is found in *namaskara mudra*. It appears to be a royal figure, which is identified with the builder king Baijaladeva by N.K. Sahu.

As mentioned earlier, the presiding deity of this temple is Vidala Nrisimha, the cat-lion form of God (the face of cat and the body of the lion). Though the inscriptional chronometry suggest a 15th century date, the architectural fragments, the ornate pillars and highly stylized door frames point to a much earlier date about 10th century AD. Very likely there was an old temple there which was completely destroyed in the vagaries of nature. But the place had not lost its religious importance and sacredness. The Chauhan king Baijalodeva, probably catering to the spiritual and religious sentiment of the populace, built the main temple and completely renovated the present *Mukhasala*, which was in an architectural mess. The place name suggests that it was the place of Lord Nrisimha. Originally, Nrisimha was the presiding deity. In this connection it is worth mentioning that a life-size image of Nrisimha made out of red stone still survives the indifferent care and callous attitude of the temple servants and administration. It is a rare and unique image of Nrisimha. It has a face of roaring lion, a human body and human legs with high boots, a characteristic feature of Sun God. That is why Prof. K.K. Dasgupta takes it as a composite image of Surya Narasimha.[55] Apparently, this image was being worshipped in the old temple.

Due to the destruction of the temple and financial constraints the worship was neglected. In course of time largely Kandhas populated this area. The Kandhas popularized the totemistic worship of cat. Keeping in view the equal respects and honour to both the religious creeds – the cult of Narasimha and the cult of cat totem – Baijaladeva, the Chauhan king thought of combined worship of the both the cults, which subsequently emerged as the cult of Vidala

Nrisimha. Accordingly, the image of Vidala Nrisimha was made with the face of a cat and body of a lion. To make it acceptable to *brahmanical* fold, its origin was attached to *Ramayana* theme. Vidala Nrimimha became the presiding deity of the temple.

What was the shape of the old temple is difficult to surmise. The present temple, in architectural features and design, is nearer to the style of the temples of Bhuvaneswar and coastal area belonging to the late Ganga Period or early Suryavamsi Gajapati Period. In this context the date arrived through the date of the inscription attached to the *Mukhasala* of the temple, which points to 15th century date for the temple, may be accepted safely.

REFERENCES

1. J.D. Beglar, *ARASI*, Vol. XIII, Report of Tour in South Eastern Provinces 1870-74, 1970, Varanasi, p. 118.
2. T.E. Donaldson, *The Hindu Temple Art of Orissa*, Vol. II, 1986, Lieden, p. 228.
3. K.C. Panigrahi, *Archaeological Remains at Bhuvaneswar*, 1961, Calcutta, pp. 158-59.
4. *Ibid*.
5. S.R. Goyal, *Religious History of Orissa*, Vol. I, 1986, Meerut, p. 241f.
6. V.V. Mirashi, *C.I.I.*, Vol. IV, pp. 306-07.
7. *Ind. Ant.*, Vol. IX, verse 19, p. 178.
8. V.S. Pathak, *History of Saiva Cult in Northern India*, 1980, Allahabad, p. 18, *Insc. of Kambaya*, p. 377.
9. *Ibid.*, *Banabhatta Harsha Charita*, Nirnaya Sagar Press, Bombay, p. 103.
10. R.D. Banerjee, "Antiquities of Baudh State", *J.B.O.R.S.*, Vol. XV, 1929, pp. 64-68.
11. J.D. Beglar, *op. cit.*, p. 118.
12. J.D. Beglar, *ARASI*, Vol. XIII, 1970, Varanasi, p. 120f.
13. *Ibid*.
14. T.E. Donaldson, *The Hindu Temple Art of Orissa*, Vol. II, 1986, Lieden, p. 263.
15. *OHRJ*, Vol. XXXVI, nos. 1 & 2, pp. 64-76.
16. N.K. Bose, *Canons of Orissan Architecture*, 1932, Calcutta, pp. 78-80.
17. B.C. Majumdar, *Orissa in the Making*, 1925, Calcutta, p. 95, pl. 1.
18. N.K. Bose, *op. cit.*, 78.
19. *Ibid.*, p. 93.
20. B.C. Majumdar, *op. cit.*, p. 182, pl. 1.
21. P.K. Nayak, "Koshalesvara Temple of Baidyanath", *Proceedings of Orissa History Congress*, 1978, pp. 37-44
22. Charles Lewis Fabri, *The History of Art of Orissa*, 1974, New Delhi, pl. XXIII.
23. *Ibid.*, p. 43.
24. *Ibid.*, pl. XXV.
25. *Ibid.*, p. 43.
26. *J.K.H.R.S.*, Vol. II, nos. 2 & 3, plate between pages 126-27.
27. C.L. Fabri, *op. cit.*, pl. XXII.
28. K.C. Panigrahi, *Archaeological Remains at Bhubaneswar*, 1961, Calcutta, p. 199.
29. *Ibid.*, p. 132.
30. *O.H.R.J.*, Vol. X, no. 4, p. 6.
31. *Ep. Ind.*, Vol. XXVIII, p. 283.
32. *Ep. Ind.*, Vol. XIX, p. 97.

33. *J.K.H.R.S.*, Vol. I, no. 3, p. 29.
34. P.K. Nayak, "The Dating of Baidyanath Temple: The Epigraphic Evidence", *The Journal of Orissan History*, Vol. XIV, 1995, pp. 61-66.
35. Collected by the Author from Late Sri Jagmohan Hota of the village *Papanga*, Dist. Bargarh.
36. T.E. Donalson, *The Hindu Temple Art of Orissa*, Vol. I, 1985, Lieden, p. 210.
37. D.R. Das, *Temples of Orissa*, 1982, Delhi, p. 48.
38. T.E. Donaldson, *op. cit.*, pp. 209-10.
39. *Ibid.*, pp. 211-12.
40. P.K. Nayak, "Dating Vaidyanath Temple: The Epigraphic Evidence", *Journal of Orissan History*, Vols. XIII-XIV, 1995, Sambalpur, pp. 61-66.
    K.C. Panigrahi, *History of Orissa*, 1981, Cuttack, p. 445.
41. D.R. Das, *op. cit.*, p. 42.
42. T.E. Donaldson, *op. cit.*, p. 209.
43. Vidya Dehejia, *Early Stone Temples of Orissa*, 1979, New Delhi, p.185.
44. Krishnadeva, *Temples of North India*, NBT, 1969, New Delhi, p. 25.
45. Percy Brown, *Indian Architecture (Hindu and Buddhist Period)*, Vol. I, 1971, Bombay, pp. 114-16.
46. Krishnadeva, *op. cit.*, pp. 25-26.
47. *Ibid.*, p. 35.
48. Percy Brown, *op. cit.*, pp. 114-15.
49. *Ep. Ind.*, Vol. XXIII, pp. 283 ff.
50. *J.K.H.R.S.*, Vol. I, pp. 229 ff.
51 *Ep. Ind.*, Vol. XIX, pp. 97-99.
52. G.C. Pattnaik *et al.*, *The Somavamsis Rediscovered*, 1990, Cuttack, pp. 10-19.
53. *IndianHistorical Quarterly*, Vol. XII, no. 1, 1936, pp. 485-486.
54. N. Senapati (ed.), *Orissa District Gazetteers, Sambalpur*, 1971, Cuttack, p. 532.
55 P.K. Mishra (ed.), *Culture, Tribal History and Freedom Movement*, 1989, Delhi, pp. 137-40.

PHASE – II: MEDIEVAL TEMPLES : TEMPLES OF SAMBALPUR

The present town of Sambalpur lies between 20o-26′ North latitude and 83o -58′ East longitudes. It is situated on the left bank of the Mahanadi. It is an old town and was famous as a trade centre in the early Christian centuries as revealed by Ptolemy in his famous work *Geographike Huphegesis*. He describes that the city of Sambalpur was situated on the bank of the river Manada in the country of Mandalai. Mandalai implies the habitat of the people of Munda tribes. The city Sambalaka and the river Manada may be identified with the present Sambalpur town and the river Mahanadi, respectively. Gibbon has referred to a town named Sumelpur, which was famous for its diamond mines. The French traveller Tavernier describes Soumelpur as a place rich in diamonds. This Sumelpur of Gibbon and Soumelpur of Tavernier may be same as Sambalaka of Ptolemy identified with Sambalpur of Western Orissa. Since the time of Ptolemy up to the present day Sambalpur has passed through many ups and downs but it has never lost its identity. It regained its past glory during the time of the Chauhan rule. Under the Chauhans Sambalpur besides being the metropolis, grew to be a centre of art and culture. The artists were patronised. A large number of temples belonging to different faiths were built by the Chauhans catering to the religious requirement of the ruled and the rulers. Sambalpur became a temple town. At present also Sambalpur contains numerous temples, which are still intact. The temples are mainly Saiva, Sakta and Vaisnava shrines.

Among the Saiva shrines, the Somanath temple at Bali Bandha, Balukesvara temple at Nandapara, Budharaja temple on the hill-top, Lokanath temple on the bank of Mahanadi, Jogesvara temple at Modipara, Guptesvara temple near the municipality office, Siddhesvara temple at the back side of the market complex in front of G.M. College, Gudesvara temple near Durgapali and Bhuvaneswar temple on the bank of the Ramsagar pond are noteworthy. The first eight temples gradually became famous as *Astasambhus* of Sambalpur town. Excepting Guptesvara, all the temples mentioned above contain same architectural components. They exhibit similar plan and programme. Each has a *Vimana*, a *Jagamohana* and an entrance porch. Every temple has the *Lingam* as its object of worship. The *Parsvadevatas* in all the shrines are same – Ganesa, Kartikeya and Durga or Parvati. The Saiva temples are plain and simple and are devoid of rich ornamentation. The temples are constructed in different periods by different persons. The Somanath temple was built by Balabhadradeva. The Budharaja temple was constructed by Chhatra Sai on the occasion of the birth of his son. Balukesvara temple was erected by the *Dewan* Akbar Ray.

SOMANATH TEMPLE

The oldest Siva temple at Sambalpur town is the shrine of Lord Somanath built by Raja Balabhadra Deva,[1] the third Chauhan ruler of Sambalpur. A beautiful legend is heard from the mouth of the people regarding the building of the temple of Samanath, popularly known as Samia Gudi. The legend says that the king of Sambalpur went to visit *Mandhata* Siva every day morning. One day in the rainy season due to heavy flood in Malati Jor, the king could not go to the temple for offering his observance. He had to wait for a night on the bank of Malati Jor to have a *darsan* of Maneswar Siva. Being pleased with the intense devotion, the Lord told the king in a dream that the Lord would manifest near his fort and the king would not have to come to Maneswar for his worship. He would build a temple for the Lord and worship Him near the fort. Accordingly, a temple was built by the Raja near the fort. The God was named Somanath as the Lord manifested on the 10th day of bright fortnight of *Asvina*, auspicious for the worship of Somanath. On this day falls the Somanath Vrata, a favorite ritual of Lord Siva.[2] The Somanath temple is situated on the bank of the Chhatra-Sagar at the gate of the fort. It consists of a *Vimana*, a *Jagamohana* and a *nandi mandapa*. A pillar is found in front of the temple. The *Vimana* of the temple stands on a plinth consisting of a low *pista, bada, gandi* and *mastaka*. The *gandi* is *pancharatha* in plan (*kanika, anuratha, raha, anuratha* and *kanika*). The *nandi mandapa* has eight pillars and a *rekha*-type *sikhara*. The *Vimana* and the *Jagamohana* are square in shape. Both are built in *rekha* order. The whole body is divided into five parts. The *pagas* run from the beginning to the *vedi*. The *sikhara* of *gandi* is topped a *mastaka*. The *mastaka* has *beki, amalaka, khapuri, kalasa* and *trisula*; all are arranged one above the other. In front of the temple a statue of Nandi and of a lion are seen looking towards the sanctum. The three sides of the *bada* contain the *Parsvadevatas* – Ganesha, Kartikeya and Parvati in the niches.

The four-armed Parvati of Somanath temple is found seated in *lalitasana* on a pedestal, holding a sword. The lower two hands hold a trident. The Ganesa image at Somanath temple is found seated in the *lalitasana*. It holds a trident and a *kuthara* in the upper pair of hands. The lower left hand holds a *mudaka* and the lower right displays *varadamudra*. In the compound of Somanath temple we can find a pair of loving couple. The image is in a dilapidated condition. The male figure is shown here holding the breast of the female figure. The male embraces the female; this type of amorous posture of the temple is not found in any temple built by the Chauhans. This piece is a rare specimen of erotic sculpture. This specimen may be a Pre-Chauhan product.

BUDHARAJA TEMPLE

The temple is built on the top of the hill commemorating the death of Budharaja, a son of Chhatra Sai. Ajit Singh completed the temple at Budharaja. It stands on a low plinth. The temple is consists of a *Vimana*, a *Jagamohana* and a *Natamandira*. The temple has a prominent *sikhara*. It is topped by the *mastaka* with usual elements. The inner wall of the temple is plain and undecorated. The *Jagamohana* of the temple is plain, undecorated and flat-roofed. There are only two images on the inner wall niches of the *Jagamohana*.

Mahisamardini Durga is eight-armed. The normal pair of hands holds a trident, which has penetrated the chest of the demon. The giant is seen issuing out of a decapitated buffalo. The right three hands from the upper to lower hold *khadga*, *chakra* and *ankusa*, respectively. The left three hands from uppermost to lower hold skull, conch and a noose (*pasa*), respectively. The goddess wears necklace, necklet, *mukuta*, *kundala*, garland, wristlet, anklet, blouse, *sari*, etc. Though she was engaged in the act of killing the demon, she does not have a fierce look.

The Siva is found in a dancing pose on a corpse. He is twelve-armed. The upper two left and right hands hold a snake over the head. The next pair (left and right) holds a *mriga* and lotus. In the third pair, the left hand holds a *pasa* and the right hand is destroyed. The fourth pair of hands is destroyed. The fifth right hand holds a spear and the left is damaged. On the right side, a bull is present. On the left side, a female attendant is found. He wears *Jatamukuta*, earring and a snake thread. He has moustaches and three eyes. The Nataraja Siva is dancing joyfully on the corpse.

SAMALESWARI AND PATANESWARI TEMPLE

The Chauhans were Sakta worshippers. Their presiding deity is Ashapur Devi, a form of Durga. When they established their rule in Patna, they transformed their deity into Pataneswari, i.e., the presiding deity of Patna state. When they started their rule in Sambalpur region they accepted Samalai, the goddess of local people as the State deity and enshrined her as Samaleswari, the presiding deity of Sambalpur. Samaleswari and Pataneswari are most popular deities of Western Orissa. Numerous temples have been dedicated to the Goddess Samalai and Pataneswari in the Bolangir-Sonepur-Sambalpur region. In the Sambalpur town also two temples have been dedicated, one to Samalai and the other to Pataneswari. Those temples were built originally by Balarama Deva, the first Chauhan ruler of Sambalpur in the last half of the 16th century AD. But later on Chhatra Sai rebuilt those. Chhatra Sai has given the present shape of the temple of Samalai and Pataneswari. Both these temples exhibit similar architectural device, i.e., high platform, *jangha*, high *sikhara* and *mastaka*. Both are placed on a high plinth. Both have a covered circumambulatory path around the sanctum. The Samalai temple faces north whereas the Pataneswari temple to the south. The *jangha* of the temple contains a number of *Parsvadevatas*. In the Samalai temple four-armed Mangala, ten-armed Mahisamardini Durga, four-headed Jwalamukhi, four-armed Narasimhi, eight-armed Bana Durga, four-armed Varahi, four-armed Chhinnamasta, four-armed Matangi, four-armed Ramachandi, four-armed Kali and four-armed Ugra Tara are found as *Parsvadevatas*. In the Pataneswari temple also the *Sangadevatas* are Narasimhi, Chhatrabauti, Kali, Vagala-Mukhi, Mangala and Mahisamardini Durga. The Kali image depicts interesting iconographical features. The Goddess is four-armed and standing on a corpse. The upper right hand displays *abhayamudra* and the upper left hand holds a *khadga*. The lower right hand displays *varadamudra* whereas the lower left hand holds a human head. She wears a garland of skulls. She has a wide mouth; long out-stretched tongue and a fearful appearance. Two animals, probably jackal, are found, carved on the lower portion of the slab. Two female deities are found at the entrance, one on each side of the sanctum as doorkeepers. The presiding deity is Kali, whose features are described above. The presiding deity of the Samalai temple hardly conforms to any anthropomorphic iconic form. It is a huge block of stone having a convex front. In the middle is noticed a raised ridge-like elevation which is regarded as the nose of the deity. The lower portion of the slab has a downward extension, which is considered as the mouth of the goddess. There is a small adjunct below the groove, which represents the chin. When properly clothed and bedecked with ornaments, it gives the look of a face of a female deity. Some people accept her as *varahi*. It was very likely a tribal deity of the locality and was transformed into a *brahmanical* goddess through the process of acculturation. Tradition speaks that the name Samalai was given to her as she was residing under a *Semal* tree. It seems appropriate as the goddesses like Dalkhai, Daltalien, Palsatalien derive their names according to their habitats.

The Pataneswari temple is a mono-structural edifice containing the *Vimana* surrounded by a *Pradaksina patha*. The sanctum measures 16′ x 16′ internally and 22′ x 22′ externally. But the temple of Samalai is spacious and elaborate in plan. It is composed of a sanctum and a pillared frontal hall, which serves as the audience or assembly hall. In between the sanctum and the frontal hall existed an opisthodomos, which permitted light and air into the sanctum. But recently this courtyard was covered with a roof. The sanctum of Samalai temple measures 21′9″ x 21′9″ internally. The perpendicular parallelopiped cube was topped with a curvilinear spire, which is surmounted by the usual crowning elements. The *sikhara* of the temple is a remarkable piece of architecture. Its vertical segments adorned with miniature temple motifs and ascending successive lotus petal designs present an architectural grandeur, prototype of which is not noticed in other parts of Orissa. Some art historians regard this as the style of Khajuraho group. But the slender shape of the *sikhara* and silhouetted contour with sparse outer decoration strongly suggest that it is a logical outcome of a regional development in the architectural style. The temple of Pataneswari and Anantasayya also belonged to the regional school of architecture. The Samalai temple rises up to a height of 65 feet whereas the Pataneswari temple rises up to 60 feet.

Besides these, many temples enshrining Durga and other deities are found in Sambalpur town. Mention may be made of Gayatri temple, Mahamaya temple and Kali temple in the Sidhesvara complex.

The initiation of Prince Bansigopal, son of Madhukar Sai, the king of Sambalpur, into the Vaisnava faith and the settlement of some Vaisnava saints in Sambalpur resulted in construction of a large number of Vaisnava shrines. Among these temples, that of Jagannath features prominently. Brahmapura temple at Jharuapara, Bada Jagannath temple at Kamlibazar, Kutha Jagannath temple at Balibandha, Bariha temple at Nandapara, Timni temple at Sansarak, Baladev Jagannath temple at Kunjelpara, Madanmohan temple at Dalaipara, Jagannath temple at Modipara, Jagannath temple at Budharaja and Dadhivaman temple are all dedicated to Lord Jagannath. It provides a clear idea about the popularity of Jagannath worship in this region. Among these, the Brahmapura temple is ascribed to Balabhadradeva. The Bada Jagannath and the Kutha Jagannath temples are constructions of Prince Bansigopal. In architectural style, these three temples are more or less identical. These temples are built after the pattern of the Jagannath temple at Puri and are composed of a *Vimana, Jagamohana, Natamandapa* and *Garuda* pillar inside the *Jagamohana*. The wooden doors of these temples are lavishly carved with the scenes of Krisna *Lila* and other *Puranic* episodes. In Brahmapura temple beautiful images of Laxmi Narayana and four-armed Vishnu are housed in the niches of *Jagamohana*. The other temple of Jagannatha cited above are erected in later dates.

The Ramji temple at Balibandha is built by Ashakumaridevi, the daughter of Narayan Singh, the last Raja of Sambalpur. Though it is small in size it is a beautiful piece of architecture. The *Vimana* is of *rekha* order and the *Jagamohana* belongs to *pidha* order. The images worshipped in the temples are of Rama, Sita and Laxmana. It contains an image of *Sesha Sayee* Vishnu in the architrave of the door. Another temple dedicated to Rama worship is found in the premises of the municipality office. It is a recent construction without any architectural importance. Recently built Hanuman temple at the hill top of Motijharana near C.S. Zilla School is a fine specimen of art and architecture. But it has no antiquarian value.

ANANTASAYI VISHNU TEMPLE

Another interesting Vishnu temple is the Ananta Sayee temple at Balibandha. In architectural style it closely follows the style of Sakta temples of Samalai and Pataneswari of Sambalpur. It comprises an imposing *Vimana* and a pillared *mandapa* in front. It is open to all sides stands on low platform; unlike other temples it contains both Vaisnavite and Saivite *Parsvadevatas* in the niches of the outer wall. Four-armed Mahisamardini Durga holding *samkha* and *chakra* in upper hands and *trisula* in two normal hands; four-armed Trivikrama Vishnu with his usual attributes like *samkha, chakra, gada* and *padma* representing Trivikraka; four-armed Varaha uplifting Bhudevi by his elbow; four-armed Nrisimha in his normal form and attributes; four-armed Kartikeya with trident and kettle-drum, riding on peacock and patting a cock; and a Govardhanadhari Krishna are housed in the niches of the exterior wall of the temple. An image of four armed standing Siva holding axe, deer, a snake and in *varada mudra* is found depicted on the wall. An important image sitting cross-legged is found above this sculpture. It is a Hari Hara image. It can be recognized only through weapons. He is four-armed and attended by two females. He holds in his upper hands *chakra* and *dambaru* and in lower hands *samkha* and *trisula*. The image is ithyphallus. This image indicates the religious syncretism between the Saivism and Vaisnavism. The images of the temples belonging to both the creeds unmistakably point to religious harmony and peaceful co-existence of the divergent cults.

The uniqueness of the temple lies in its presiding deity. The presiding deity is Ananta Sayee Vishnu. Another Ananta Sayee Vishnu is found as a part of the decorative programme of the temples but nowhere in Orissa is found Ananta Sayee Vishnu as the presiding deity. The image is four-armed and reclining on the coil of the seven-hooded Ananta. He rests on the right side keeping his head on the right hand. The other three hands hold *chakra, sankha* and designed *gada*. His head is canopied by the hood of the snake. Brahma is seen on the *Navikamala*. Laxmi is found massaging the left foot of the Lord. The image is said to have been brought by the Surguja princess along with her after her marriage with Balarama Deva, who built a temple for the deity. The present temple is ascribed to Bansigopal.

Bansigopal is also known to have constructed the Gopalji temple of Sambalpur town whose presiding deities are Radha and Krishna. Another temple enshrining Gopinath is found in Sakhipara. The temple is known as Sakhi-Gopinath. The building of the temple was started by Abhaya Singh and completed by Jayanta Singh. It was a simple structure without any remarkable ornamentation. The best among the Chauhan temples of Sambalpur is the Gopilji temple. It surpasses all Chauhan temples except Nrusimhanath in artistic representation of cult icons, flora and fauna, with high aesthetic properties. It is considered as the cream of the Chauhans' art.

GOPALJI TEMPLE

Sambalpur was the principal seat of Chauhan rulers of 16th/17th century AD who trace their origin to the celebrated Chauhan hero, Prithviraj Chauhan. They adorned the capital with beautiful temples and monasteries of *brahmanical* faith. Gopalji Math is one of the significant monasteries, which includes the temples, the residence of the mendicants and a Sanskrit toll. Gopalji Math, a Vaisnava *Vihara*, is situated on the left bank of the river Mahanadi at Kamli Bazar. Its compound begins from the end of the weekly market and extends up to a distance of 150 meters. The *math* faces the east. There is another entrance to the north. In the front is found a spacious square courtyard with the Garuda pillar in it. In the premises of the *Vihara* there are two shrines. One is dedicated to Lord Jagannath, Balabhadra and Subhadra and is called Badajagannatha temple. Lord Gopal Krishna with his eternal consorts Radha and is famous as Gopalji temple.

Gopalji temple is constituted of a *Vimana* and a *Jagamohana*. The *Vimana* is square in shape and is flanked by two square structures. The *Jagamohana* is oblong. It houses a few images in the niches of the interior wall. The floor is made of marble plaques. The shrine is approached by a flight of steps through a pillared porch topped by a *rekha mastaka*. The elevation of the *gandi* of the *Vimana* and *Jagamohana* is unique in Western Orissa as it displays the *khakhara* pattern of architecture. Both the halls contain three-tiered vaulted roofs topped by two *khakhara mundis* on the vaulted roof of the *Vimana* and two on that of the *Jagamohana*. But now the *khakhara mundis* are replaced by only *amalaka*, *khapuri* and *ayudha*. The *mundis* were placed separately, not one above the other. There is no other *khakhara* temple in Western Orissa belonging to this period. The storehouse and the kitchen also have semi-cylindrical roofs. The outer walls of the temple are adorned with niches containing cult images of Hindu pantheon. The *Jagamohana* has three entrances on the wall of which the middle one belongs to the sanctum. The main entrance is on the front wall.

The other shrine dedicated to Jagannath, Balabhadra and Subhadra is bigger than the Gopalji temple. It stands on a high platform and consists of a *Vimana*, a *Jagamohana* and an oblong verandah in the front, which is attached with a flight of steps. The *Vimana* is of a *rekha* order. It is *pancharatha* in plan having a *panchanga bada*. The *pagas* are sub-divided into many vertical segments. The outer walls contain the niches for housing the *Parsvadevatas* and other cult icons. The *gandi* is surmounted by a *rekha mastaka* with its necessary elements. The *Jagamohana* is square and is connected with the sanctum by a covered vestibule. Two rows of columns are found inside the *Jagamohana*. The niches of the interior walls also shelter the figures of divinities. The *Jagamohana* is designed in the *bhadra* style. The verandah in front of it seems to be a later addition. It preserves two panels of sculpture. One is *Dasavatara* and the other a *Ramabhiseka* panel attached with other *brahmanical* images.

The walls of Bada Jagannath and Gopalji temple are decorated with a number of *brahmanical* sculptures. The doors and door-jambs of the entrances of *Jagamohana* and sanctum of the Gopalji temple are found lavishly carved with the sculptures of flora and fauna, cult images, incarnations of Vishnu, Ganga, Yamuna, activities of child Krishna and some folk sculptures.

On the lintel of the entrance of the sanctum is a beautiful image of Ananta Sayee Vishnu. Here Vishnu is shown reclining peacefully on the body of Ananta, Laxmi massaging his left leg and Sarasvati playing the *Vina*. The god is four-armed. The two right hands hold *sankha* and *gada*. One of the left hands has a *padma*, the other supports his head. The god is decorated with other usual features like *vanamala*, *mukuta*, *kundala*, *hara*, *srivatsa lanchhana*, etc. The Naga Ananta is seven-hooded.

The lintel of the *Jagamohana* gateway contains an image of Gajalaxmi with four arms, the upper pair of which hold lotuses while the lower ones display abhaya and *varada mudra*. She is flanked by two elephants pouring water on her head. A lady attendant is seen near her. Not far from this image are carved the images of Garuda and Ganesa. The scene of *Kaliya dalana* is carved elegantly on the same slab. The child Krishna is depicted here dancing on the head of the seven-hooded Kaliya holding the flute on the right hand and the tail of the snake on the left. The scene is remarkable for it evokes a sense of vigour and dynamism. The architraves contain the representation of animals like lion, tiger, jackal, monkey; of birds like peacock, pigeon, parrot, swan; and of cult images like Sarasvati, Durga, the Kalki and so on. The creeper bond and the filigree works surround the entire door frame. At the bottom of the door jambs are found the graceful representations of Ganga and Yamuna standing on their respective vehicles, crocodile and tortoise, each holding a water pot.

The entire door is embellished with carvings of *Krishna lila*. Among them mention may be made of *Dadhimanthana, Putanavadha, Yamalarjuna bhanga,* the slaughter of *Vatsa, Sakata, Kesi, Mustika* and others. Along with this it preserves a remarkable piece of art depicting hefty man with a slightly protruded belly comfortably smoking a *hukka*. The man is sitting in a slanting pose, the body rests on a cushion, which is kept vertically on the wall. Both the knees are raised upward. The head is probably wrapped around with a thin piece of cloth. The sculpture appears to be a figure of a king, or a royal person due to its muscular physique with latent vigour and seemingly royal attire. The sitting posture and the style of smoking *hukka* point to the prevalent court life under the Chauhans.

The niches in the outside of the wall contain some interesting cult images besides the *Parsvadevatas*. The *Parsvadevatas* are unusual. In place of Varaha and Vamana, the images of *Bansidhari* Krishna and Ganesa are found in the north and south, respectively. Narasimha occupies a place in the rear west wall. The figure of a ten-armed Nataraja is noticed on the exterior front wall of the temple. Nataraja is dancing on the *Apasmara purusa*. The god is wearing a *jata mukuta, sarpa upavita, sarpa kundala* and crescent on the head. He is holding *sarpa, trisula, dambaru, danta, mesa* (ram) *parasu, ankusa, varada mudra* and *dhanu* in his hands. The god is attended by Brahma in the right and Visnu in the left. While enjoying the dance they appear to be participating in the dance with their *mridanga* and cymbals. The presence of the *Apasmara purusa* suggest Southern influence but the position of the same does not tally with the Southern iconic trait. Certainly it bears the stamp of the local school of art.

An image of four-armed Mahisamardini Durga can be seen on the left exterior wall. The goddess is standing on a lion holding conch, disc and trident. The normal pair pierces the body of the demon with the trident. The demon is presented here as emanating from a decapitated buffalo. The Goddess, though engaged in fighting, does not look fierce. Inside the *Jagamohana* there is an image of four-armed Siva with a bull to the right. Brahma is shown on the left side with folded hands. Siva holds a *parasu* in his upper right hand and a *mriga* in his lower left hand. The rest two display the *varada* and *abhaya mudra*. A proto-type of this is also found in the Bada Jagannath temple.

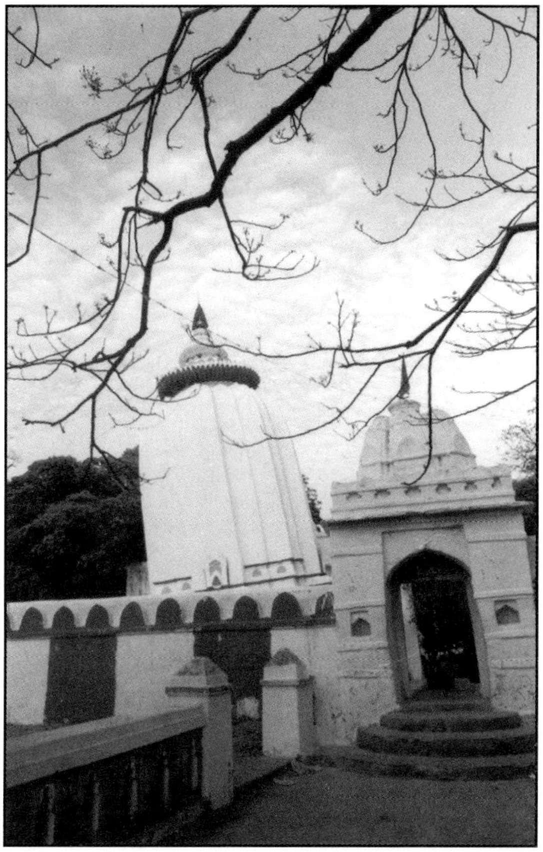
Pl. 1. Leaning Temple of Huma.

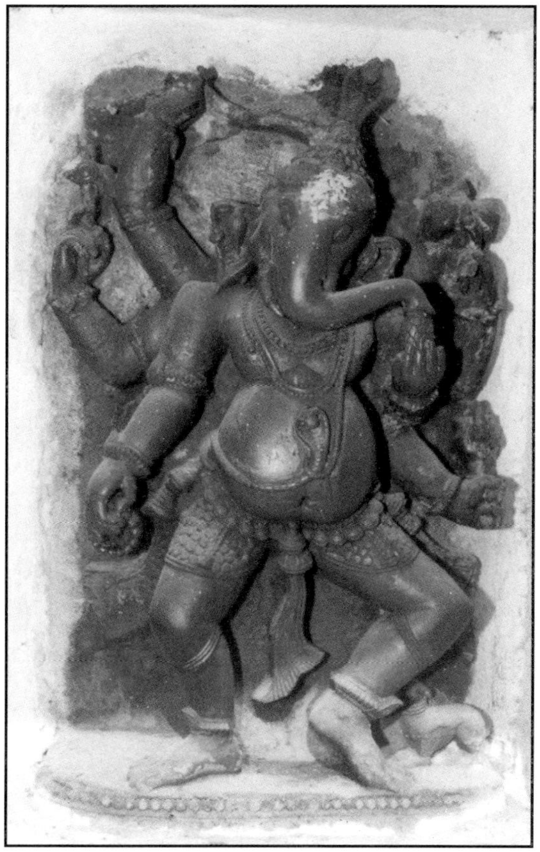
Pl. 2. Ganesa, Gopalji Temple.

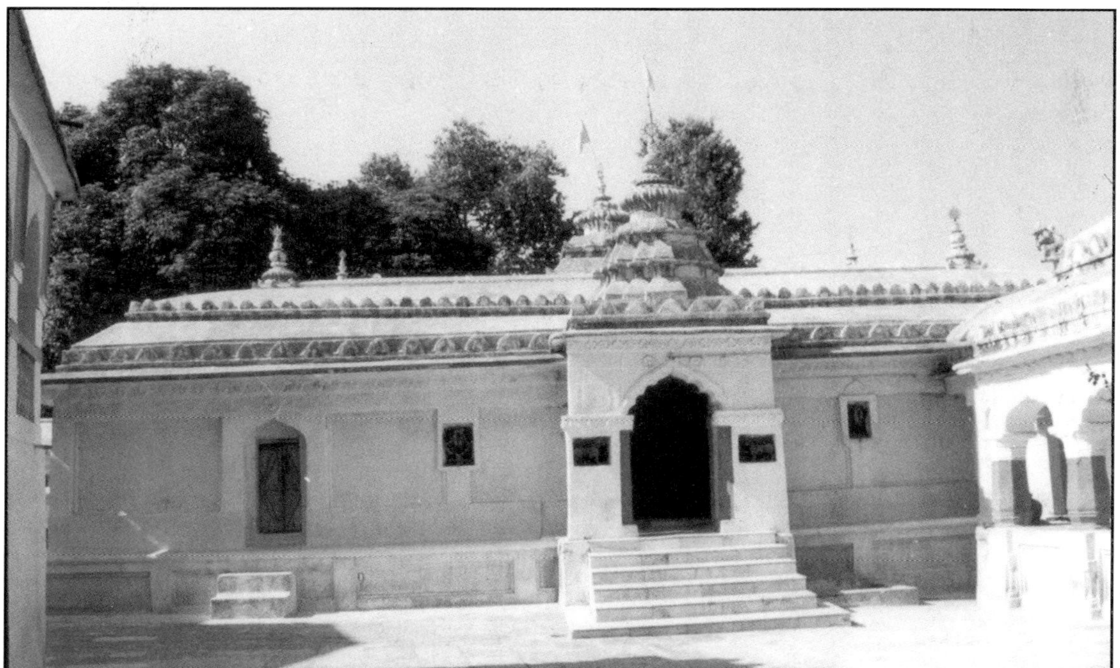
Pl. 3. Gopalji Temple, Sambalpur.

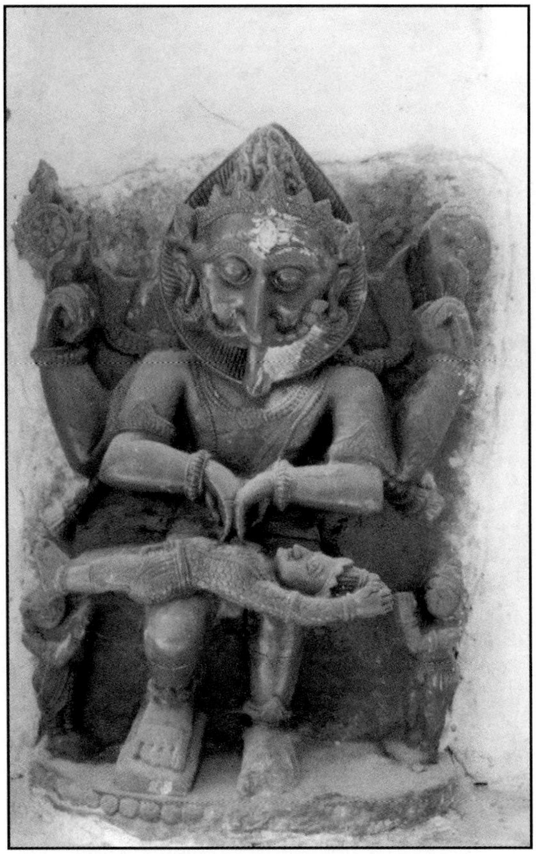

Pl. 4. Nrisimha, Gopalji Temple.

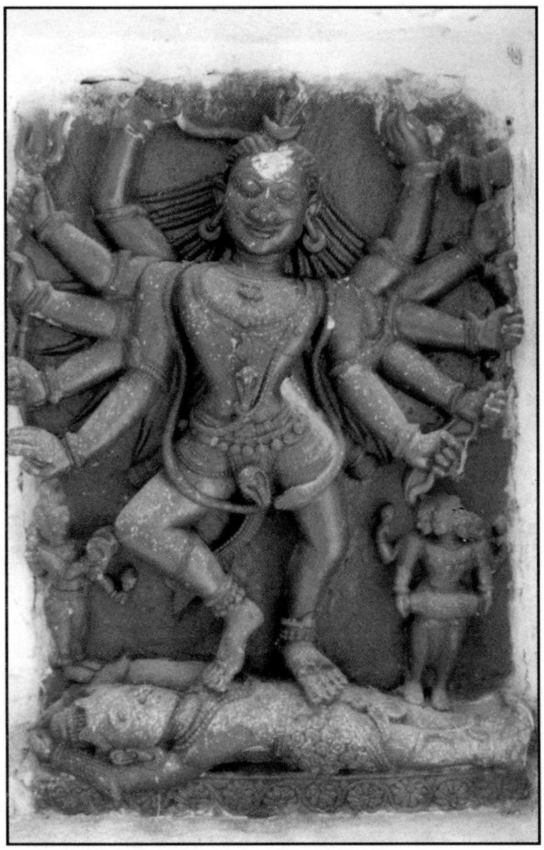

Pl. 5. Ten armed Nataraja, Gopalji Temple.

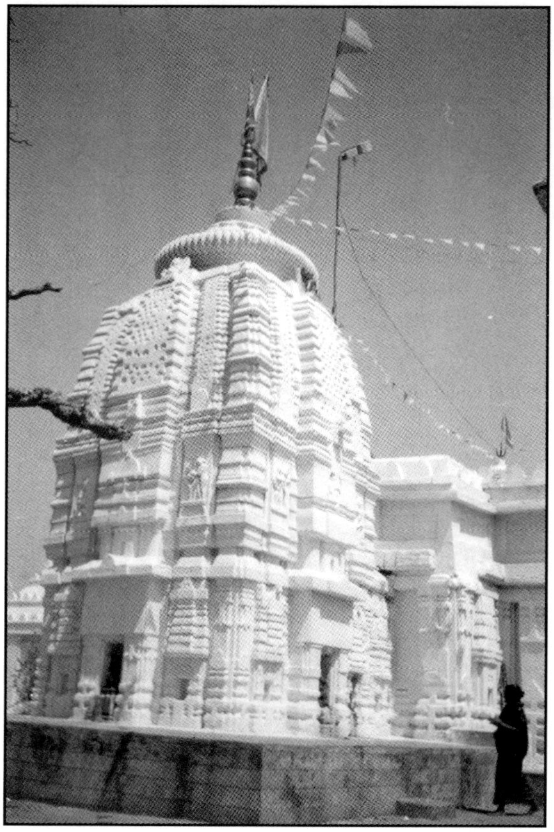

Pl. 6. Kapilesvara Temple, Charada.

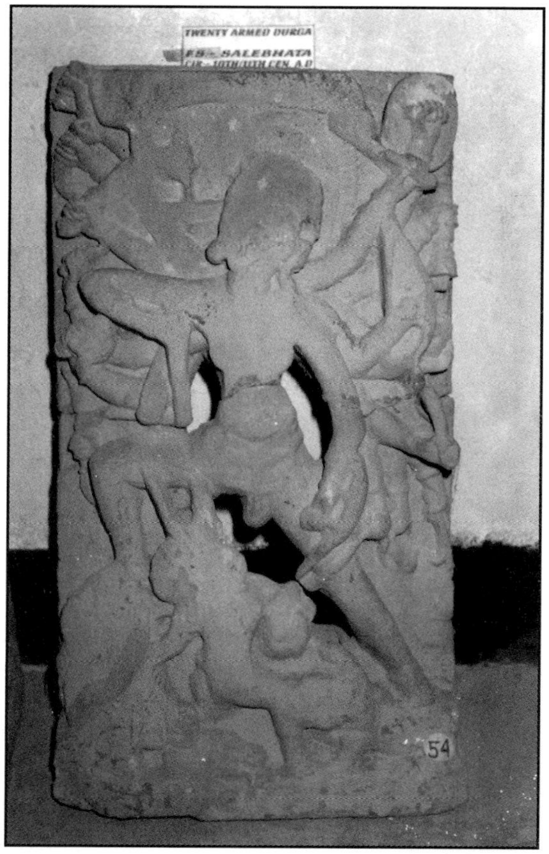

Pl. 7. Twenty armed Durga, N.K. Sahu, Museum.

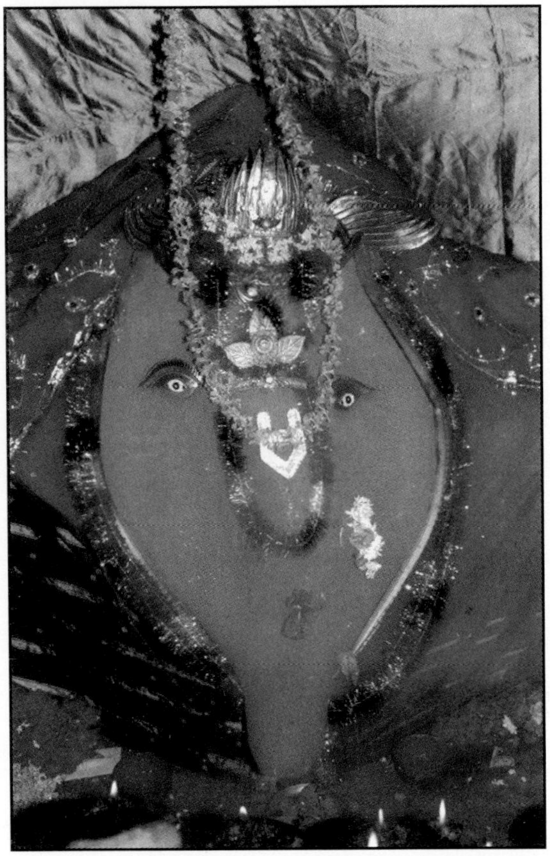

Pl. 8. Goddess Samalai, Sambalpur.

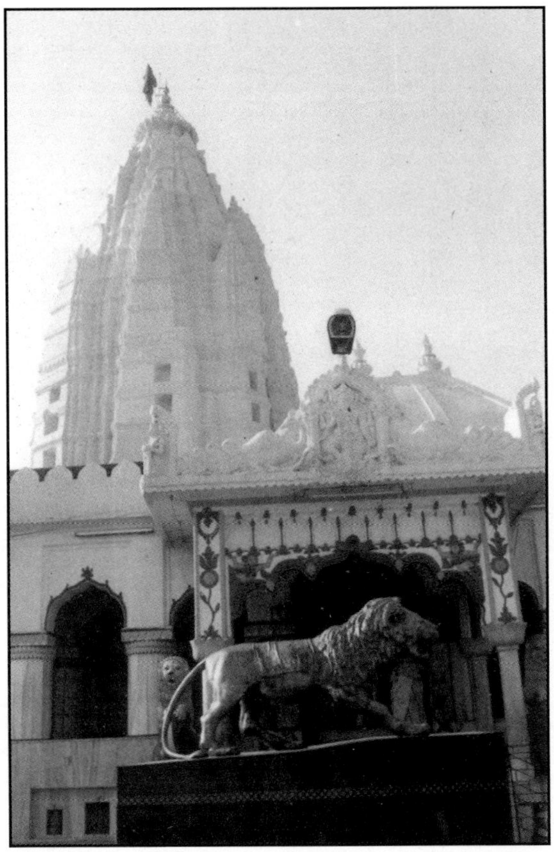

Pl. 9. Samalai Temple, Sambalpur.

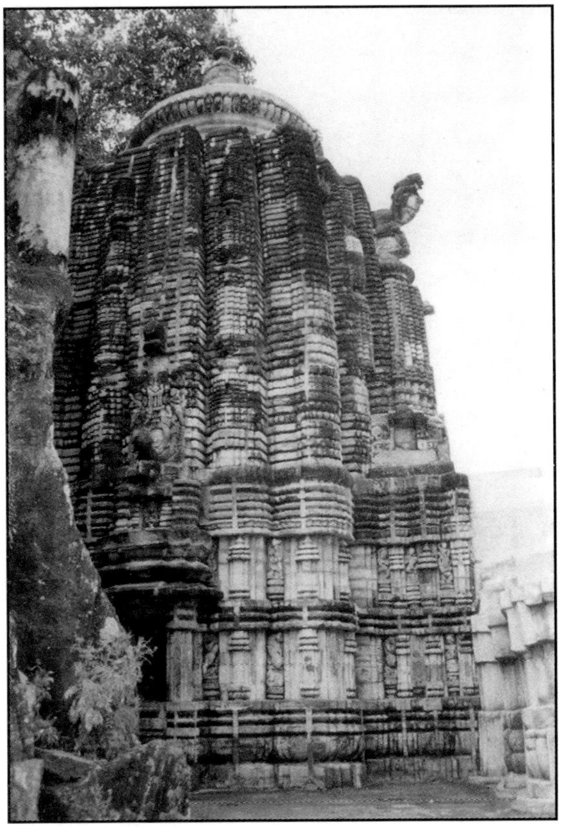

Pl. 10. Narsinghnath Temple, Narsinghnath.

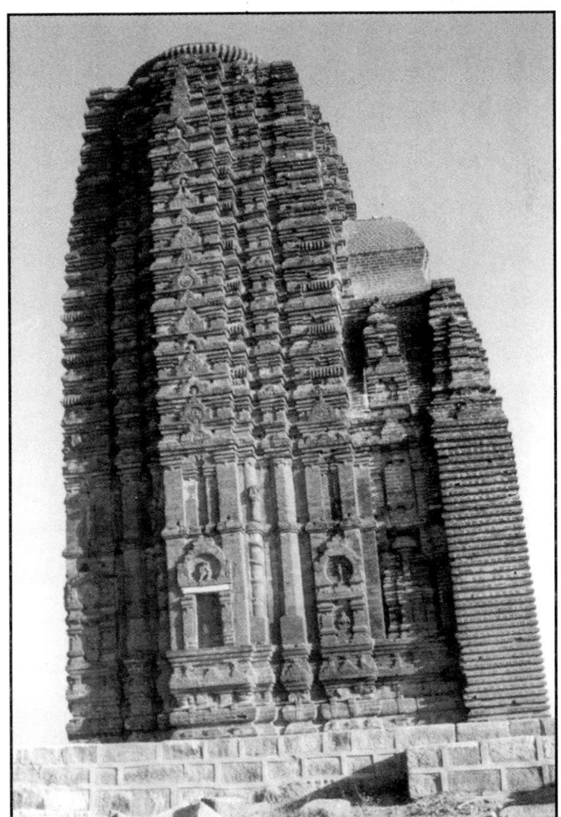

Pl. 11. Indralath Temple, Ranipur-Jharial.

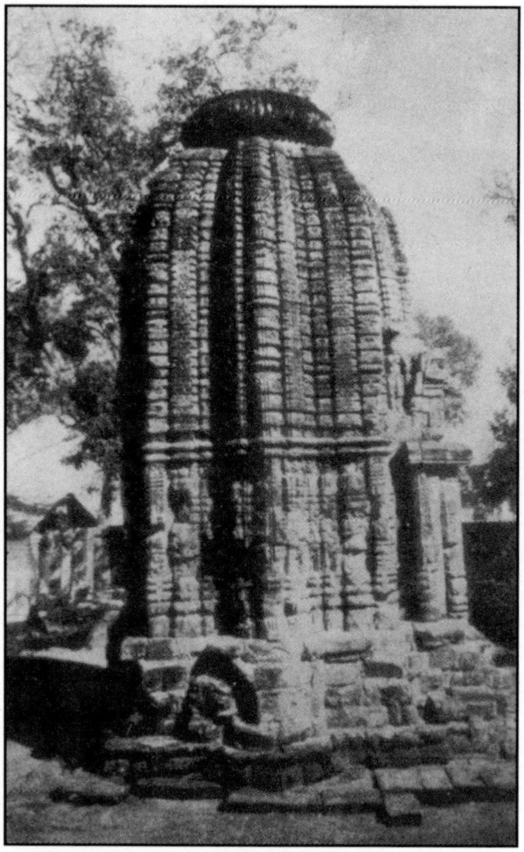

Pl. 12. Baudh Temple, Baudh.

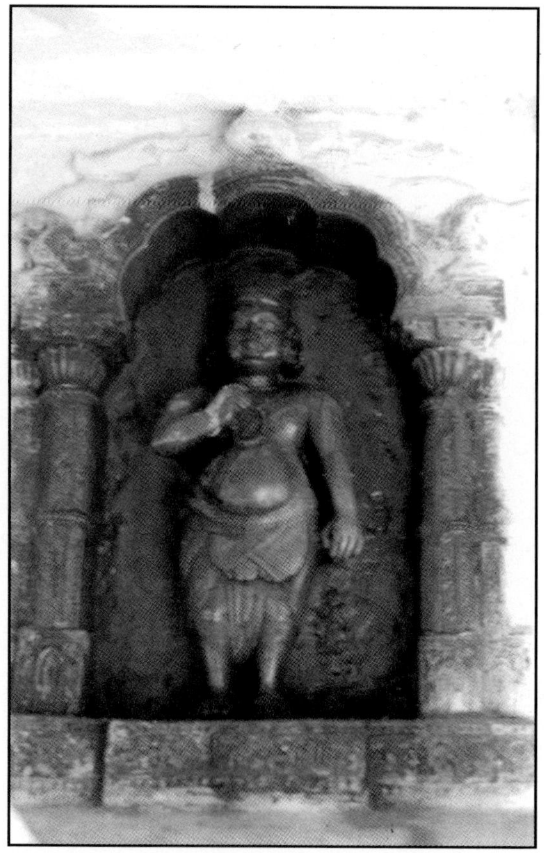

Pl. 14. Statue of Bansigopal, Gopalji Temple, Sambalpur.

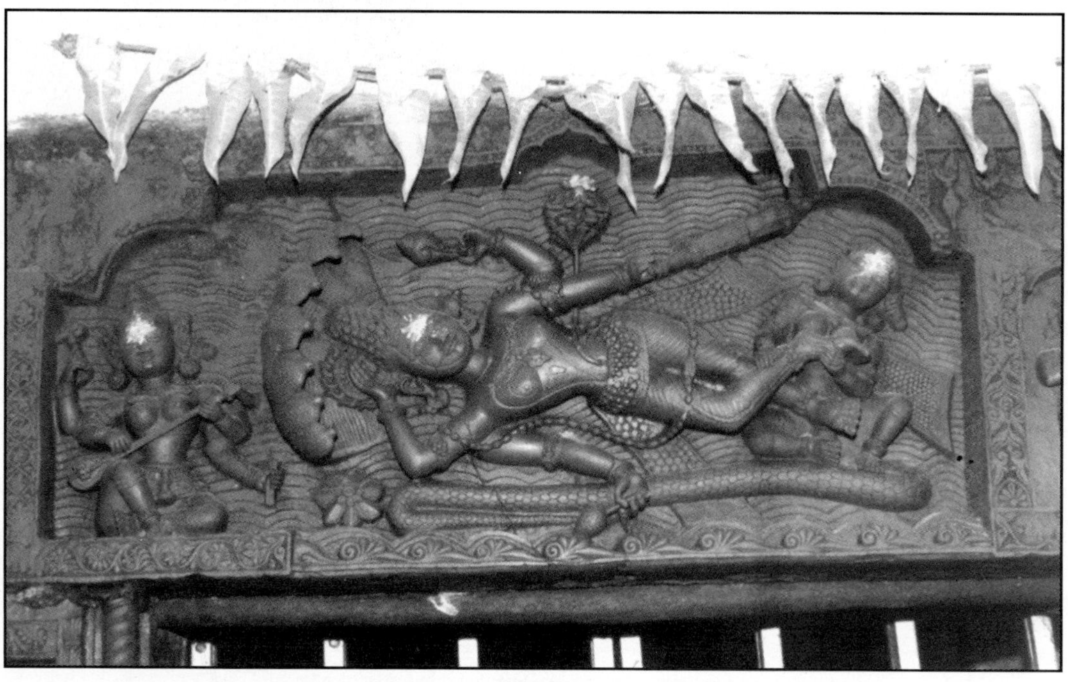

Pl. 13. Ananta Sayana, Gopalji Temple, Sambalpur.

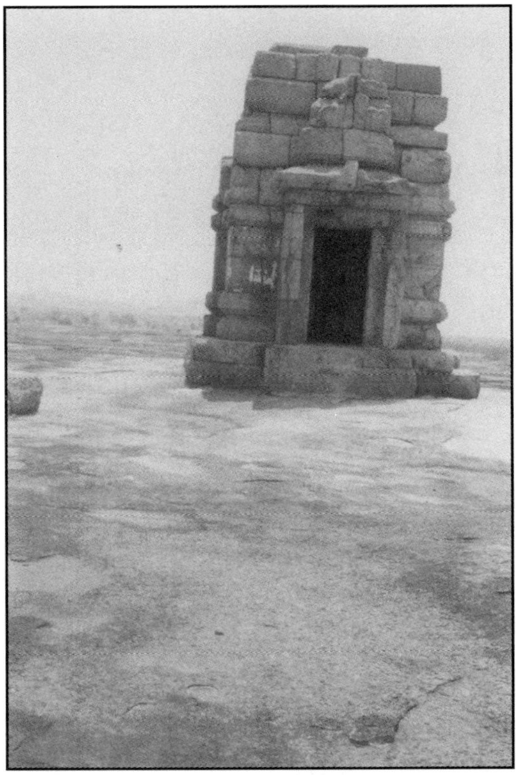

Pl. 15. Khakhara Temple, Ranipur-Jharial.

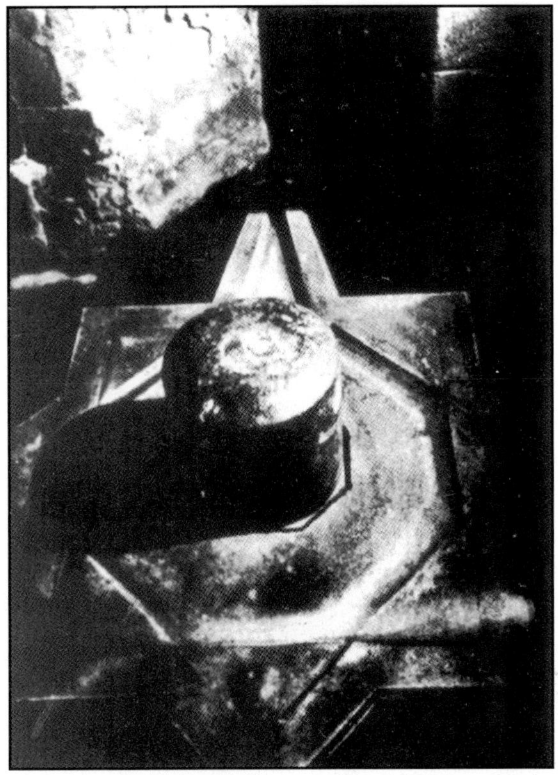

Pl. 17. Lingam, Baudh Temple, Baudh.

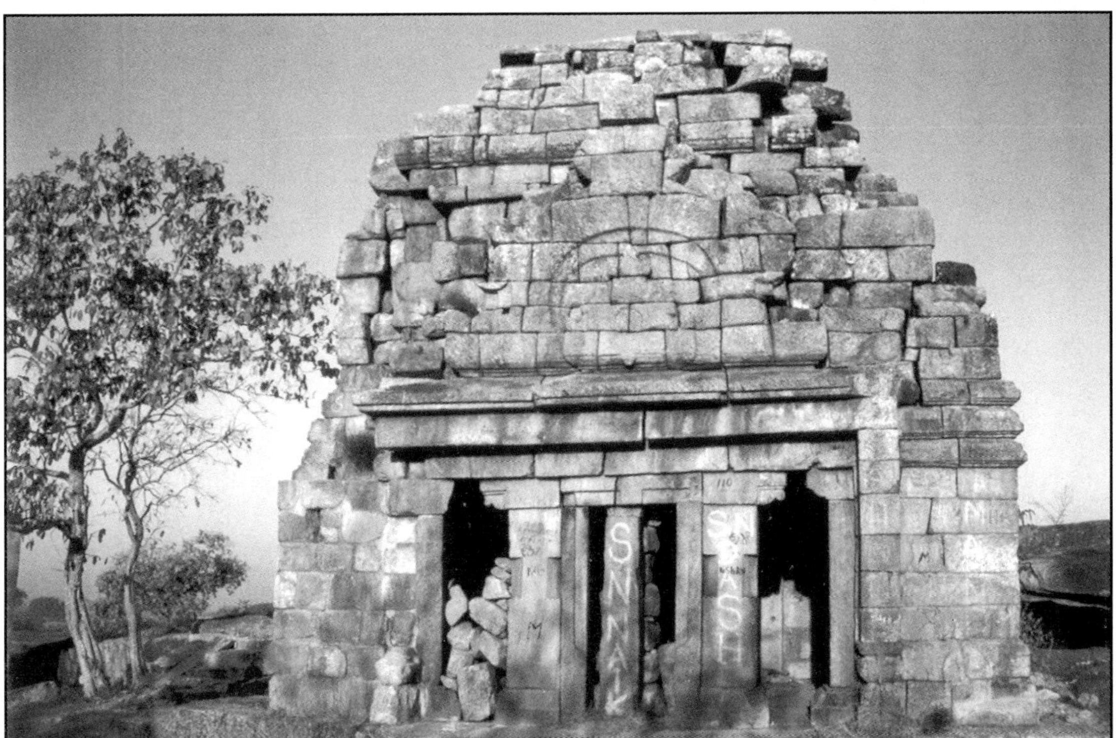

Pl. 16. Liyahari Temple, Ranipur-Jharial.

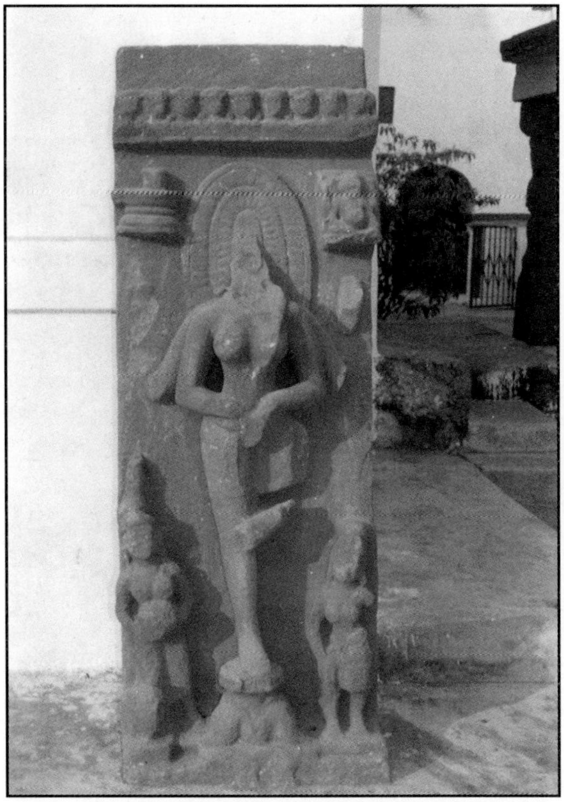

Pl. 18. Tapasvini Parvati, Patnagarh.

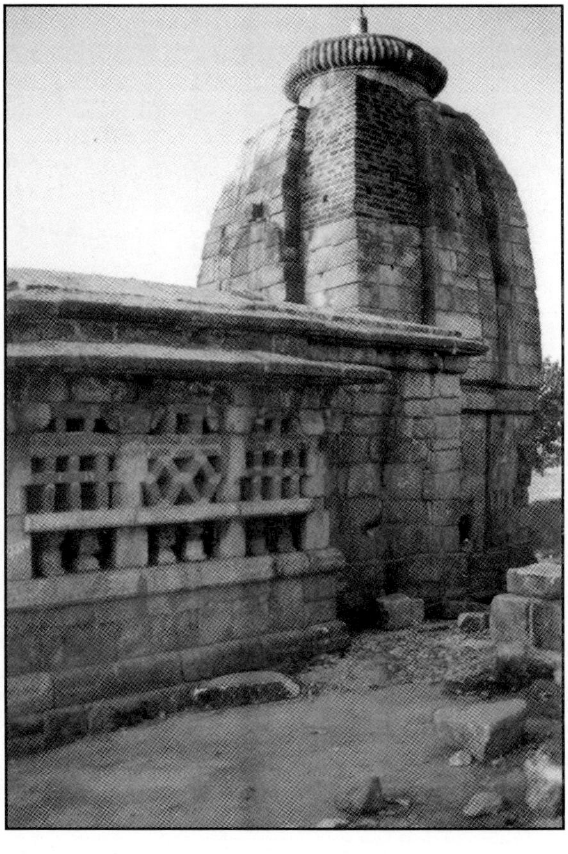

Pl. 19. Somesvara Temple, Ranipur-Jharial.

The temple of Bada Jagannath, which is situated in the same complex, preserves some significant motifs, like Krisna flanked by Gopis, Narasimha, Gajalaxmi, six-armed Ganesa, Krishna killing Vatsasura and others.

A fine specimen of a composite image of Krishna is carved on a block of red sandstone on the exterior back wall of the temple. The images are six-armed, standing on a lotus pedestal in an attitude of *tribhanga*. The uniqueness lies in the attributes held by the god. The god holds bow and arrow in the upper hands. The normal pair of hands is shown playing the flute. The lower left has a *Kamanadalu* while the lower right holds a *musala* (pestle). This was taken as a *parasu* by Prof. K.K. Dasgupta[1] and Dr. J.K. Sahu.[2] The pestle is interpreted by them as *parasu* probably because of its shape as it looks like a handle of an axe. It may be taken as an axe also. The figure contains the characteristic cognizances of Vamana (*kamandalu*), Balarama (*musala*) or Bhargava Rama (*purasu*), Rama (bow and arrow) and Krishna (flute), thus assimilating the four *avataras* in one person. Further, the central figure here is Krishna in *tribhanga* pose suggesting that he is the supreme god and the others are his incarnations. Lord Krishna is presented here as the *Avatari Purusa* or *Purna Brahma* and the others are *vibhava* or *avataras*. The huge bulk of *Gaudiya Vaisnava* literature unequivocally treats Lord Krishna as the Supreme God-head, which is expressed here iconically. In fact, both thematically and iconologically it occupies a prominent place in Indian iconography. In this connection the remarks of Prof. K.K. Dasgupta is noteworthy who observes "undoubtedly this is a hitherto unknown type of composite image, the parallel of which has found no where in India."[3] It is an image of *Sadbhuja Gauranga*, a divine form of Lord Chaitanya, which conceives. Chaitanya is identical with the four gods and is a combination of four gods. Anyway the synchretic concept is praiseworthy. These type of images emerged in the art history in the Medieval Period. So Dasgupta would be taken as right if his observation is limited to the ancient period.

Another interesting image is found on the northern wall. This is a small statue of the royal prince Bansi Gopal. He is portrayed as a dwarf, hefty, pot-bellied man, with moustaches, a turban on the head and a mark of *tilak* on his forehead. He is standing. There is a legend at the bottom, which reads as "*Sri Maharaja Madhukra Sahankar beta Sri Bansigopal Deva*". (Bansi Gopal, the son of *Maharaja* Madhukar Sai). The *tilak* mark on the forehead indicates that he is a Vaisnava initiate and apparently Gaudiya Vaisnava. The fixation of the figure of Bansi Gopal on the wall of the temple may be connected with the building of the temple as he was the builder of the temple. This sculpture may be employed as an evidence for dating the temple.

Maharaja Madhukar Sai was a Chauhan king of Sambalpur.[4] He has five sons. The eldest was Baliar Singh who succeeded Madhukar Sai. Bansi Gopal was the third son of Madhukar Sai[5] who took to asceticism. A court poet of Baliar Singh named Gangadhar Mishra has written a *Kavya* entitled '*Kosalanandam*'.[6] This *Kavya* was completed during the reign of Baliar Singh. Gangadhar Mishra has recorded the date of the work in the Chronogram as "*Kalou Kala Chala Yuga*", i.e., Kaliyuga era 4764 which corresponds to 1663 (4764-3101) when Baliar Singh was ruling.[7] So this would be the date of Bansi Gopal also whose image is found in the temple and who was a brother of Baliar Singh. Therefore, the temple in question was probably constructed during this period. This monument is ascribed to Bansi Gopal who is known to have borne the entire expenditure of the building. Hence, his statue figures on the wall of the temple of Bada Jagannath.

The sculptures of Bada Jagannath were slightly different in execution from those of the Gopalji temple. The icons of the Bada Jagannath temple are dwarfish, flat in treatment and are not as refined as those found in Gopalji temple. The images of male figures of Gopalji temple are endowed with moustaches. Adding moustache to the male divinities is a distinctive feature of Chauhan art. Another feature is the pointed nose, which is observed in almost all the images of Chauhan period. These features are noticed not only in the temple reliefs of Sambalpur but also in those of Sonepur. The art of Gopalji temple in general expresses a regional iconoplastic idiom.

There is a beautiful legend regarding the construction of the Gopalji temple.[8] In the early days this area was infested by the aborigines and tribals. They were sacrificing human beings in honour of their goddess Samalai. It was prevalent during the early Chauhan kings also. Once a Vaisnava saint was brought forcefully for the sacrifice. When he was taken to be sacrificed he pleaded and requested the king that the butchers appointed for the purpose should not kill him. He should be closed alive in the temple of the goddess. If the goddess wants, let her kill and devour him. The king was Baliar Singh. He agreed the proposal of the mendicant and accordingly the latter was closed inside the chamber of the goddess and all assembled in the morning before the temple. To their surprise, the saint was found in good health when the door of the temple was opened. The king came and informed the public that he had a dream last night when the goddess appeared before him and told that she was the mother of the world and of all beings. How can she kill them for her food? She is not satisfied by animal sacrifice. Hereafter, she should be provided with milk, dessert, cakes, fruits, etc. The saint was Bihari Das and he belonged to Gaudiya Vaisnavas sect. Bihari Das was honoured for his wisdom and was accepted by the royal family as the royal preceptor. Bansi Gopal, who had religious inclination beforehand, kept the *matha* in charge of Bihari Das. Bansi Gopal constructed the temples and the monastery out of his own share. The legend though appears to be simple, it has deeper meaning. It speaks about the abolition of long-standing human sacrifice by the powerful influence of the teaching of the Vaisnava tenets. The goddess was also included in the *brahmanical* cult, the greater tradition of Devi, and accepted as the universal mother. She is now worshipped in Bhuvaneswari *mantra*[9] and commands honour and worship from the people.

Beside the temples of Sambalpur town, some important temples are also seen in the ex-state of Sambalpur. Some of them are;

BIMALESVARA TEMPLE OF HUMA

The village Huma is situated at a distance of 30 km from Sambalpur town to the right side of the State Highway running from Sambalpur to Birmaharajpur. It is 5 km interior to the right side of the road. Once upon a time Huma was well known and the kingdom was called after his name as Humarajya, Humadesa, etc.[10]

There is a famous temple dedicated to Bimalesvara Siva constructed at the end of the village, on the left bank of Mahanadi. The temple is reknowned for its peculiarity. It is in a leaning condition. The temple has a *Vimana* and a *Jagamohana*. The main temple has tilted towards left in approximately 84 degree inclination for some unknown reason. At present a high thick wall is closely attached to the temple wall which covers the *bada* portion of the *Vimana*. It was built around the *Vimana* obviously to support the temple to prevent it from falling down. The interior space of the *Vimana* also was made high accordingly. As a result, the *linga* which was on the original floor, now remained under the present floor. However, a hole was created while constructing the recent floor in such a way that the devotee could see the *linga* through the hole. The original placement of the *lingam* is very well detected from the original spout of the *saktipitha*, which is noticed on the outside wall of the temple. It is a wonder that the temple still exists in its tilted shape like the leaning tower of Pisa of Italy. Now it is better preserved. Two small temples were built in leaning way imitating the inclination of the main temple.

Tradition ascribes Anangabhima Deva as the builder of the present temple. According to the genealogical list of the priests the temple may be dated to the time of Baliar Singh, or at best to that of Balarama Deva, the Chauhan kings of Sambalpur who were ruling in the 16th/17th century AD. The temple is almost plain and devoid of sculptures. It is built of sizely cut stones. Iron bars and hinges are used in the building. The simplicity and plainness of the temple reminds us of temples of Somavamsi Period in Western Orissa, viz, at Surda and Ranipur-Jharial. Now it is difficult to date the temple accurately without any dependable evidence.

The temple is of moderate height. It is 40' high. The *vimana* is square and belongs to *rekha* order. The plinth and the *bada* portion have been covered by a thick wall, which serves as a protective support. The temple inclines towards the north-western corner. It is more felt when one enters the temple for the lintel of the entrance has also bent. The cracks in the door jamb and lintel is clearly visible. Now the *gandi* is visible. Nothing can be ascertained about the shape and size of the *pabhaga* and *jangha*. On the right wall of the temple traces of moulding of the *baranda* is noticed. It is not visible on the left wall, as the side has gone down due to the tilting of the temple. The *gandi* has moved upward straight and taken a sharp bend near the *bisama*. The *sikhara* or *gandi* is *pancharatha*. On the wall above the *baranda* is seen the miniature shrine which contains niches. The niches are vacant. They were probably occupied by the *Parsvadevata* images, which are not there now. The right side corner of the *nandi mandapa* contains broken images of Mahisamardini and Ganesa. The *mastaka* is found above the *bisama*. Astonishingly the *mastaka* stands straight. It has no sign of inclination. It suggests that the *mastaka* was added after the leaning of the temple or a new *mastaka* might have been substituted after the falling of the *mastaka* due to the tilting of the temple. The *mastaka* has its usual parts like *veki*, large *amalaka*, *khapuri*, a full blown lotus design, *Kalasa*, *ayudha* and *dhvaja*.

The *Jagamohana* is also square and contains pillars inside. It has a plain interior. Small niches are found on the wall, which are occupied by votive sculptures. On the right side corner a small panel of three images are attached on the wall. The doorways are made of long stone slabs. The door lintel contains four-armed Ganesa. There is a *navagraha* panel on the entrance of the *Jagamohana*. On the top of the lintel of the entrance to the sanctum is found a figure of beautifully carved Gajalaxmi seated in *lalitasana*. One leg of her is hanging down the pedestal while the other is kept on it. She holds a lotus stalk in her hand and is flanked by elephants pouring water on her head. The lintel also contains figures of Brahma, Vishnu and Siva. In front of the *Jagamohana* is a *nandi mandapa*, which was constructed much later. The entrance door jamb of the sanctum contains the creeper designs and foliage works.

Inside the premises are found two small leaning temples – Bhubaneswara and Kapileswara. There is a big temple dedicated to Bhairava. The sikhara of the Bhairava temple has been built by large bricks of probably early Medieval Period. The presence of an *Astagraha* Slab on the base of the eastern wall and a bust of a beautifully carved *Sadbhujā* Durga in the nearby field strongly suggest of the existence of an Early Medieval temple there. Very likely the temple complex of Huma has developed in three stages. There was a brick temple belonging to 9th/10th Century AD. After its destruction another temple was built using stones probably during the time of Anangabhima III. It was developed into the present state by the Chauhan rulers of Sambalpur. At present other deities like Jagannath, Balabhadra and Subhadra are being worshipped in a temple built very recently. The temple of Huma is the foremost among the *Asta Sambhu* temples of erstwhile Sambalpur State.

KEDARNATH TEMPLE OF AMBABHANA

Dakshina Rai, the Dewan of Raja Ajit Singh of Sambalpur, constructed the temple. The temple is constructed on a high platform in the middle of a pond. The temple is composed of a *Vimana* and a *Nandimandapa*. The *mandapa* consists of four pillars topped by a semi-domical roof. The porch is open at four sides. The *Vimana* is of *rekha* type. It raises from the *pista* up to the *vedika*. The body of the temple is divided vertically into three parts. In the *raha paga* of each side small projected niches topped by miniature *rekha mundis* are noticed. Near the *vedi* in the *raha paga* is noticed the representation of inverted lotus petal device. The *mastaka* consists of *veki, amalaka, khapuri, padma, kalasa, ayudha* and *dhvaja*. The *linga* is enshrined in the *garbha griha*. The temple displays the features of Chauhan art. The niches of the three sides of the *jangha* accommodate the *Parsvadevatas* – Ganesa in the south, Parvati in the north and Kartikeya in the west. The temple faces east[12].

VISVANATH TEMPLE OF DEOGAON[11]

Deogaon is situated 8 km from Bargarh town. The temple stands on a low platform near a small pool. It has two structures. It consists of a *Vimana* (sanctum) and the *Jagamohana* or *Mukhasala*. In front of the *Mukhasala* is found a porch.

The porch is topped by a small *rekha sikhara* surmounted by a *rekha mastaka*. It serves as the entrance to the temple and is approached by a flight of steps. The *Mukhasala* contains the image of the bull, the favourite mount of Lord Siva. The temple is built of stone, fixed with lime mortar. The sanctum of *Vimana* can be divided horizontally into four sections, *pista, bada, gandi* and *mastaka*. The *bada* consists of *pabhaga, jangha* and *baranda*. The *pabhaga* has three mouldings and the *baranda* has one moulding. The upward tapering of the temple is noticed from the very beginning. Practically there is no distinction between the *gandi* and the *jangha*. It seems the *gandi* continues from the lower-most portion of the temple to the *veki* at the top on which the *mastaka* rests. The whole body of the temple is divided vertically into seven segments. The projected middle one which is called the *raha paga* contains a niche for the accommodation of the *Parsvadevatas*. The whole of the body of the temple is seen adorned with a number of horizontal mouldings. The temple is plain both externally and internally.

The *Parsvadevatas* installed in the niches of its three sides are Ganesa, Kartikeya and Durga. Ganesa is standing. His trunk is found turned to the left. Durga is found seated on the lion; Kartikeya is also in a standing pose with his traditional *ayudha sakti* and mount peacock.

The crowning elements of the temple consist of *vedi, veki, amalaka, kalasa, chakra* and a flag made of cloth. The temple exhibits the style followed in other Chauhan temples. The temple is facing to the east and the presiding deity is the *linga*, emblematic of Lord Siva[13].

BALUNKESVARA TEMPLE OF GAISAMA[12]

Gaisama is situated 13 km to the south-east of Bargarh. The Balunkeswar Siva temple of Gaisama contains three components. The entrance portico, *Jagamohana* and the *Vimana*. The portico has four entrances and has a *bhadra mastaka* on the top. The portico leads to the *Jagamohana*. The *Jagamohana* has a square hall surmounted by a *rekha sikhara*. The *Jagamohana* has an entrance to the sanctum. The *Jagamohana* houses the bull. The *linga* is enshrined in the sanctum. Like Niljee and Ambabhana temple this temple also contains projected niches at the four sides of the *gandi*. The three *Parsvadevatas* – Ganesha, Kartikeya and Parvati – are found in their respective position. The *mastaka* has *amlaka, khapuri, kalasa, ayudha* and the *dhvaja*. There is a *navagraha* panel on the lintel. The image of Nandi and Bhringi are found at the entrance gate of *Vimana* of Balunkeswar temple.

One image of Ganesa, which is inside the *Jagamohana* is more or less in damaged condition. On the right hand the god holds an *ankusa*. This image has been made out of hard stone.

Towards the backside of the *linga* are found the images of Siva-Parvati, a pair of Laxmi-Narayana and a pair of Sita-Rama. The temple faces east.

MANDHATA TEMPLE OF MANESWAR

Maneswar is situated 7 km from Sambalpur town. The temple is situated on the bank of river Malti. The temple displays the style of the later period. It originally consisted of the *Vimana* and a *Jagamohana*. The other parts have been constructed in later period. The *bedha*, boundary wall, is erected on hard rock around the temple. The four sides of the enclosure are unequal.

The temple is 31 feet 6 inches in height. It is made of quarried stone from the river-bed of Malati. The *linga* is underground unlike other Siva temples. A copper snake of nearly one meter height is installed in the *sakti pitha* encircling the *linga* and covering it with its wide hood.

The temple stands on a low platform and has two components – *Vimana* and *Jagamohana*. The *Vimana* is square and is of *rekha* order. The *Vimana* has four horizontal divisions – *pista, bada, gandi* and *mastaka*. The temple rises upwards reducing in size from all sides. *Pabhaga* contains three moulding. The *jangha* is plain and simple. The *baranda* is divided into five vertical segments. The middle one, which is called the *raha paga*, has one shallow niche in every side excepting the front one. The niches have the respective *Parsvadevatas* – Durga in the north, Kartikeya in the west, Gajalaxmi in the south.

The *sikhara* is terminated on a small platform at the top. It is crowned by the usual prescribed elements of the *mastaka* like *veki, amalaka, khapuri, padma, kalasa, ayudha* and *dhvaja*. *Jagamohana* is also of *rekha* order. There is a vestibule between the *Jagamohana* and the sanctum. The *nandi mandapa* where the bull is fixed and worshipped contains a number of votive images of small bulls. The *Jagamohana* has three entrances inclusive of a small exit. Lattice windows are also found on the sidewall in the *Jagamohana*.

The *dvarapalas* are found standing with folded hands on both sides of the entrance. On the lintel is noticed a four-armed Ganesa. In the sanctum are found three *nagas*. In the middle of the coil of the *naga* is found a hole within which the *linga* is said to have gone down the floor.

Independent images of Siva, Durga, Parvati and Laxmi are noticed inside the temple. Siva is four-armed and is in *sthanaka* pose. He holds a *trisula* and *dambaru* in the right lower and left lower hands, respectively. The upper right hand holds a *Parasu* while the left one catches a *mriga*. Parvati also is four-armed. The upper pair holds *parasu* and *mriga* whereas the normal pair shows *varada* and *abhaya* posture. Laxmi is also shown here as four-armed. The *ankusa* and *pasa* are seen in the upper right and left hand, respectively. The lower right displays *varada* whereas the left exhibits *abhaya*. An eight-armed image of Mahisamardini Durga is also found there.

VISVESVAR TEMPLE OF SARANDA

Saranda is situated 3 km to the west of Godbhaga. The temple mainly consists of three structures – *Vimana, Jagamohana* and entrance portico. The entrance portico is a small one, open to four sides and topped by a *rekha sikhara* and *mastaka*. In the portico is found a bull fixed on a pedestal. The *Jagamohana* is a square hall having a flat roof with a *pheni* decoration in the upper parapet. The *Vimana* is composed of a *jangha*, a *gandi* and a *mastaka*. It has a *pancharatha jangha* and a *pancharatha sikhara*. The *pagas* of the former closely align with that of the latter. In the *jangha* we find three niches in three sides. The niches housed the respective *Parsvadevatas* – Ganesa, Kartikeya and Parvati. The *sikhara* of the temple terminates at a small *vedi*. It is crowned by *beki, amalaka, khapuri, kalasa, ayudha* and flag (*Dvaja*). In the front side of the *Jagamohana* two perforated windows are found.

The image of Ganesa installed on the southern niches is four-handed. The upper two hands hold *kuthara* and *ankusa*. The lower right hand holds a *modaka* and the lower left holds a rosary.

In front of the main temple, three subsidiary structures dedicated to Goddess Durga, Bhairavi and Laxmi are found. The temple faces east.

NILAKANTHESVARA TEMPLE OF NILJEE[13]

Niljee is located around 20 km north-west of Bargarh town. The temple consists of *Vimana, Jagamohana* and a *Pravesamandapa*. The *Vimana* is of *rekha* order and is square in size. The *Jagamohana* is also square in size. It is a house-like structure having a flat roof. In the front of it is the entrance. It has a portico surmounted by a *sikhara* and *mastaka*. The temple is approached by a flight of steps. The *mastaka* of the porch is composed of *amalaka, khapuri, kalasa* and *ayudha*. The *Vimana* (sanctum) is vertically divided into three parts. On the body of the *paga* also are found vertical sub-division. The *raha paga* of each side of the temple contains two niches. The projected one is found at upper portion of the *gandi* and the shallow one is found in the *jangha* portion. The niches are found empty. The body of the *Vimana* from the plinth up to the *vedika* is horizontal, divided into sixteen parts. The *gandi* terminates at the *veki*; it contains a high *veki*, which is crowned by double *amalaka, khapuri, kalasa* and *ayudha*. A bull (Nandi) is found in the *Jagamohana* facing the *linga* and in the shrine the *linga*. The temple faces east.

A temple of Bhairava is situated to the right side of the main temple. The image of Bhairava is in standing pose. He holds a *trisula* in his right hand and the left hand is positioned downward.

TEMPLES OF SUVARNAPURA

Suvaranpura, literally meaning the "town of gold", was the nucleus of political gravity for centuries. Located on the bank of the well navigable river Mahanadi, it served as an important "*pattana*" or port and hence was a famous centre of trade and commerce. It has passed through political vicissitudes under the rule of various dynasties. But notwithstanding its fluctuating fortune, it had never lost its identity and survives till today as a modest town. A populous and prosperous town as it was, people's religious sentiments combined with the economic affluence resulted in the construction of numerous religious edifices and temples. The art activities were cultivated to such an extent that it was described as Varanasi (the temple city of North India) in *Kosalananda Kavyam*.[14] Thus, Sonepur or Suvarnapura was a city of great antiquity with a rich cultural and architectural heritage. At present also Sonepur contains a large number of temples and justifies its comparison with Varanasi. In that context a study of temples of this place becomes imparative. For a convenient study the temples of Sonepur are divided into two groups – Pre-Chauhan temples and Chauhan temples.

The temples belonging to Pre-Chauhan Period are not physically traceable. But the epigraphical records refer to many important temples, which were in existence during Somavamsi Period. The Sonepur plate of Janamejaya I[15] refer to a donation of the village Goteikela by the Merchant Association of Kamalavama (*Kamala vana vaniksthana*) to the Kesava and Aditya temple (*devakula*). This copper-plate grant belongs to the 17th regnal year of Janamajaya I. The Gopalpur copper-plates (2nd set) issued in the 10th regnal year of Janamejaya records the grant of the village Jollamura to Sri Sadharana which was divided into eight shares. Three shares out of the ten shares were donated to God Jalasayana Narayana Bhattaraka (obviously Ananta Vishnu or Sesa Narayana) for his *vali, charu, naivedya* and *puja*.[16] The first set of Gopalpur plates of Janamejaya issued in his first regnal year mentions *Talasanatha* Panchamvari. The Jatesinga-Dunguri plates of Yayati II refer to the Goddess Bhagavati *Panchamvari*[17] Bhadrambika. Panchambari of Gopalpur plate may be identified with the Panchamvari Bhadrambika of Jatesinga-Dunguri plates. If this is accepted, then a temple of Panchamvari was there at Suvarnapura.[18] And that temple was nearer to the river Tel (Telasanatha). Another ancient goddess is Stambhesvari, which finds mention in the Terasingha plate of Parvatadvaraka king Tustikara.[19] The Sulkis of Kodalaka *mandala* and the Bhanjas of Kheinjili *mandala* often describe themselves as the favourite devotees of Stambesvari (*Stambhesvari labdhavara prasada*).[20] It is known that the Baud-Sonepur region was being ruled by the Bhanjas of Khinjili *mandala* at the advent of Somavamsis. Therefore, it is not impossible that Stambhasvari was also being worshipped at Suvarnapura. All the evidences show that there were a number of temples existent at Suvarnapura during and even before the time of Somavamsi kings. In fact, Jatesingha-Dunguri plates[21] aver that Suvarnapura had many temples, *mandapas* and *udyanas* built by many persons. But unfortunately, even the ruins of the said temples could not be traced till now in Sonepure. So it is not possible to determine the actual size and shape of those temples. The temples, which may be considered as contemporary or near contemporary to the early group of temples of Sonepur, are still extant in the vicinity of Sonepur and Baud. These are the Siddhesvara and Nilamadhava temples at Gandharadi, Ramnath group of temples at Baud, Baidyanath temple and Charada temple. But these temples do not possess stylistic homogeneity. Each group differs from the other in architectural features. The Gandharadi group has corbelled window and oblong *mukhamandapa*. The Baud group reflects a stellate ground plan without any *Mukhasala*. In Baidyanath the *Mukhasala* is square having a quadri-pillared *vedika* in the centre with intersepts on sidewalls. The Charada temples, though undergone alterations, reveal a similar style. The only feature seemingly similar is the height. All temples are of small height. So the only guess can be made of the architectural features of the early temples of Sonepur that they were probably of moderate height. But they were of considerable importance as attested to by their occurrence in royal and official charters.

The temples of Chauhan Period form a separate and significant chapter in the art heritage of Sonepur. The temples constructed by them are numerous. Sonepur has the credit of having *Asta Sambhu*, *Asta Chandi* and *Asta Vishnu* temples in addition to other temples. A detailed discussion about all the temples cannot be accommodated in a limited article. A general survey of some of the important temples is made here. The temples of Sonepur exhibit the Orissan style of architecture. The *rekha* and *bhadra* are the popular types of temple style in Orissa. The *khakhara* style is sparingly used by the Orissan architect. So is the case with Sonepur. *Bhadra* and *rekha* temples are noticed abundantly in Sonepur. *Khakhara* style is partially adopted in the Gopalji temple of Sonepur. All temples excepting a very few, are multi-structured building. Some contain two components, i.e., *Vimana* or the main temple and the *Jagamohana* or the frontal hall. It is also called *Mukhasala*. The temples of Sureswari, Brindavan Bihari, Dadhi Vaman, Gokaneswara, Sitalai, Rama Chandi, etc are bi-cellar. In others we find an additional structure, i.e., a *mandapa* or a pillared porch. Most of the temples of Sonepur fall in this category such as Suvarna Meru, Ramesvara, Paschima Somanath, Samalesvari, Manikesveri, Jagannath, Gundicha, etc. Among the mono-structural temples mention may be made of Hanuman, Rudresvara, Sashisena and Budhisamalai. The *mandapa* in some temples are separated from the main plan. In Sonepur the *mandapa* is often called Chandana *mandapa*. Variations are noticed in temple compositions. Usually in a temple complex the *Vimana* belongs to *rekha* group and the *Jagamohan* to *bhadra* group. Along with this, other compositions are also found in Sonepur. Suvarnameru, Ramesvara, Paschima-Somanatha and few others that contain *rekha Vimana,* and *bhadra Jagamohana* exhibit the first variety. The second group contains *Bhadra Vimana* and *Bhadra Mukhasala* or *Jagamohana*. Temples like Jagannath, Dadhivaman, Brindavana Bihari, Siddhesvara and Lokanath belong to the group. The third category has a *Rekha Vimana* and an oblong *Mukhasala* having a vaulted roof. This characteristic is seen in Sureswari and Samalai temple. The Gopalji temple has a tri-cellar *Vimana* and an oblong *Mukhasala* with vaulted roof. It is built after the style of the Gopalji temple of Sambalpur and the builder is the same person, Prince Saint Bansi Gopal. Sobha Singh subsequently renovated it.

The architects of Sonepur have adopted the broad and common features of the temple. The temple has been divided into four parts – *pista, bada, gandi* and *mastaka*. Sonepur temples display *panchanga bada* both in *rekha* and *bhadra* temples. The *rekha gandi* or trunk of the temple exhibits *pancharatha* plan. The *mastaka* with all its elements prescribed in the cannon are found in the temples. The *gandi* of the *bhadra* temple of Sonepur is composed of two tiers and in some cases of three tiers. The premises of some temples like Suvarnomeru, Ramesvara and Jagannath are found teemed with small temples dedicated to different deities. The walls of the temples are not over-laden with sculptures. Only cult images are found housed in the niches of the outer and inner walls. The entrance lintels are often depicted with the Gajalaxmi figures. In Suvarnameru and Ramesvara temple, the representation of Ananta Sayi Vishnu is noticed in the beam of the architrave. In Saiva temples the *Vimana* wall contains the *Parsvadevatas*. The *Parsvadevatas* found in Siva temples are Ganesa in the south, Kartikeya in the west and Durga in the north. Sometimes Durga is substituted by Parvati. Varaha, Nrisimha and Trivikrama are found as *Parsvadevatas* in the Vaishnava temples. Vamana, sometimes substitutes Trivikrama. In the Jagannath temple we find a beautiful representation of both the aspects of Vishnu, i.e., Vamana and Trivikrama in a single slab.

The temples of Sonepur are plain and free from ornamentation. Only cult images are found in the temples and a few stucco erotic images are depicted on the exterior of some temples. Among the temple sculptures the cult images feature prominently. The Saivite images include Nataraja, Siva, Parvati, Chandra Sekhara, Ganesa, Kartikeya and the door-keepers. A Nataraja icon is noticed in Suvarnameru temple. It is a four-armed image dancing on *Apasmara purusa*. It holds a trident and kettle-drum in the major hand and a battle-axe and a deer in its upraised hands. A large serpent hood canopies the head adorned with a crescent moon. He looks forceful with bulging eyes and matted hair. He wears *sarpo pavita, sarpa kundala, sarpa keyura*. He is attended upon by Visnu on the right and Parvati on the left. His mount Bull is also seen watching the dance. Another dancing image of Siva is placed in the Khambeswari temple as a *Parsvadevata*. The icon is eight-armed holding a thunderbolt, trident, sword, small shield, bow, arrows, battle-axe and an indistinct object. He wears a garland of skulls, a snake around the neck, and a loincloth with a girdle. This image is later in date than the previous one, which belonged to the 17th century AD. The images of Siva are found in Chandra Sekhara, Nrisimha and Dadhivamana temples. Siva in the last named one has an additional feature of crescent with falling of the celestial river Ganga on his matted hair.

Parvati, Kartikesvara and Ganesa are depicted as *Parsvadevatas*. The image of Parvati is shown in sitting and standing position. She has four arms. The normal pair holds *pasa* and *ankusa*. The other pair exhibits *varada* and *abhaya mudra*. Kartikeya is found in standing posture. Both two-armed and four-armed images of the God are found. He is found associated with cock and peacock. He is represented in *Shanmukha* (six-headed) aspects. The Yaudheya coins portray the heads in two rows of three each. In some, the five heads are placed around the central one. In the Medieval Period only five heads are visible around the central one. The head on the back is not portrayed. In Sonepur the heads of Kartikeya are arranged horizontally in a single row. The icons of Ganesa are represented as an elephant-faced pot-bellied dwarf. He is shown in four-armed and eight-armed and in sitting as well as standing posture. In some temples we find *Shakti* Ganesa, i.e., Ganesa with his consorts sitting on the lap.

The icon of Vishnu is very popular among the Sonepur artists since the Somavamsi Period. The iconic tradition of the reclining image of Vishnu is traced to the time of Somavamsi Janamejaya I. The Ananta Sayi panel of Sonepur is simple and not crowded with accessory associates. Bhudevi is substituted by Sarasvati, which is not found in the early Indian images. The Sayana panels are found in the entrance lintels of the sanctum. The standing images are not rare in Sonepur. It is found in all Vaisnavite temples. The lord Vishnu is depicted with all his attributes and features. The images of man-boar, man-lion and dwarf-cum-tri-strider incarnation adorn the three sides except the front one of the Vishnu temples. The man-boar incarnation has a human body topped by a boar head. Likewise, the man-lion figure is depicted as a lion-faced man. Lord Vishnu in his *nrivagraha* form is portrayed as standing in an archer posture with upward glance. He holds his usual attributes. He is shown pulling up the uplifted hand of Bhadevi and keeping her on the raised left elbow of the God. Nrisimha is an *ugra avatara* of Vishnu. He is portaryed as a lion-faced human being of fierceful look having mighty claws and sharp teeth. He is shown tearing the body of the demon Hiranya Kasipu. This type of image is found in Gundicha, Jagannath and Gopalji temples. A beautiful brass icon of Laxmi Nrisimha has been enshrined by King Prataparudradeva in the Gundicha temple as its presiding deity in the place of the broken original image. Here the Lord is seen seated in *lalitasana* with his consort Laxmi on his left lap. Both have been decorated with their usual ornaments. Though he is represented in pacific form, his lion head, bulging eyes and projected tongue generate fear in human mind. He is eight-armed holding wheel, sword, club and arrows in his right hands and conch, lotus, mace bow in his left hand. It is a fine specimen of Chauhan art.

The Chauhan temples of Sonepur adorn their exterior walls with the narrative plaque of Balivamana episode. The plaque depicts the scene of giving the gift by Bali to Vamana, receiving of the gift by Vamana and assumption of Trivikrama form by Vamana. Such depictions are found in Ramesvara, Jagannath and Gundicha temples. Donaldson dates the portraiture of Ramesvara to 11th century AD and of Jagannath to 13th/14th century AD. But the close similarities of images of both the temples suggest that they may belong to the same age. Probably these images were collected from the ruins of ancient temples once situated on the bank of river Tel. Gopinath Panigrahi also gives some hints of building temples by using the stones of old temples. Besides these, images of Gajalaxmi, child Krishna, Garuda and Hanuman are noticed in Vaisnavite temples of Sonepur. Wood carvings on the doors of the temple depicting the activities of child Krishna and other scenes also constitute an important aspect of Chauhan artist. The doors of Gopalji temple were replete with such carvings.

The Sakta temples of Sonepur provide some notable examples of Chauhan art. Among the Sakta images, that of Mahisamardini figures prominently both as *Parsvadevata* and presiding deity. She is noticed in her four, eight and ten-armed varieties. She is depicted as a Warrior Goddess in her usual demon destroying posture. Goddess Durga also is represented as a pacific deity in Khamveswari and Budhisamalei temple. In Budhisamalei temple she is eight-handed and mounted on a tiger. In Khambeswari temple she is with her lion mount. Here she is depicted as eight-armed and fourteen-armed goddess. The fourteen-armed icon of Mahisamardini is an unfrequented and uncommon variety in Orissan as well as Indian art. The Khambeswari temple has the credit of possessing an image of this variety. She stands here on a *Visvapadma* cushion. In her normal hands she holds a *shakti* and a *kapala*. Among other weapons distinguishable are lotus, *vajra*, dart, trident, *parasu*, conch, bow, *kartri*, etc. She wears heavy garment and a tiara at the base of her coiffure. She is flanked on either side by a *chauri*-bearer. The treatment is stiff and static. The Samaleswari temple contains some good examples of *Matrika* images which are depicted here in their warrior aspects. The *Matrikas* are Vaishnavi, Varahi, Rudrani, Indrani, Kaumari, Narasimhi, Chamunda and Kali. All are four-armed. Along with the *Matrikas*, Hanuman and Mahisamardani Durga are also housed in the niche of the *Mukhasala*. Among the *Matrikas*, Varahi, Dakshina Kali and Chamunda deserve special mention. Varahi stands in an *alidha* pose with pendant breasts and upward gaze holding *samkha*, *kartri*, sword and by the remaining left hand she is devouring a demon through her gapping mouth. Dakshina Kali is seated in *lalitasana* and engaged in sexual congress with the ithyphallic *Purusa* (Siva) who lies on his back with folded hands above his head.[22] Chamunda is the principal deity among the *Matrikas*. She is here eight-armed and dancing on a prostrate *Urdhavalinga* corpse who has his hands on his head in *anjali mudra*. She has an emaciated body, flowing hairs, garland of skulls, bulging eyes and thus a ferocious look. Her major right hand displays *abhaya* with rosary and the left *charchchika mudra*. The other hand holds *kartri*, arrows, sword, bow, *kapala*s and an indistinct object. A jackal is depicted to the left near her feet. Bhuvanesvari and Bhairavi images are also noticed in the Sakta and Saiva temples.

Another interesting image is that of Sitalai thakurani. Her icon is noticed in the Gundicha temple and Sitalai temple. She is four-handed. The upper right hand displays *varada* and the lower left *abhaya mudra*. The lower right hand holds a club and the upper left catches a pitcher. She is seated on a horse. The peculiarity is found in her headdress. In place of a *mukuta*, her head is adorned with a winnowing fan. The big stone slab the carved portion of which lies littered on the ground, is called by the people Dasamati deity. Probably Dasamati is a corrupt form of Dasmurti or the images of ten deities. Either it may be a *Navadurga* slab which contains nine Durga with the central one or a *Dasmahavidya* slab where ten *mahavidyas* are engraved. Nothing can be said with certainty at present. Lankesvari and Khamvesvari, though famous, are originally aniconic deities.

Thus, the temple art of Sonepur carves a comfortable niche in the mighty fabric of Orissan art tradition.

Some of the information are based on the author's field study conducted during 1976-1978. In recent years, the temples have undergone changes due to total renovation, heavy plaster and colour wash. Even new structures have been added. Narayani temple complex has been renovated completely. Gopalji temple was restored by necessary repair and replacement. Suresvari temple underwent changes due to modern masonry and colour wash. Some of the important temples are described below.

SAIVA TEMPLES

SUVARNAMERU TEMPLE

The location of Suvarnameru temple is different from that of the other temples of this town. It is situated on the left bank of river Tel towards the south-west of the confluence of river Mahanadi and the Tel. It is situated outside the town proper. The temple was built by King Madan Gopal at the request of the legendary Neuli Sahu, a trader.

The temple of Suvarnameru is a *pancharatha rekha* deula facing towards east. It stands on a raised platform. The *pabhaga* of the temple have five mouldings of different shapes, out of which four are plain.

The *Vimana* is a square structure. It stands on a low platform and rises through the *bada* topped by a curvilinear *sikhara*. The *Vimana* is a *rekha* structure. The temple has a *panchanga bada*, having five horizontal segments. Also, it shows a *pancharatha* plan. The division is made by the pilaster-like projections on the body of *bada* and *gandi*. The niches are created on the *tala-jangha* to accommodate the *Parsvadevatas* in the temple. The *bandhana* which separates the lower *jangha* from the upper *jangha* has three simple mouldings. The *baranda* contains five mouldings. The figure of lions are fixed projecting outward on the *raha* of the *gandi*. A *rekha* replica or *anga sikhara* is seen on the *raha* of the eastern side. Different types of erotic sculpture in stucco are found in the *gandi* portion of the *Vimana*. A projected lion is found above the *anga sikhara* of the eastern side. The *gandi* ends with the *bedi* followed by *beki, amalaka, khapuri, kalasa, ayudha* and the *dhvaja* above the other.

According to legends the *linga* of Suvarnameru is a touch-stone, which if comes in contact with any metal, changes that into gold. The *linga* is kept within a brass cover and is not visible now.

Neuli Sahoo, who brought the God from the other side of the river Tel, is also worshiped here. There is a Gajalaxmi image in the middle of the lintel of the *Vimana*. This frontal hall is a *pidha* deula. The *bada* of the same is horizontally divided into five parts. They are *pabhaga, tala-jangha, bandhana,* upper-*jangha* and *baranda*. The *bandhana* consists of three mouldings. The pyramidal elevation of the *Mukhasala* contains three *pirhas*. Above the *gandi* there is the *mastaka* containing a circular *beki, amalaka, ghanta, kalasa* and *ayudha*. The *Mukhasala* has two gates in the east and the north. Besides *Jagamohana*, a *bhoga mandapa*, a *yajna mandapa*, and a *chandana mandapa* are found in the temple complex of Suvarnameru.

There are some other shrines within the compound. One is dedicated to Bhubaneswari facing to north. The deity is four-handed holding *pasa* and *ankusa* in one pair and displaying *barada* and *abhaya* in the other pair of hands.

The other one is a *pancharatha rekha* deula, where Hanuman is enshrined and worshipped. The Parvati temple, which is also present within the compound, was built by Biramtrodaya Singh Deo in 1927 AD. This temple exhibits a *pancharatha* plan and *rekha* design. Other miniature shrines like Lanchesvara, Santesvar and Hara-gauri are found within the Suvarnameru campus. These are of recent date and of little architectural value[23].

RAMESVARA TEMPLE

The temple of Ramesvara is built at the confluence of river Mahanadi and Tel. The temple is situated within a compound facing east. The compound has three gates in the south, west and north corner. The temple of Ramesvara is the oldest one of the Sonepur town. Tradition attributes Ramachandra as the builder of the temple and he installed the Siva *linga* inside it before his marching against Lankapuri.

The Ramesvara temple is composed of the *Vimana* and the *Jagamohana* or the frontal hall. The former is of *rekha* type whereas the latter is built in the *bhadra* style. The temple of Ramesvara rises up from a low platform. The plan of the *garbha griha* is square. The cube or *bada* of the temple is divided horizontally into five parts, viz, *pabhaga, tala-jangha, bandhana, upara-jangha* and *baranda*. The *pabhaga* is composed of seven mouldings. The *tala-jangha* section of the *raha* contains the niches for housing the *Parsvadevatas*. The *bandhana* which is the demarcating line between the lower and the *upara-jangha* has three horizontal mouldings. The *upara-jangha* ends with the *baranda* having seven mouldings. The *bada* again is divided horizontally into five sections. The temple has a *gandi* of *pancharatha* plan. It has five vertical divisions. Those divisions of *gandi* are completely aligned with those of the *bada*. The *gandi* portion contains some erotic sculptures of later date. The *raha-paga* of each side of the *gandi* has a projected lion (*jhapa-simha*). The *gandi* is terminated by the *mastaka* with its necessary elements, like *vedi, beki, amalaka, khapuri, kalasa* and *ayudha* arranged one on the other.

The *Jagamohana* of the temple is a *pidha* deula. The *Vimana* is linked with the *Jagamohana* by an *antarala*. The vestibule and *Jagamohana* were renovated in 1983 and hence no sculptures of early date are found. The *Vimana* or the *rekha* deula has been left untouched. It reveals a thick lime mortar. There are found some erotic figures in stucco in the body of the *Vimana*. But the *gandi* of *Jagamohana* is devoid of sculptures. The *Jagamohana* has three *pirhas* or tiers. Like the *Vimana*, the *Jagamohana* also has a *mastaka* having a *beki, amalaka, khapuri, kalasa* and *trisula*. It is interesting to note that an image of Ananta Sayi Vishnu is carved on the lintel of the entrance door of the frontal hall. A Vaisnavite image on the Saivite structure, though not uncommon, are not much frequented. This reflects eclectic attitude of the ruling king and patrons.

Like other temples the Ramesvara temple also has a *nandi mandapa* and *chandana mandapa* besides the *Jagamohana*. They all are linked with each other.

There are as many as nine shrines, small and big, found within the compound of the Ramesvara, which have no antiquarian importance. Among them, the Durga temple is situated in front of the Ramesvara temple. Here the ten-handed Durga is worshipped as Parvati. The compound of the temple and the other shrines were built by a fisherman, named Tila Taria, a great devotee of Lord Siva[24].

VAISHNAVA TEMPLES

JAGANNATH TEMPLE

The temple contains a sanctum and a *Mukhasala*. Both the *Vimana* and *Mukhasala* are built in *bhadra* style. The *Vimana* is small and the *Jagamohana* or *Mukhasala* is a big one. The *bhadra bada* of the *Vimana* is a *panchanga* one. The *tala-jangha* contains the niches meant for *Parsvadevatas*. The *Parsvadevatas* are Tribikrama, Varaha and Nrisimha. The *Mukhasala* also has a *panchanga bada*. In the upper *jangha* are found the decorative motifs and in some niches a few erotic sculptures are noticed. The *gandi* of the *Vimana* is made of three *pirhas* whereas the *gandi* of the *Mukhasala* contains two *pirhas*. On the upper top of first tiers there are projected lions on *raha* in the north, west and south side but there is a *gaja-simha* over the second tier on *raha* of some portion.

Above the *gandi* rises the *mastaka* section. The *mastaka* consists of a circular *beki*, a bell-shaped *ghanta* (again a *beki*), an *amalaka* and *khapuri*, a metal *kalasa* above which is a *chakra* and a *dhvaja*.

The sanctum is a square chamber. Lord Jagannath, Balabhadra and Subhadra are installed on *ratna simhasana*, which is close to the western wall. The lintel of the door has a Gajalaxmi image in its centre.

In front of the *Mukhasala* there is a pillared *mandapa* which has a flat roof supported by four pillars in its centre. The *garuda-stambha* stands to the north east of *Mukhasala*. A courtyard is also noticed in between the *mandapa* and *Mukhasala*.

In the premises of the Jagannath temple, shrines for Lokanath, Sarasvati, Lakshmi, Hanuman, Sun God, Siddhesvara, Ganesa and Radha-Krishna are found. Among these shrines Lokanath temple and Siddhesvara temple are prominent.

The temple of Jagannath was built by the Maharaja Raja Singha Deva in the middle of the 16th century AD. Its *mandapa* was constructed by Raja Biramitra Deo[25].

GUNDICHA TEMPLE

Gundicha temple is situated on the right bank of the Mahanadi in the heart of the town. It is named after Gundicha Devi, the builder of the temple. She was the queen of Prithvi Singh. The temple is known as Mausi mandir as it is reported that during the Car festival Jagannath, Balabhadra and Subhadra were staying here. Gundicha Mandir and Mausi Mandir are synonymous. The presiding deity of the temple is Laxmi Nrisimha. A number of votive images are found around the presiding deity. The image of the presiding deity is made of brass and is of full size. Nrisimha is sitting on a high pedestal. His one leg is on the footstool and the other is on the pedestal. On the left Laxmi, his consort, is found seated on his lap gracefully. The image of Laxmi Nrisimha is known to have been installed by King Prataparudra of Sonepur.

The temple is composed of two structures. The first one is the *Vimana* or sanctum where the presiding deity is enshrined and the next is the *Jagamohana*, in front of the *Vimana*. The *Vimana* is a *rekha* temple having a *panchanga bada* and a *pancharatha gandi*. The *Jagamohana* is a *bhadra* temple and is square in plan. In front of the *Bhadra* temple there is a porch topped by a *bhadra mastaka*.

The temple stands on a raised platform. It is of *rekha* type and is designed in *pancharatha* plan. The *bada* is divided into five parts horizontally. The *pabhaga* has five mouldings. In the *tala-jangha*, three niches are found where *Parsvadevatas* are housed. The niches are topped by *rekha mundis* which touch the *bandhana*. The principal niche is flanked by two other small niches. The upper-*jangha* is plain. The *upara-jangha* is terminated by the *baranda* which consists of five mouldings. The *gandi* is a curvilinear tower having five *ratha*s. But the *ratha*s or *pagas* are not roundish but flat, pilaster-like projections. On the *raha paga* above the *baranda* are found the projecting lions on three sides. A shallow recess is found in between the *kanika* and *anuratha* and another is found between the *anuratha* and *raha paga*.

The northern niche contains the image of Tribikrama. The side contains a Govardhanadhari Krishna and an image of a female sitting on the shoulder of a male. The southern niches have the deity Varaha. The two side niches contain an erotic sculpture and two male figures in *bhanga* pose. The *gandi* portion ends with *beki* on which is found the *amalaka* topped by a *khapuri* holding the *kalasa*. Above the *kalasa* the *chakra* and the *dhvaja* are present.

The *Jagamohana* has a square *bada* and a *bhadra gandi* consisting of *pirhas*. The crowning elements of the *Jagamohana* are *beki*, *amalaka*, *khapuri*, *kalasa* and *chakra*. The *Jagamohana* and the *Vimana* are connected with an *antarala*.

This temple is the tallest of all the Vaisnava monuments built in Western Orissa having a height of 114 feet.

SHAKTA TEMPLES

SURESVARI TEMPLE

The temple of Suresvari is one of the famous temples of Sonepur. The temple is situated on the left bank of the river Tel towards the north of Suvarnameru and south-east of Ramesvara temple. Goddess Suresvari is installed in the temple and is worshipped everyday with proper rites and rituals. She stands on a decorated *pitha*. She is six-armed and stands on a corpse. The image is completely blurred. The objects are not distinct at present.

The Suresvari temple is a *pancharatha rekha* deula facing north. The temple stands on a raised *pitha*. There are three niches on three sides of the *bada* of the temple. The niches are adorned with the images of ten-handed Durga, eight-handed Ganesa with his consort on the left lap and the mount below the pedestal and a four-armed Varahi in the east, south and west, respectively. Above the *bada* there is *baranda* having five mouldings, on which rises the *gandi* of the temple. It touches the *beki*, which is situated above it. The vertical projections of the *bada* and the *gandi* are same. Above the *beki*, there is *amalaka*, surmounted by the *khapuri*, *kalasa* and *ayudha*. The *ayudha* of the temple is a *trisula*.

The temple of Suresvari has a frontal hall. The *Jagamohan* of the temple is connected with the *Vimana* by a vestibule. The *Jagamohana* is oblong and has a vaulted roof with *rekha mundi* at the top. There is a small-latticed window in the middle of the north wall of the frontal hall and it is told that the people, whose entrance to the temple is prohibited, used to see and worship the goddess through that small window. There is a portico in the east gate of the frontal hall. It seems to be a later addition. Further, there is a *yajna mandapa* towards the east of the temple where rituals are performed.

The Goddess Suresvari is offered fish everyday. It is a must for her *bhoga*. The same practice is prevalent in the Varahi temple of Chaurasi.[26]

SAMALESVARI TEMPLE

The Samalesvari temple of Sonepur is situated on the right bank of river Mahanadi towards the south-east of the royal palace. The temple consists of a deula, a *Mukhasala*, and a pillared *mandapa*. It is built on a strong and high platform. In plan, the *Vimana* of the temple is *pancharatha* and has a *bada*, *gandi* and *mastaka*. The *bada* has *pabhaga jangha* and *baranda*. There are three niches where four-handed seated Ganesha in the south, Varahi in the east and Narasimhi in the west are housed as the *Parsvadevatas*.

Rising above the *baranda*, the *gandi*, which is curvilinear in shape, is severely plain. It has five *pagas*, which terminate below the *bisama* or *vedi*. There are projected lions in every side on the *raha* of the *gandi*.

Above the *bisama* rises the *mastaka* section, which consists of a circular *beki*, a *ghanta*, again a *beki*, an *amalaka*, *khapuri*, *kalasa*, the *ayudha* and the *dhvaja*.[27]

The *garbha griha* of the temple is a square chamber with indented sides. The floor of the sanctum is below the *Mukhasala* level and it takes one step from the vestibule to reach the same. Close to the southern wall the deity Samalesvari is found standing having four hands. There is an image of Gajalaxmi in the centre of the lintel of the entrance.

The deula is connected by a vestibule with its *Mukhasala*. The *Mukhasala* is a rectangular chamber. It has a two-tiered vaulted roof. Two *bhadra mastaka*s are found on the top of the vaulted roof. Inside the *Mukhasala* there are twelve niches where the images of the different Sakta goddesses are found. All the goddesses are four-armed. Varahi is seen devouring a human being. Narayani is seen on the Garuda. Four-armed Jayadurga is sitting on a lion. Ferocious looking Chamunda stands on a corpse with *khadaga* and *kapala*. Rudrani is found on her mount bull. Kaumari on Mayura is kept in the niche. Indrani on an elephant and an eight-handed Kali are found in the other niches. Two Vaisnavite *dvarapalas* are found on the side of the entrance with Vaisnavite *ayudha* in hand.

In front of the *Mukhasala* there is a pillared *mandapa*. It has a flat roof supported by sixteen pillars. Samalesvari is the *Kula Devata* of the Chauhans but Suresvari is the presiding deity of Sonepur.

The deula and its *Mukhasala* were built by King Sobha Singh and the pillared *mandapa* by Maharaja Sir Biramitrodaya Singh Deo Bahadur in 1932 AD.

TEMPLES OF SUNDARGARH

Sundargarh became a district in 1948. It is constituted of the ex-States of Banai and Gangpur. The copper-plates discovered from this area suggest that it was under the Varaha, Tunga, the Paramara and Kadamba rulers.

The district contains a number of temples. Most of the temples were built during the Late Medieval Period. Among them Siva temples are pre-dominant. Here also are found Astasambhu temples, which include Banesvara, Kopesvara, Svapnesvara, Ksiresvara, Jhadesvara, Langulesvara, Balkalesvara and Jatalesvara. All the temples were built within a radius of 10-12 miles of Banesvara temple. But unfortunately none are in existence except Banesvara and Kopesvara. Besides these, temples of Lord Dhavalesvara are found in Subdega, Tildega, Deogaon, etc. Belsargarh, Sukhabandh and Panposh also contain Siva temples of religious importance.

The temples of Gopalji, Bansidhari, Radhakrishan, Ramji, etc speak of the popularity of Vaisnavism in Sundargarh. Jagannath temples are found in a large number of villages, which evince the devotion of the people towards Jagannath.

Sakta temples are not less in number in Sundargarh. Samalesvari temple in Sundargarh indicates the influence of Samalesvari cult and its spread. Temples have been built for the famous goddesses like Kumari, Basuli, Sikharavasini, Jagadhatri, etc. As most of the temples were constructed in Late Medieval Period and early 20th century AD, they do not display super architectural skill or artistic excellence. But some temples are quite interesting. Even at places sculptures of Early Medieval Period are traced.

BANESVARA TEMPLE

Of all the extant temples Banesvara is the oldest one. It is situated near Banaigarh. A legend ascribes Banasura, the demon of Puranic fame as the builder of the temple. But it seems that the Varahas have initiated the construction, which was renovated later on by the Kadambas. Udaya Varaha in the Bonai copper-plate inscription has been described as Parama Saugata, a Buddhist king. His successors might have caused the temple to be built. As they are Buddhists by faith, the people of *brahmanical* faith probably portrayed them as demons and attribute the building of the temple to the demon Banasura. Later on Bhanupratap Deva who established the Kadamba rule in Banai, declared Banesvara as Sthanesvara and made provisions for worship of the Lord.

The temple of Banesvara is monocellar one with a projected entrance. There is a cemented *mandapa* built very recently in front of the temple which was previously a straw-roofed cottage. The temple has a boundary with a beautiful gate. The temple faces east. Banesvara *lingam* is the presiding deity. The temple contains the four fundamental parts which are *pista*, *bada*, *gandi* and *mastaka*. The *bada* of the temple is *trianga*. The *pabhaga* has three plain mouldings. The *jangha* is divided vertically into five segments. The *baranda* consists of two mouldings. The *sikhara* ends at *bisama* which is surmounted by the *mastaka*. The *mastaka* possesses the *beki*, large *amalaka*, *khapuri*, *vikasita padma*, small *khapuri*, *kalasa*, *ayudha* and *dhvaja*. The *beki* accomodates the *Deulacharinis*, projected lions as *bharbahakas*. Though the *trianga bada* and *Vimana* without *Mukhasala* suggest an early date, the elaborate *mastaka* with *amalaka* and *vikasita padma* indicates a late date. These features are noticed in Chauhan temples of Sambalpur, which belong to the 17th century AD. If tradition is to be believed then there was an early temple and the present temple have undergone heavy renovation during the time of Kadambas. The temple is built by sizeably cut laterite stone joined with locally made mortar. The use of iron plates, hinges, nails, etc is noticed in the temple. The temple has the usual *Parsvadevatas* housed in their respective niches, i.e., Ganesa in the south, Kartikeya in the west and Durga/Parvati in the north. A strange image of Astika Jaratkaru is seen in the premises of the temple. Jaratkaru, the sister of Vasuki, is found seated on the pedestal in *lalitasana*. On the lap of her is sitting a young boy. In the middle the coiled snake is carved. Two devotees are seen in folded hands to the right of the image. Not a second one of this image is found in the area. It is difficult to date this image, as it is a scattered piece.

A beautiful dancing image of Ganesa occupies the southern niche of the temple. The image is eight-armed and dancing on the back of his mount mouse.

The upper pair of hands holds the snake, which is carved in the shape of an arch. The left hand of the normal pair displays *gajahasta mudra* while the right carries the *danta*. The right of the third pair shows *karana mudra* and the left catches the *laddupatra*. The fourth pair of hands holds *ankusa* in the left while the right exhibits *varada mudra*. He wears a crown, snake festoons around the temple, necklaces, wristlet, armlets, snake-sacred thread, etc. The flying *Gandharvas* are carved on the top corners and the drummers with cymbal players are carved at the bottom of the slab. The image is sculpted in high relief and is a fine specimen of dancing Ganesa. Stylistically this image may not be dated earlier to 11th century AD. Kartikeya is in standing position. He has four hands. The hair is arranged in three braids. He wears crown, necklace, earring wristlet, armlet, anklets and girdles. He is playing with the *mayura* and carrying a *kukkuta* in his left hand. To the left is carved a female figure which may be identified with his consort Devasena. The northern niche is occupied by the image of Mahisamardini Durga. The image is eight-armed and is shown in *alidha* pose standing on her mount lion. The normal pair of hands is shown piercing the trident into the neck of the demon. The hands carry *ankusa, dhanu, sarpa, khadga, chakra, trisula* and *khetaka*. Another hand is engaged in pulling out the arrow. Her body is bedecked with fine jewellery from top to toes and is clad in a *sari*. It is a good example of medieval art. On the entrance lintel is found a six-armed image of Nataraja.

Apart from these images, some scattered sculptures are housed in a recently built room in the premises of the temple. Figures of Varaha incarnation, Krishna fighting Kesi, Kalki, Uma Maheswar, four-armed Kartikeya, four-handed Ganesa, crouching bull, etc. A standing image of Bhairava having four hands is also seen near the temple. S.S. Panda refers to two peculiar sculptures. A stone slab containing a depiction of *khakhara* temple having a sketch of *Triratna* symbol of Buddhism in its *jangha* portion. The temple motif is flanked by two female *chauri*-bearers. The second one is a lady warrior riding on a galloping horse holding sword is carved on a stone pillar near the temple. The stone pillar is considered to be a commemorative pillar like Sati pillar or hero stones.

KOPESVARA TEMPLE

Kopesvara temple is situated about one kilometer from Banaigarh fort and near the General Post Office of the town. The place where it is now was in early times known as Raghunathpur Patna. The place was gradually destroyed. At one particular spot there was a big hole looking like a small well (*kupa*). Tradition says that a black cow of the village headman used to visit the hole everyday. She stood above the hole and milk flowed spontaneously from her teats. After being reported about this recurring incident the village headman followed the cow and saw the same scene. He could not restrain himself, went there and searched the hole. To his astonishment, he discovered a *lingam*, which was worshipped by him. Nata Sarangi, a village man, being ordered by the lord in dream, built a temple during the rule of Narahari Chandra Deva (1680-93 AD) As the *lingam* was discovered from the kupa, he became famous as Kupesvara. Kupesvara later on was pronounced as Kopesvara

The temple has a single structure. The bull is placed on a pedestal in front of the temple. It faces east. It has a *pista, bada, gandi* and *mastaka*. The *Vimana* rises from the ground with uniform inward inclination from all sides till it meets the *bisama*. But the *Vimana* of the Banesvara rises straight up to certain height and it has taken a sharp bend at the top. The *bada* is *panchanga* and the *Vimana* is divided into nine segments vertically. The *sikhara* is topped by the *mastaka*, which contains a *beki, malaka* attached with full blown lotus petals above it. Then the usual elements like *khapuri, kalasa, ayudha* and *dhvaja* are found. The *beki* has snakes as *bharabahaka*. The *Parsvadevatas* are a four-armed Ganesa, an eight-armed Mahisamardini and a four-armed Kartikeya. Other images like that of Bhairavi and eight-armed Chamunda are also noticed near this temple. This temple is one among the Astasambhu temples of Sundargarh area.

KUMARI TEMPLE

Kumari is a mother goddess. She is considered as the protectress of Banaigarh state. There was no temple for this goddess. She was housed in a mud cottage. Pratap Chandra Deo, the king of Banai after being instructed by the goddess, built a temple for her. This temple is not constructed according to the norms of the *Vastusastra*. It is a square-shaped room surrounded by a processional path. Architecturally the temple has very little importance. Around the temple a large number of loose sculptures are found scattered. Among them, the images of Mahisamardini Durga, Trivikrama (incarnation of Visnu), Nataraja Siva, Haraparvati, Ganesa and beautiful female figures are worth mentioning. The image of Ganesa is four-armed. Here the proboscis of the deity is turned towards right the examples of which are very less. Besides a four-armed Durga, an icon of six-armed Durga is also traced from among the ruins near the temple. All hands are broken. Her body is bejewelled with ornaments. Peculiarities noticed here are that the goddess not only wears a *katimekhala* but also *udarabandha*. The four-armed image of Mahisamardini stands in *alidha* pose. The upper pair of hands carry *khadga* in the right and *sankha* in the left. The mount lion is in crouching position. The deity is piercing the trident into the body of the buffalo demon who is represented in the theriomorphic form. The representation of the animal form of Mahisasura suggests an early date. This image may belong to circa 9th/10th century AD.

It is told that the Kumari temple and Basuali temple were near the temple of Baneswar.

TEMPLES OF PATNAGARH

As discussed earlier Patnagarh contains many sculptures. The Somesvara temple have been covered in the temples of early phase. The other extant temples belong to Chauhan Period.

JAGANNATH TEMPLE

Another temple is situated 3 km away from the main town at Brahmapura, a suburb of Patnagarh town. It was a Brahmin *sasana*. The temple is dedicated to Lord Jagannath, Balabhadra and Subhadra. The architecture is similar to that of Patneswari. It is composed of a *Vimana* and *Jagamohana*. The temple is about 40 feet high. It has the fundamental elements like *pista, bada, gandi* and *mastaka*. It is a *pancharatha* temple. The *pagas* of *bada* are aligned with that of the *gandi*. The *baranda* has five mouldings. The *raha, anuratha* and *kanika pagas,* each are divided into a good number of horizontal mouldings. The *raha* in the *jangha* portion has only one niche and in the *gandi* portion has two small niches. The *mastaka* has a square *vedi,* on which the *beki* is there. The *beki* is surmounted by an *amalaka* above which is *khapuri* attached with a *kalasa, chakra* and *dhvaja* in succession. The *mandapa* is square and displays a similar style having the same type of parts. All these temples belong to the Medieval Period and are products of the Chauhan school of art.

PATANESVARI TEMPLE

The temple is situated near the old temple known as Kosalaswera/Somesvara temple in the fort area. The temple enshrines the tutelary deity of the Chauhans of Patna. The deity is famous as Patanesvari, the presiding deity of Patnagarh.

The temple had only a sanctum but later on a *mukhamandapa* was added to it. The *mandapa* was open to all sides through arched entrances. But afterwards except the front entrance, all openings were blocked by iron railings. The sanctum is a square of 12 feet. The temple rises from the ground, which tapers upward. It has three prominent parts – a *bada, gandi* and a *mastaka*. The whole body of *gandi* is surrounded by a number of horizontal mouldings like *bhumi varandikas*. The *mastaka* contains in succession *beki, amalaka* and *kalasa*. On the rim of the *kalasa* is an *amalaka* topped by a small *khapuri,* which holds the trident and *dhvaja*.

The presiding deity is a life-size image of Mahisamardini Durga. The image is eight-armed with usual weapons. The deity still commands respect and honour of the people from Patnagarh and its vicinity. Besides this there is another temple about a forlong away from Patnesvari temple, which is dedicated to the Goddess Samaleswari. It has a *Vimana* and a *mandapa*. The *mandapa* is open and the other openings of the *manadapa* are blocked. The temple stands on a raised platform. The entrance doorframe has beautiful figures. The doorframe is highly ornamented. The deity is worshipped in the shape of a block of stone like Samaleswari of Sambalpur.

TEMPLES OF KHARIAR

The town Khariar in the district of Nuapara was the political headquarters of Chauhans of Patna. Later on a branch of Chauhan family was assigned to rule this area. Khariar possesses many temples of the Chauhan Period.

BADA DADHIVAMANA TEMPLE OF KHARIAR

The *Bada* Dadhivamana temple is the biggest temple of Khariar. It consists of two components – *Vimana* and *Jagamohan*. The *Vimana* is a square one of *rekha* order. The *Jagamohana,* which appears from the present look, might have been a pillared *mandapa* having rows of pilasters along the side-walls and the four pillars at the centre as that of Charada and Vaidyanath. The door frame of the sanctum contains an Ananta Sayi Visnu panel. The placement of the panel is similar to that of Charada and Baidyanath temple. The temple has undergone repairs/renovations many times during the ruling period of the Khariar Rajas and finally by the Department of Archaeology, Government of Orissa. Whether the lithic frame of the temple was there from the inception or the temple was completely renovated by the rulers utilising the ruins and materials of the old temple, is now difficult to determine. But it is certain that the image of Ananta Sayi Visnu, and the pillars are of an early date, may be late contemporary of the temple of Charada and Baidyanath.

Besides this temple, Khariar contains many other temples among which Jagannath temple, Samaleswari temple, Raktambari temple, Laxmi temple, San Dadhivamana temple and Kanaka Durga temple are noteworthy. These temples display a similar type of elevation and belong to the late 19th or early 20th century AD.

BRICK TEMPLE OF KOMNA

Komna is an important town situated in the district of Nuapara. It has a brick temple. The temple is a *rekha* deul. It rises from the ground like the Bhumij temple. It has three horizontal divisions – the *bada, gandi* and *mastaka*. The *bada* is divided into five parts – *pabhaga, tala jangha, badhana, upara-jangha* and *baranda*. The *gandi* exhibits *triratha* plan. The *kanika pagas* contain the *bhumi amalakas* and *vedi*. Then *mastakas* start, which have a *beki, amalakas,* double lotus intervened by small *khapuris*. Above it, there is a *kalasa* attached with the *ayudha* and *dhvaja*. It was heavily plastered by lime. J.P. Singh Deo is of the view that the temple was originally a Siva temple but subsequently it was transformed into a Jagannath temple.

TEMPLES OF KALAHANDI (JUNAGARH)

LANKASVARI TEMPLE

Junagarh was the old capital of Nagavamsi ruler of Kalahandi. Afterwards it was shifted to Bhawanipatna whose old name was Bhandesvarapur. It is told that Satyanarayan Deb shifted the capital form Junagarh to Bhandesvarapur. It was Fateh Narayan Deb who established Bhavanishankar *linga* in Bhandesvarapur and renamed it as Bhavanipatna. It was he who brought finally the Goddess Manikesvari from Junagarh to Bhandesvarapur. So Junagarh is an important town in the Kalahandi district. The town has a number of temples, namely, Lankeswari temple, Kanaka Durga temple, Gopinath Mandir, Balaji temple, Ramasvami temple, Somesvara Mandir, Nilakanthesvar Mandir, Dadhivaman temple, etc. In Kalahandi Ramasvami temple are found in Bhawanipatna, Junagarh, Khariar, Komana and at many other places. Probably the followers of the deity had a wide diaspora and belonged to an influential community.

Lankeswari was the presiding deity of Nagavamsi rulers. Later on Manikesvari was accepted as their presiding and family deity. Lankesvari temple consists of a *Vimana* and a *Jagamohana*. It stands on a platform. It has a moderate height. The sanctum is square and composed of seven platforms, which are receding upward. The temple has a panchanga *bada*, namely, *pabhaga, tala jangha, bandhana, upara-jangha*, and *baranda*. The *gandi* exhibits a pyramidal elevation. The outer wall contains niches. In the northern and southern niche Ganesa is placed as the *Parsvadevata* and in the western niche Mahisamardini Durga has been housed. The sanctum faces east. The presiding deity is Lankesvari. She is seated cross-legged in a blissful gesture. She has four arms. The upper right possesses a mace while left holds a conch. The main right displays *abhaya mudra* and the left is shown in *varada* pose. She is shown in purely Vaisnavite features.

The sanctum has direct access to the *mukhamandapa* without any vestibule. The *mukhamandapa* is also square. It is also built in *bhadra* style. Both the sanctum and the frontal hall belong to the *bhadra* order of architecture. The temple is built of stones. Now the temple is plastered and pasted with lime and colours. On the *upara-jangha* are found some female figures and erotic sculptures. The *tala jangha* contains some animal figures. All these are in stucco. In front of the temple at a distance, there is place called Jenakhel where goats are sacrificed. Previously Jenakhal was near the High School under a Semal tree as reported by the priests. For some project work a bulldozer was employed for levelling the space and in the process the tree was uprooted from below the earth. Under the tree a number of human skulls were found. It indicates that human sacrifice was prevalent here.

DADHIVAMAN TEMPLE

The temple was built by the ceaseless efforts of Aranyaka brahmins and at present also it is managed by a trustee. The temple is of *bhadra* order. It is square. In front there is a *Mukhasala*, which also belongs to the *bhadra* category. There are two other rectangular halls after the *Mukhasala*. These temples contain *bhadra mundis*. The sanctum and the *Jagamohana* have the similar architectural features like *pista, bada, gandi* and *mastaka*. On the outer back wall is carved a royal figure on a galloping horse. It may be identified either with Udit Pratap or Yugasai Deo as it is a solitary figure with royal dignity. Both the kings had contributed much to the temple. In the rectangular hall is found an inscription of Yugasai Deo in Oriya belonging to Kaliyugabda – 4819, i.e., 1718 AD. The temple faces east and it is also heavily plastered. On the lower portion of the brass image of Laxmi also there is an inscription, which records the name of Udit Pratap.

All other temples of Junagarh exhibit the same structural plan with *bhadra* elevation. None have any other architectural or antiquarian values.

TEMPLES OF BHAWANIPATNA

Bhawanipatna is located in 19° 54' N and 85° 10' E. It is the present headquarters of the Kalahandi district. The town possesses a good number of Late Medieval and modern temples. The temples of Bhandesvara, Manikeswari, Kali and Taratarini are famous. The Bhandesvara temple is the oldest one. It situated on the bank of a pond in between the college and Manikesvari High School. Tarini temple is on a small hillock and Kali temple also on a mound. These temples are of moderate height and lack architectural elaboration. Manikesvari temple is within the area of the royal palace. This temple is the tallest temple of the town. The temple has no *Jagamohana*. It displays *rekha* order of architecture. The temple rises from a low platform. The platform is so low that it appears to have risen from the ground. It goes up straight with gradual inward inclination from all sides up to its terminal points at *bisama*. The temple has seven vertical segments, thus may be termed as *Saptaratha*. There is no clear distinction between the *bada* and *gandi* except the niche meant for *Parsvadevatas*. The horizontal *barandis* surround the *bada* and *gandi* with a uniform spanning of space. It has a squeezed *beki* topped by a heavy *amalaka* above, which is a thin *khapuri*. It is found that five round finials (substance) are arranged in succession from big to smaller one above the other, the top-most of which contains a *trisula* and a *dhvaja*. The exterior as well as the interior walls is severely plain. The presiding deity is Manikesvari whose image is made of some wax-like adhesive substance. The deity is two armed and holds a trident. She is adorned with crown, nose ring, earring, armlets, necklets, necklace, the upper garment, girdle and a saree. It is told that "the head of the deity is changed every year in Dasahara." Small temples, which were built after its style, surround the main temple. The lower portion of these small temples have opening to all direction. There is a *bhadra* temple adjacent to the main temple, which housed the Goddess Bhairavi. The three small shrines found on the three sites of the main one, probably serve the purpose of niches meant for *parsvadevatas*. Thus, in totality, it may be termed as a *shakti panchayatana* temple if the Bhairavi temple is included in this complex. *Shakti panchayatana* is unique in Orissa.

MADANPUR RAMPUR TEMPLE

Madanpur-Rampur is connected with a road from Bhawanipatna, the district headquarters of Kalahandi. It is a place of archaeological importance. A few years back a gold coin belonging to the Sarabhapuriya Dynasty was reported from this place. A Saiva temple known as Rameswara temple is found at the end of the village, which stands near a small pond. The temple is built of stone. The *Jagamohana* is rectangular. It is destroyed and a house of wooden pillars and straw roof has been constructed in its place. The *linga* is worshipped in the sanctum. The local people say it to be a *svayambhu* (self-created) *linga*. The circumference of the *linga* is about 3¢ and the height of the *lingam* is 1½¢.

Near the sanctum is found a huge mound of bricks and stones. Pieces of broken *amalakas* also are traced there. The stones are sizely cut and bricks are of various designs. Excepting the bull, not a single sculpture is noticed in the surface of the temple area. The temple may be ascribed to the 15th century AD.

CONCLUSION

Western Orissa, as the survey report goes, contains varieties of temples. In other words, most of the types of temple are noticed in this tract of land. Temples of Gandharadi is an excellent example of identical twin structure on the same platform rare in India. Then the temples having eight-pointed ground plan and the elevation of the *Vimana* which form a style recognised as stellate group of temples are also found in Western Orissa. These star-shaped temples are seldom noticed that too in a restricted area in India. The three temples of Baudh exhibit this style in its fullest form. The next variety is the circular sky-roofed structure meant for sixty-four Yoginis. Circular Yogini temple are not many. One can count the number in fingers. It is a valuable specimen in possession of Western Orissa. Another type of shrines are available in Western Orissa which is almost absent in coastal belt except one or two. This group is characterised by a temple with a pillared *Jagamohana* having lateral transepts on sidewalls. The nascent examples are noticed in the Central Province under Pratihara rule and in Rajasthan. In Western Orissa these kind of shrines are present in Baidyanath, Charada, Ranipur-Jharial, Patnagarh, ruins of Sauntpur and even at Narasinghnath where the renovated *mandapa* is a pillared one. In some the lateral transcpts were closed later on. These groups of temples were built and discontinued afterwards. Temples without *Jagamohana* are not unknown in this area. Rectangular *mukhamanadapa*, an uncommon practice rarely followed in Orissa, also exists in this zone. Baud temples, Narla temples and Surda temples are good specimens of this category. Surda temples exhibit a *Panchayatana* plan. If the report of Beglar is accepted then Baud group can also be considered as *Astaparivara* and *Panchayatana* temples. But a final decision requires further evidence. *Rekha* and *bhadra* order temples are available in plenty in Western Orissa. But *khakhara* shrine is not available barring two or three instances in this region. The Liyahari temple near the Somesvara temple and a small *khakhara* temple near the sixty-four Yogini temple are found at Ranipur-Jharial. Another feature noticed in Western Orissa is brick temples. The gigantic temple of Indralath at Ranipur-Jharial and the temple at Budhikomna come under this category. In the Medieval Period the vaulted roof is adopted in the Gopalji temple complex of Sambalpur. Not only the Gopalgi temple but also the store and other buildings contain barrel-vaulted roof. The Manikesvari temple may be included in the *Panchayatana* category. This is unique in Western Orissa, also in Orissa. Shakti or Devi temples are very rarely met with. In Western Orissa, *bhadra* style is adopted both in the *Vimana* and *Jagamohana*. A large number of temples are of this plan. The Samaleswari, Patanesvari and Anantesayya temples reflect a hybrid style of construction, which may be taken as a distinct regional style.

Like in all temples, the temples of Western Orissa also adopted cult icons, secular images, erotic and amorous scenes, *Alasakanyas*, filigree work, floral designs, animals, birds, etc as decorative motifs. Gajalaxmi, Ananatasayi Vishnu, sometimes Ganesa and *Navagraha* panels form important constituents for decoration of *dvaralalatbimva*. The door jambs contain floral design, animal or human bands, *dvarapalas*, etc. Ganga and Yamuna are depicted at the bottom of the entrance. The *Anga sikharas* or miniature temples of *rekha, bhadra* and *khakhara* orders are used as a part of ornamentation of the temple. *Yaksa, Naga, Nagini, Gandharvas, Vidyadharas, Deulacharinis, Chauri*-bearers, *Bharavahaka* and other such elements adorn the body of the temples. Interestingly, representations of the domestic life and hunting scene of the tribal people are carved very naturalistically in the balcony railing of the temple at Baidyanath. At Patnagarh also fragments of such depictions have been discovered recently. This type of secular sculpture is not noticed in the eastern part of Orissa. Thus, the temples of Western Orissa with their peculiarities and regional variation, contribute significantly to the domain of art and architecture of India.

REFERENCES

1. K.K. Dasgupta, "Iconographical Notes", *Journal of Ancient Indian History*, Vol. XII, 1978-79, Calcutta, pp. 112-15.
2. J.K. Sahu, "Temples of Sambalpur Town", *New Dimension of Tourism in Orissa*, 1976, Bhuvaneswar, p. 37.
3. K.K. Dasgupta, *op. cit.*, p. 114.
4. S.P. Dash, "Sambalpur Itihas" (Oriya), 1969, Sambalpur, pp. 250-51.
5. *Ibid.*
6. N. Senapati (ed.), *Orissa District Gazetteer*, Sambalpur, 1971, Cuttack, pp. 62-63.
7. J.K. Sahu *et al.* (ed.), Kosalanada Kavyam.
8. Collected from Mahant Nilambara Das of Gopalji Math in 1976.
9. S.P. Dash, *op. cit.*, p. 253.
10. *Ibid.*, p. 357.
    P.K. Nayak, "Huma Gramara Vakra Deula", *Smaranika, Saradiya Vesesanka*, (Oriya), 1976, Sambalpur.
11. D.S. Naik, "Astasambhu Temples of Western Orissa", unpublished M.Phil Dissertation, Dept. of History, Sambalpur University, 1994, p. 19f.
12. *Ibid.*
13. *Ibid.*
14. Gangadhar Mishra, *Kosalananda Kavyam*, 1929, Sonepur, canto–17, verse–55, p. 93.
15. *E.I.*, Vol. XXIII, pp. 248-255.
16. *O.H.R.J.*, Vol. XXXIX, nos. 1-4, pp. 119-32.
17. Gorachand Patnaik *et al.*, *Somavamsi Rediscovered*, 1990, Cuttack, p. 4, line-13.
18. *J.B.O.R.S.*, Vol. II, pp. 45-55.
19. *E.I.*, Vol. XXX, pp. 274-78.
20. *Ins. Qrs.*, Vol. VI, pp. 65-124. The Sulkis of Kodalaka mandala and the Somavamsi feudatories like Devapya and Jayarnama call themselves devotees of Stambhesvri.
21. *J.B.O.R.S.*, Vol. II, pp. 45-55.
22. T.E. Donaldson, "The Hindu Temple Art of Orissa", 1986, Leiden, pp. 733-35.
23. K.C. Darjee, "Temples of Sonepur", Unpublished M.Phil Thesis, Dept. of History, Sambalpur University, 1987, pp. 33f.
24. *Ibid.*, pp. 36f.
25. P.M. Nayak (ed.), *P.L.S.S.* (Oriya), 1981, Sonepur College, p. 141.
26. K.C. Darjee, *op. cit.*, p. 55f
27. K.C. Darjee, *op. cit.*, p. 57f.
28. *Orissa Review*, Vol. LI, no. 10, May 1995, Bhubaneswar, pp. 22-25.